A Calm Temperament
Expectant of Good

A Calm Temperament Expectant of Good

A Memoir

Don Perkins
and
Betsy Perkins Hill

Adams Press

For Jane, who has kept me young at heart for over twenty years; and for our merged families, whose love for me and each other gives me great joy, and for Jeremy Jefferis Hill, my oldest grandson, whose tragic death at the time this book was at the printer reminded each one in our family how fleeting life is.

TABLE OF CONTENTS

PREFACE

I have long admired and therefore aspired to live up to these words of an unknown sixth-century Chinese philosopher:

A leader is best
when people hardly know he exists,
Not so good
when people obey and acclaim him,
Worse when they despise him.
But of a good leader
Who talks little
When his work is done
His aim fulfilled
They will say:
"We did it ourselves."

With such a creed, why would I agree to participate in this memoir? The simple answer is that I have a strong-minded and persistent daughter. Betsy came to me in 2002 and asked for my cooperation to help her write this book. She thought that the effort might help my progeny understand how lucky I have been and how I have tried to live as an example for them.

I questioned that. She said that she thought the book might lead to future commissions for her to write biographies of others. She was getting to me. And finally she added, "I *want* to do this!" So I agreed. Some 50 hours of tape-recorded interviews later, and following an immense amount of compiling, rewriting, and editing, this is the result. I hope that others will look past the contents to admire the writing skill of my daughter, the author.

These are events of my life as I remember them.

DON PERKINS

INTRODUCTION

My father will tell you that the writing of this memoir was my project. I gladly take credit for the initiative that enables his story to appear in writing. I recall that he was both amazed and pleased when I told him I wanted to write about him. He told me that he had frequently thought that he should capture some of his memories for his grandchildren, but never found the time to do it. He could not fathom that this was really something I wanted to do, especially since I already had a full-time job at the time. I'm pretty sure that I have managed to convince him since that my interest was, and is, genuine.

During the course of the project, we spent a lot of time talking. I decided at the beginning that I would concentrate and listen better if I weren't madly taking notes while we talked. So I recorded our conversations. Those were special hours. In fact, I began to think that my siblings might be jealous of all the time I was spending with him. We laughed a lot—my father is a good storyteller—and even the very familiar stories took on added depth.

My father was also a ready subject when it came to sharing his speeches, clippings, and other memorabilia. The scrapbook that his late mother, Edna Meinert Perkins, had created when he was a boy preserved the details of many events that would otherwise be vague memories—such as his high school commencement speech and the narrative of the 14-mile hike he took as a Boy Scout.

Another absorbing source of insight into the time before my personal recollection was his correspondence with his mentor Don Booz during his 10 weeks as a Jewel trainee. It was fascinating to observe my father's business philosophy beginning to form. It was also just plain fun to read about a time when TV tables were new and Gene Autry guns were a fading fad. The collection of memorabilia provided a wealth of detail that human memory could not.

I discovered as we started to work that I had trouble organizing and keeping track of all of his many activities, boards, awards, and involvements. Maybe it was the influence of my business training, but the only way I found to match the chronology with the variety was to put it into a spreadsheet. The idea of putting a life into a spreadsheet still makes me laugh, but I can only guess how many times I went back to that spreadsheet to check dates and the chronological relationships among events.

As we wrote and rewrote, we also recognized the need for an editor. That role was ably filled by my long-time friend, Catherine J. Votaw, with help from her father, David F. Votaw, Jr.

When most successful businesspeople write books, they are usually about their business achievements. My father's business accomplishments could fill a book on their own, but it would hardly provide an accurate picture of his life; his business accomplishments, as admirable as they are, are only one part of who he is.

His story is, in truth, many stories. It is the story of merit and hard work overcoming the handicap of poverty and achieving success—the epitome of the promise of America. It is a business story—the growth of a major U.S. corporation responding to and leading its market. It is the story of a manager and leader, driven by his fundamental respect for others—who grew a business by leveraging the strengths and aspirations of individuals, not by treating them as fungible, commandable resources. It is a story of corporate governance and board relationships—both prescriptive and a reassuring example of the many counter-examples to the unfortunate corporate scandals of recent times. It is the story of someone determined to make a difference in his community, and who recognizes that his community is, increasingly, the world. Finally, it is the story of a loving and beloved father.

While my father had trouble believing at first that I wanted to tell his story, his natural humility makes it at least as difficult for him to imagine that others will be interested in reading about his life. His modesty is exemplified by the number of times (more than I can count) that he changed the word "I" to "we" as we edited. I trust and hope that others will find his story as compelling as I do. I am profoundly grateful to have had the opportunity to play a role in the telling.

BETSY PERKINS HILL

A Calm Temperament
Expectant of Good

CHAPTER I

EVERYTHING THAT EVER HAPPENED TO ME IN MY LIFE

E verything that ever happened to me in my life has been the result of education or volunteering. Of course, that isn't literally true, but since so many of the good things I have experienced in my life, and so many of the people I have met, can be traced back to either volunteering or education, I can forgive myself a little exaggeration. I think about the events of my life as representing a decision tree with branches. Education or volunteering started each major new branch; they all started growing distinctly, but end up in a bramble of connections.

One of the earliest branches was one I could not appreciate at the time—in 1935, I skipped the third grade. But more about that later.

I was born in St. Louis on March 22, 1927, at the Missouri Baptist Hospital. My parents, Edna Ann Meinert and Arthur Sheldon Perkins, had been married the year before and had moved into a house given to them by my mother's father, a contractor and builder. That house, at 4962 Walsh Avenue, was my first home and was one of the many ways in which Grandpa and Grandma Meinert would help our family over the years. They also helped my parents with our second home, at 4431 Wallace Avenue, where we moved between the birth of my brother Bob in 1929 and the arrival of my sister Joan in 1932.

My father had been named Sheldon Arthur Perkins, but he didn't like the fact that his initials spelled "SAP." Unfortunately, he wasn't educated enough to recognize the equally unfortunate implication that resulted from reversing his first two initials. Arthur or Al Perkins, as he liked to be called, was a womanizer and a wanderer. The first time my father left the family was while my mother was still in the hospital after my sister's birth.

The Depression was on; times were tough. The value of the house on Wallace Avenue had been lost somewhere along the way. So my mother, with three small children—Joan still an infant—had to move back to her parents' house at 3838 Botanical Avenue. My earliest memory is of riding a tricycle there, and I started kindergarten while we lived with Grandpa and Grandma Meinert. I also recall that my mother worked at home doing typing for an insurance salesman, earning money while watching over the three of us. It was also there that I learned to play pinochle as a four-year-old by watching the adults play.

My father came and went over the years. He worked mainly on the West Coast painting houses, but never sent any money home between 1932 and 1937. He would leave us for good in 1943.

In 1935, Grandpa Meinert set up a house for my mother, Bob, Joan, and me on our own at 6417 S. Kingshighway, and we moved out of my grandparents' home. That was when I had the grade school achievement that changed my life. When I switched from Sherman School, where I had attended kindergarten through second grade, to Gardenville School, I went from the second grade to the fourth. Skipping that year of grade school meant that I would graduate from high school at 17, instead of 18. And in 1944 when I finished high school, being 17 instead of 18 meant the difference between starting college and immediately being drafted into military service. Gardenville School really did me a favor.

But at the time, any notion of college was years away and the possibility of war, to say nothing of military service, was far from my experience. I was more concerned with getting my homework done and whether there would be anything besides white beans to eat each day.

Moving to the house on Kingshighway also meant that my mother had to get a job. She came home one day, sat with us, and told us that she had found a job—as a secretary at the St. Louis sales office of the J. I. Case Company, manufacturers of farm equipment. While my mother had not finished high school, she was proud of having attended Brown's Business College where she had become adept at bookkeeping, shorthand, and other secretarial skills. She also had an uncanny ability to spell, a talent she failed to pass on to me.

When she told us about the new job, she admonished us never to contact her at work. If anyone from work contacted us when she wasn't there, she said, "Tell them I'm your aunt, not your mother." They would not have hired a married woman, to say nothing of a woman with children.

Still, she and we were grateful for that job, because it put coal in the furnace and more white beans on the table. Day after day we ate those bland-tasting white beans—soaked for twenty-four hours and then cooked. Rarely, as a special treat, we would have meatloaf. Breakfast was cold scrambled eggs, which my mother would cook before she left for work in the morning.

My mother's new job and the house my grandfather provided also brought us the Meyer sisters, from Valmeyer, across the river in Illinois. I can't remember their names, but the first sister came to live with us in 1935, just for room and board—her family was happy to have one less mouth to feed at their table. She made one more at our table, but she was there to look after us when we got home from school. The first Meyer sister was replaced by a second and then a third, as the elder left and a younger arrived. The second two made a little money, but not much. We didn't have much.

The house on Kingshighway was one in a long string of one-story houses on 25-foot lots, deeper than they were wide. Coal was delivered and dumped on the street in front of the house; we had to shovel those large chunks of coal down the coal chute. It would have cost $2 more to have the coal distributor put it down the chute. I learned how to shovel coal down the chute and into the furnace not long after I learned to read.

The ice man also made deliveries, as ice was needed every few days for the ice box. Getting a sliver of ice to suck on from the ice man, when he delivered his 25-, 50-, 75-, or 100-pound blocks of ice, was a treat we looked forward to. The ice man knew how much ice to bring from his truck by reading a sign placed in our window showing how many pounds of ice we needed.

My father returned when we had been living in the Kingshighway house for a few years. I would help him with the chores, like shoveling coal and going to the store to buy him Muriel cigars for 5¢ apiece. I sometimes went with him to paint houses on weekends. My father also pushed me into my first selling experience. When I was about 11, he baked two dozen cupcakes, arranged them in a cardboard tray, and sent me into the neighborhood to sell them for 5¢ each. Instructed not to return until they were all sold, I did just that, bringing back $1.20 a few hours later.

One Thanksgiving time, when I was in the fifth or sixth grade, my teacher asked all the students to bring canned goods to school for the needy. I don't think I brought anything for the food drive because we didn't have anything to spare. At the conclusion of the drive, the teacher said, "If anyone knows of a family who needs food, let me know." I walked right up to her after class and said, "We do." She drove me home with a box of canned goods from the collection. My father thought that was a great coup. I would have been embarrassed to tears in his shoes, but he thought it was wonderful. He took the box into the house and picked out the items we would use. He put the rest back in the box and sent me to the store to exchange them.

When my father lost his job selling paint at Sears (accused, probably justly, of selling paint on the side), he got a job running an automobile glass repair business. I would sometimes accompany him to the repair shop at 21st and Pine, and even learned how to install window glass in a car. The owner of that automobile window installation business was named Carl Gissler. His wife's family owned some apartment buildings, and Mr. Gissler offered my father a job as maintenance man in one of them, the building at Kingsbury and Clara.

From our basement apartment there, we looked out of windows that were only half above ground. I helped my father with his maintenance duties by replacing burned-out light bulbs in the building, loading coal into the furnace hopper, and picking up trash.

When I was in the seventh or eighth grade at Hamilton School, my teacher seated the students in her classroom in order from those receiving the highest scores down to the lowest. At that age, I certainly didn't want to be singled out as the smartest one around, so I managed to screw up just enough to get down to the third or fourth seat.

I went to the Mt. Calvary Lutheran Church every Sunday with my mother. The church was important to her. She had few friends and didn't do much besides work, attend to her children, and go to church. At the appropriate age, I went to confirmation classes, two afternoons a week one year and three afternoons a week the next year. I would ride my bicycle to the church to listen to Reverend Jesse, a nice old man who counseled us that in order to go to heaven, you had to be Lutheran ... and preferably Missouri Synod.

It was a sin to pray in another church, according to Reverend Jesse. I suppose it would have been a sin to pray in a synagogue too, but the Catholics were more the enemy for him. I asked questions like, "What about all the people who lived in the world before Luther?" And, "What about all the people in Africa right now that nobody's ever gotten to?" I memorized what I was supposed to from the Catechism and was confirmed, but the only answer I ever got to my questions was, "Well, you've got to have faith." It didn't do much for my appreciation of the Missouri Synod Lutheran Church.

Reverend Jesse's efforts were more successful where my brother Bob was concerned—one of the many ways we were different. Unlike me, Bob always struggled in school. I believe now that his difficulty reading was dyslexia, but, at the time, I couldn't attach a name to it. I just knew that I was asked to help him with his reading. He would look at a word. I would say that the word was "bad." He would say it looked like "dab" to him. I did my best, but I was no reading teacher.

My memories of my sister Joan as a little girl are mainly of going to her dance recitals. Mom, with admiration for Shirley Temple, had Joan dancing from the time she was three or four years old. Bob and I were commanded to sit quietly through her dance lessons and recitals.

My mother never owned a car, nor did she know how to drive. She used public transportation to get to work, and I used my bicycle to get everywhere I needed to go, whether it was confirmation classes or Boy Scout troop meetings. My mother made sure I joined the Boy Scouts. I remember a jamboree for which we studied Indians (today we would refer to Native Americans), built a teepee and totem pole, and danced around an imaginary campfire. Another time we studied skiing and built a ski slide eight feet tall, coated with wax to make it slippery.

The Boy Scouts also gave me my first experience away from home and family. I spent two weeks at Boy Scout Camp two summers in a row. One of those years, I remember, my mother packed a nice fancy lunch for me in a brown paper bag to take on the trip to camp. I set it on the bumper of the van I was helping to load. Later, when I got hungry, I realized that was where I had left it. I felt so bad because food was too precious to waste.

One of the things I had to do as a Boy Scout was take a 14-mile hike—from the camp to the local town. I wrote the following account of the journey when I returned.

> Calvin Miller and I took a hike from Irondale Boy Scout Reservation to Bismark, Missouri (7 miles) and then we hiked back (a total of 14 miles). The hike was over a dirt road, covered with rocks. The main landmark was a granite pile near a granite quarry. We saw a mashed rabbit, evidently run over by a car, and a mashed snake which probably met with the same mishap. We left camp about 6:30 in the evening and we got to Bismark at about 10:00 in the evening. We got the postmaster's signature in the morning, after sleeping on the community church lawn. We left Bismark at 6:00 in the morning and returned to camp at 9:30.

Those 14 miles seemed very long back then. It would be the equivalent of three rounds of golf today.

Boy Scout camp had all kinds of crazy competitions. One involved a tripod with a pie pan hanging from it. The pie pan could be raised and lowered. The contest was to see who could kick the pie pan at the highest point. I won because of one decided advantage—my feet were the longest! When I was going into eighth grade, my mother took me to buy shoes. The shoe salesman measured my foot and informed my mother that I needed a size 13 shoe, the biggest size they had in the store. My mother looked at the shoe salesman in dismay, worried about

what would happen the following year when I was certain to
need shoes again, and asked, "Do they make them any bigger?"
Fortunately, a size 13 was as large as my feet would get, and we
never had to try to find larger shoes.

My career in the Boy Scouts lasted as long as it took to
become a Star Scout. By then, I was old enough that girls
seemed a lot more interesting than merit badges.

Other than Boy Scout camp those two summers, I had few
other occasions to be away from home. Sometimes, we would
go across the river to Illinois to visit Grandma and Grandpa
Meinert's families on their farms. Grandpa Meinert drove us
there. I remember that we ate well and used the outhouses.
When I realized how much physical labor was required, I
concluded that I would rather not live on a farm. I don't think
we ever stayed overnight, but it was a good day's journey by the
time we drove there, had lunch, and came home.

The other family trip—maybe we went twice—was to visit
my father's family in Wilkes-Barre, Pennsylvania. My father
drove us there in one of the series of used cars he had when I was
young—I remember a Pierce-Arrow and a Packard. In Wilkes-
Barre, I recall meeting my cousins and my grandmother—my
paternal grandfather had died about the time I was born. Most
of my father's family worked in coal mines, and the most
prosperous member of the family sold insurance. The sad thing
is that I have no lasting impressions of my father's mother. I can
picture her as she looked in Wilkes-Barre and when she came
to visit us later at the apartment at Kingsbury and Clara, but I
can't recall a single meaningful conversation with her.

Other than those visits to relatives, the only trip I remember
from my years growing up was the time my mother used her
vacation from J. I. Case to take Bob, Joan, and me to the
Chicago World's Fair. The Fair opened in 1935, so our trip,
without my father, would have taken place in 1936 or so. The
thing that impressed me the most was taking a boat across the

lake to Benton Harbor, Michigan, where there was something called the House of David.

The House of David, originally founded as a colony for Christian Israelites, was famous for its baseball team. The players all had beards and long hair, even the team players who were not members of the colony. At the time, I was aware only of their baseball team—watching them play the game was memorable. However big and impressive the Chicago World's Fair was, that trip across Lake Michigan and the House of David are what stuck in my mind.

St. Louis was a baseball city when I was growing up. We had no professional basketball or football teams, but we had two major league baseball teams—the Cardinals and the Browns. My friends and I all knew the names of the players on both teams and their histories. Both teams played at Sportsman's Park (which has since been demolished). I had the good fortune to work as an usher at Sportsman's Park for the Cardinal's World Series games in 1942 and 1943, because I had been working for a firm that supplied ushers to events throughout the city during my high school years. It was great to be paid to be at those World Series games! But even when I wasn't ushering at baseball games, I could walk down the streets of my neighborhood and never miss a play. In those days before air conditioning and portable pocket radios, everyone had their windows open and their radios blaring while they listened to the games.

Baseball was also a game to be played. My friends and I played ball across the street from our apartment in the Vacant Lot. It never had any other name—it was just the Vacant Lot. We played football there, as well as baseball and corkball, a game played with a broomstick-sized bat and a soft one-inch ball (or a bottle cap). Corkball was a game peculiar to St. Louis.

I wasn't really much of an athlete, but I played a fair amount of basketball in a church league. I was tall enough to have an advantage for a time. In high school, I wasn't good enough to be on the track team, so I became the manager. However, staying off the field wasn't as safe as it might have seemed. I once dropped a shot put on my foot and broke my toe.

Roller skating, another favorite activity, also proved to carry a risk of injury. Near our apartment was a big sports facility called the Winter Garden. It was used for ice skating in the winter and roller skating in the summer. When I fell and broke my arm, my father happened to be around at the time, and he figured out that the incident was probably worth a few dollars. He never told me how much he settled for. I just knew that *he* got the money and *I* had the broken arm.

My first paying job was in the seventh grade when a friend and card-playing buddy of my father's, Vern Fry, who owned an independent grocery store on DeBaliviere, hired my brother Bob and me to shell peas. The two of us sat and shelled peas for six hours. I think we earned 50¢ apiece, although it could have been 50¢ between the two of us. After that, I was always trying to find something to do to earn money.

One summer, I worked at a lumberyard. My job was to count the pieces of lumber as they were unloaded from the railroad car. As I watched the men unloading the lumber, I realized that they worked at a constant rate. I figured out how many pieces they could unload in an hour, kept track of how long they worked, and estimated the amount of lumber. My estimates were accurate and I had time to do other things. My employer was happy with me and I continued to work there during the school year on weekends.

When it came to high school, I had a choice. For reasons known only to them, the St. Louis Board of Education maintained two high schools only a couple of blocks apart— Blewett and Soldan. I chose Blewett because a lot of my friends were going there. The school was named for Benjamin Blewett, a former superintendent of the St. Louis school system. Its chief claim to fame was that the building had formerly been the Smith Academy, where T. S. Eliot had gone to school.

It had probably been Blewett High School for 20 years when I entered as a freshman and, in the history of the school to that point, only one graduate had gone to an Ivy League School. He had gone to Columbia about seven or eight years before I would go off to Yale.

During high school, I spent a lot of time at my desk doing my homework and developed the habit of getting things done on time or early. I was also always trying to figure out how to do something more or better than others did it. The habit paid off during the competition for the editor-in-chief's job for my high-school yearbook. A few people showed up to apply for the job, but I was the only one who came in with an 8½-by-11-inch mock-up, showing how it could be organized.

One Sunday afternoon—December 7, 1941 to be exact—as I sat in my room doing my homework with the radio on, the program I was listening to was interrupted by a special news report. I went to my mother to report that the Japanese had bombed Pearl Harbor. "What does that mean?" she asked. "I think it means we're at war," I told her. I was 14 and thought that there was no chance the country would still be at war when I turned 18.

In high school, I tried to do everything, and the list of activities next to my name in my senior yearbook includes so many that I can't remember precisely what some of them were. Some stand out, though. Throughout my years at Blewett, I was on or ran the student council. By my senior year, I got bored and started to wonder what the student governments were like in the other high schools around St. Louis. Somehow I managed to get support for a city-wide student council meeting—the first that anyone remembered. All the leaders of the various student councils around the city gathered at Blewett.

The biggest surprise for me was to understand, for the first time, that two of the city's 10 high schools were black high schools—Sumner and Vashon. The student leaders who came from those high schools were just as impressive as the white kids that came from all the others. Some of them even lived in the same neighborhoods as the rest of us, but they had to go across town to Sumner or Vashon. It was my first experience with racial segregation. It dawned on me that while there were a few blacks in our neighborhood, I had never seen a black person in school or at church.

While I was in high school, and while we were still living in the apartment at Kingsbury and Clara owned by Carl Gissler's family, I worked in Gissler's law office for a time. He had me filing and doing other administrative work in his office, and I continued to work there after my father left home again. One day he offered to take me out to lunch. We went over to the restaurant at Famous-Barr, the department store. I looked at the menu and saw things I had never had before. I asked him what scallops were. Gissler said, "They're good." So a kid whose idea of a special meal was meatloaf and whose family never ate seafood had his first scallops that day. They *were* good!

In the summer of 1943, I had just turned 16 and was about to begin my senior year in high school. That was when I had my last conversation with my father.

Neither my father nor my mother had more than a year of high school education, which is not surprising given that he was born in 1899 and she in 1902. In other respects, however, they were polar opposites. My mother was a devout Lutheran who went to church every Sunday; my father never went to church. My mother had few friends outside our family; my father was gregarious. My mother held one job for all of her 25-plus years of working life; my father never held any one job for more than a few years. My mother lived with the cards she was dealt … my father kept shuffling the deck.

I never saw a show of affection or heard words of love between my parents. In many ways, I may have become the symbol of their drifting apart. My father's frequent absences served to focus my mother's attention and affection on her children. Her attention focused especially on me because I was the oldest, a good student, responsible, and the closest thing there was to the man of the house when my father was gone. I could always feel my mother's love, but I can't recall a single hug or word of love from my father. He had a sense of humor, but was an adult-oriented person. I obeyed more than loved him.

On a summer afternoon in 1943, my mother told me the news. My father was leaving the next day. He had been doing some work down in the Ozarks and had apparently met a woman he planned to marry—his reason for leaving my mother.

I thought carefully about what I would do, and finally went into the living room where he was sitting in his undershirt, reading the *Post-Dispatch*, then the evening paper. I had decided to put my words in the form of a question: "Why are you doing this to our family?" I asked. My father hardly looked up from his newspaper to respond, "I don't have to answer to the likes of you."

He left the next day. We never spoke again.

Things changed quickly. Because my father was no longer the maintenance man in the apartment building, we had to move. We found a two-flat a few blocks away at Kingsbury and Cabanne (5601 Cabanne), again with the help of Grandpa Meinert. It was a block or so away from the famous 5547 Kensington Avenue address in the musical *Meet Me in St. Louis* starring Judy Garland.

Shortly after my father left, his bills started coming in. My mother couldn't pay them, and she was told that the only way to get out from under them was to get divorced. She learned for the first time during the divorce process that my father had been married before and had two children in Pittsburgh. I remember her being terribly hurt when she learned about the previous marriage, but I don't remember her ever saying anything negative about my father.

I don't know how my mother found her divorce lawyer, Judge Mix (a cousin of Tom Mix, the cowboy movie star), but it was an important event for me. He seemed ancient to me at the time—he would have been 63 in 1943. He took an interest in me and talked to me about college. The most important advice he gave me was, "You only come this way once. Why don't you try for the best?" The best, according to Judge Mix, was his alma mater—he was a 1902 graduate of Yale University.

Impressed by Judge Mix, I applied to Yale, as well as to Washington University in St. Louis. The only way I was going to be able to go to college was if I got a scholarship, and I thought that it was unlikely I could get a scholarship to Yale. There was a scholarship to Washington University designated for a Blewett High School student, and I thought I would have a shot at getting that.

Part of the Yale application process involved an interview with a member of the local alumni association. Yale assigned me to a man named Sam Capen. Sam was the third generation of an insurance brokerage family from St. Louis, and he lived on an estate on a bluff overlooking the Missouri River. I was told later that Sam had left Yale after his second year. But Sam was so proud of having gone to Yale at all that he became active in the alumni association. When we met for my interview, he became intrigued with me. He supported my application to Yale and would continue to help me get summer jobs over the years, throughout my time at Yale, and later when I went to the Harvard Business School.

Yale accepted me for the class starting in June of 1944. Just as importantly, they were offering me a regional scholarship, which would cover tuition, books and some expenses. I would also be eligible for a "bursar's job," which would cover room and board. The prospect of going to Yale made me very different from my gang of friends. I refer to my friends as a gang because we tried to fashion ourselves as a gang. We invented secret signals and assigned ourselves numbers that we would use instead of names when we wanted to avoid identification. I was "Number Three."

It was mostly a nice group of kids, although one did end up going to jail. It turned out that the car he was driving us around in was stolen. I had had no idea! Each member of the gang stenciled the Greek letters Omega, Alpha, and Sigma on our jackets. We thought, incorrectly, that we were translating the English letters OAS, which stood for Order of the Athletic Supporter, not understanding that Omega was not an "O."

Shortly before I was to leave for college, my gang was standing on one side of the street exchanging insults with a rival gang across the street. Finally, one of my friends hurled what he thought was the ultimate challenge, "Well, you don't have anyone going to Yale!" It was the first time in my teenage years that my peers showed respect for rather than belittling academic achievement.

Because of that fateful skipping of third grade, I was now 17 as I was finishing high school. Had I been 18, I would have had to go directly into the service, as most of my classmates did. It helped that Yale was trying to maintain a civilian class and had to create one largely out of 17-year-olds. When the acceptance from Yale arrived in the mail, I rushed to get ready to leave home. My first semester would start in July since Yale was operating year-round.

I cringe now to look back at the speech I gave at my high school commencement, and wonder at the temerity of a 17-year-old addressing the topic, "Wisdom, the Key to Happiness." I had enough insight to distinguish between what my classmates and I had learned from textbooks or classroom lectures, and the kind of wisdom that relies on "common sense" and "the knowledge of how to live among our fellow men." I referred to life's obstacles still to be overcome and the role those would play in developing wisdom. I spent far too much time in the speech trying to reconcile the old axiom, "Ignorance is Bliss," with my chosen theme.

I would use different words today, but I still agree wholeheartedly with my youthful assertion that, "Man does not shun common sense or knowledge when given the chance to learn. This is a law of human nature." More than 60 years later, I am even more certain than I was then that curiosity—the passion to know and learn and grow—are what make us and keep us vital human beings. If we stop learning and growing, we stop living.

As I was graduating from Blewett High School during the second week of June, 1944, and getting ready to go off to Yale, U.S. troops were invading Normandy and being killed on Omaha Beach. I would be in New Haven before the Fourth of July, and felt happy and excited at the prospect of starting at Yale before I would be drafted. I was also hopeful that the war might end before I finished my second freshman semester at Christmas time.

CHAPTER 2

REASONABLY GOOD
AT A LOT OF THINGS

I boarded the Pennsylvania Railroad in St. Louis with two large suitcases containing almost everything I owned. In one of the suitcases were the double-breasted blue suit I had worn for my high school graduation—my only suit—and a pair of big thick-soled cordovan (red) shoes called Threadneedles—my only pair of non-sports shoes. Threadneedles were popular in St. Louis then but, like the rest of my clothes and their owner, they would be distinctly out of place at Yale.

The Pennsylvania Railroad took me to New York, where I knew I had to switch train lines. I was to take the subway from Penn Station to Grand Central Station, where I would catch the train to New Haven, Connecticut. The closest I had ever been to New Haven was Wilkes-Barre, Pennsylvania, where we had visited my father's family.

I had never been to New York before, and figured that, as long as I was there, I should see the skyscrapers. I climbed up out of the bowels of Penn Station—lugging my two big suitcases with me—took a "now I can say I've seen New York" look at the skyscrapers—and then lugged those suitcases back down the stairs to the subway and Grand Central Station. Next stop: New Haven.

On the advice of Judge Mix, I arrived several days early at Yale and Calhoun College, my freshman year residential college, to give myself a chance to find my way around. At that time, Yale was housing a naval V-12 program in the residential colleges and an Air Force training program on the Old Campus. Only three of the 10 colleges, Calhoun among them, were maintained as civilian colleges; the students housed there were either 4F's or those like me who had graduated from high school at 17 and had not yet been called up.

It was fascinating to be there when the military students were marching down the streets and singing songs to the cadence of their marching. Glenn Miller was a part of the Air Force program at Yale, and we could hear his band playing as we walked past their dining hall at lunchtime.

I shared a third floor walk-up with two roommates, one of whom was from a nearby Connecticut town and went home to see his mother every weekend. I didn't relate to him. The other, Robert Rogers from Memphis, Tennessee, was a nice guy. Even before my roommates arrived, however, I started to meet some of the other students at Yale. They were so impressive—their backgrounds, what they had done, how smart they were ... It was the first time in my life that I had to question my abilities. I started saying to myself, "You're not going to be as good as any of them in their special strength, but maybe there is a place in the world for someone who is reasonably good at a lot of things but not outstanding at any one."

My freshman "year" at Yale would be crammed between the Fourth of July and Christmas 1944. That was enough time to realize how ill-prepared I was academically. I had sailed through high school with virtually all "A"s, which was the level of performance I was accustomed to. At Yale, I took a European history course, although I had never studied European or world history in high school. There were so many dates and facts to learn that I only managed to get a

"D" in the course. Later, I got much smarter … at least about which courses I took.

Besides trying to adjust to the academic challenge of college-level work, I started to try to figure out what I was going to do when I entered the service. I would turn 18 in March 1945, and it didn't look as if my hope for an end to the war before Christmas would be realized, although the war was beginning to wind down. The draft was still in effect and I expected, like all young men of the day, to be drafted as soon as I reached my birthday.

I thought I was being smart and looked into the only officer training program that was still open—the Merchant Marine Cadet Corps with its Academy at Kings Point on Long Island, New York. The Navy's V-12 program had closed, as had the Army and Air Force officers' programs. Scores of my classmates were competing to get into the very few available spots in the Merchant Marine Cadet Corps. I worked hard at getting into the program, including having Sam Capen help me get a letter from my congressman.

I was the only one I knew who got into the program. Ironically, all those who were not accepted were drafted instead and were back at Yale in six months because the war ended. I outsmarted myself. I had made a 21-month commitment to the Merchant Marine and would be away from Yale for two years and three months.

Just before I left Yale in December 1944, I went to the headmaster at Calhoun and asked him what I should be reading while I was gone, because I felt the need to make up for my lack of academic preparation. He said to me, "Just read whatever you enjoy." He also suggested that I might be smart to keep my attendance at Yale to myself while in the Merchant Marine.

I returned to St. Louis to wait for my orders and got a job at the Scullin Steel Company. Working in the safety department, I handed out goggles and the security badges I was assigned to make. I developed the pictures for the badges in the darkroom—a wonderful place to work, I thought. I could doze off there from time to time.

In February, as the time for my departure grew closer, I received a touching send-off letter from the Yale Club of St. Louis, orchestrated by Sam Capen.

> We regret that because of your age, your college activities must necessarily be suspended for a short time, and we are sure that your accomplishments in the armed forces will be as great as your collegiate career. We hope that you will be able to return to university life very soon.

Very soon thereafter, the time came for me to report to Pass Christian, Mississippi, for basic training. Marching around in the summer heat of Pass Christian, we were dropping like flies. It was sweltering! There was one highlight. We got the weekend off for VJ (Victory over Japan) Day and went into New Orleans in our uniforms. On that weekend, civilians would offer to pay for whatever we ate or drank.

After basic training, the Merchant Marine program required a year at sea. On September 25, 1944, I was assigned to SS The Cottonwoods, an oil tanker on which construction had been completed exactly a month prior to my assignment. The Cottonwoods was 523.5 feet long and weighed 6,134 tons (net), very small by today's standards. The main engine had 7700 horsepower and the tanker could travel at a maximum speed of 18 knots.

I learned (and then forgot) all these facts because one of my cadet assignments aboard The Cottonwoods was to complete my Sea Project. This Sea Project was a self-study book which would have to be filled out and turned in when I reported to the Academy at Kings Point. Besides learning the location and function of every piece of equipment on the ship, I had to answer questions about safety procedures, navigation, crew responsibilities, and a host of other information regarding the management of a Merchant Marine vessel.

Sometimes the questions didn't relate directly to the operations and procedures on a tanker. But usually, common sense would serve—as in my answer to a question about walking under slings of cargo. "Although I have never been confronted with such a situation, I would say that this is an extremely unadvisable practice."

Some of the answers seemed rather obvious. For example, the question, "On what instrument do sailing vessels sound fog signals?" Answer: "On the fog horn." But others demanded more work as I calculated longitude, drew diagrams showing how to splice mooring lines, and learned all about the pumps and how to keep the ship balanced during loading and unloading.

On my first trip, we left Gulfport, Mississippi, took on our oil cargo in Mobile, Alabama, and headed for the Panama Canal and Hawaii. When we left the Panama Canal, the Pacific Ocean was like a piece of glass, the wake of the ship the only visible ripple. I could understand how the Pacific Ocean had earned its name.

Coming back through the Panama Canal on the return trip from Hawaii was not as peaceful, however. When we reached the Pacific entrance to the canal early one morning, the captain didn't want to call the crew because he would have had to pay them overtime. As the cadet on the ship, I wasn't entitled to receive overtime pay, which is why I was the one at the wheel as we entered the canal. The captain was on one wing of the wheelhouse and the pilot was on the other.

As we maneuvered at the canal entrance, one of them yelled, "Hard right!" At the same moment, the other yelled, "Hard left!" We backed into a buoy and seriously damaged the propeller. The damage caused the ship to shake like crazy whenever the propeller turned. So, before I had finished my first round trip on a tanker, I was part of an accident inquiry conducted by port officials.

Once the inquiry was behind us, we crept back to Galveston, Texas, for propeller repairs with only six aboard, including the cook. But we weren't quite there yet. Just off Galveston, we ran into fog. One of us had to ring a bell 10 seconds out of every two minutes (the bell, not the fog horn, mind you). Twenty-four hours later, the fog finally lifted, and we were able to finish limping into port in Galveston.

We stayed in Galveston awhile waiting to get back on the ship while the repairs were being made. We were there long enough that I was able to use the local library to supplement the collection of paperback books I had assembled. Reading "what I liked" spanned subjects from philosophy to every book Damon Runyan ever wrote. I also saw every movie that played in all five movie theaters in Galveston during that time, and even managed a quick trip up to St. Louis to see my mother. But instead of getting back on The Cottonwoods in Galveston, I received orders to report to Biloxi, Mississippi.

When my new tanker, The Choctaw Trail, was loaded with oil, we crossed the Atlantic to the Adriatic coast of Italy, unloading half of the oil at Bari and half in Ancona. The war had been over for less than a year, and I could see the bombed-out vestiges of the village that had been Ancona rising on a hillside. It was hard to distinguish a single standing building or wall.

While the oil was being unloaded, I could leave the ship. I would take cigarettes (free to crew on the ship), despite the fact that I didn't smoke, and trade them for money on shore. A kid came up to me once and offered me a better exchange rate than anybody else. I gave him a dollar. He gave me the lire he had shown me and ran away. He had the money folded in such a way that it looked like more than it was. Big, smart American college student … outwitted.

After we had unloaded the oil in Italy, we proceeded into the Arabian Sea to Bahrain to pick up more oil. That meant going through the Suez Canal. We were in Bahrain in early 1946 and were ordered to take the oil to Okinawa and Japan. I had my 19th birthday in the China Sea in the middle of a typhoon.

When we arrived in Okinawa, I got very bold. Although I did not have the authority to do so, I signed out a jeep from the local Army installation and drove around. My cadet uniform made me look like an officer. Okinawa was just like Ancona— absolutely devastated. I think by then there were no longer any Japanese soldiers hidden in the caves, but I was aware of the stories of U.S. forces who had used flame-throwers against the enemy who had hidden there. The same typhoon that had affected us in the China Sea had done still more damage to Okinawa. On top of the destruction wrought by the war, the typhoon had thrown a startling collection of ships up onto the beach.

While the captain of The Cottonwoods had been a nice guy, the captain of The Choctaw Trail turned out otherwise. One of the crew members was mute; he could hear, but never spoke. One night in Okinawa, the captain, who carried a gun, came back to the ship drunk, got mad because the mute wouldn't speak, and hit him over the head with the gun. The mute, whose name was Daniel Boone , was carted off to the hospital. The rest of the crew was ordered back on board and we went more than three miles out to sea so that the captain would be beyond the reach of the Coast Guard and the local authorities. He was never charged in the incident.

We went from Okinawa to Yokosuka, Tokyo's seaport, to unload the rest of our oil. We stayed there for a time and, when I was able to go into Tokyo, the Japanese were extremely deferential to their American conquerors. I rode the streetcars for free; people stepped aside when a uniformed American walked down the street. By the time I had seen some of Tokyo, it was time for me to head back to the Merchant Marine Academy at Kings Point, so I got a berth on a Liberty Ship coming back from Tokyo to Seattle. I had been around the world, but as anyone who has sailed an oil tanker knows, the places I saw were far from attractive.

My tour of duty in the Merchant Marine would be over in another six months or so. I had gotten through basic training and the mandatory 12 months on a ship; I could finally get back to more formal academic pursuits. I was co-editor of the *Cadence*, the Academy newspaper. Academic courses included Navigation, Spanish, English, and Economics. I had taken economics at Yale, so I was the class expert. It wasn't hard to do well at Kings Point, and my high academic standing meant that I got to wear a star on my sleeve and stay out two hours later than other cadets on Saturday nights.

At the time I joined the Merchant Marine, leaving Yale for more than two years seemed like a huge delay in my career, even if I was getting one semester's academic credit for that service. It was certainly a challenge to be around shipmates who used the "f" word between syllables. But despite its challenges, that maturing experience has made me an advocate for some type of national service for most if not all young people.

When at last my Merchant Marine service was up, I had a few months before a new semester would start at Yale. I needed some civilian clothes so I got a job at Boyd's, a men's department store in downtown St. Louis, because I could get a discount by working there. I made friends with another employee in the store, a jazz trumpeter named Fred Schiller, a bright guy coming out of the service just as I was, who would end up being a professor at Princeton. We dated a pair of friends and had a great time while we waited for a new term to begin.

My first semester back at Yale, I had a choice of living in a Quonset hut, where the school was transitioning returning servicemen, or in one of the residential colleges. Calhoun, where I had lived as a freshman, was already filled, but I chose the residential college option and was assigned to Saybrook. I met my new roommates then. The first of the three was Ted Heckel from Massapequa, Long Island, who would be best man at my wedding several years later. The two Bobs were Bob Coulson, from Marblehead, Massachusetts—intercollegiate sailing champion, and future lawyer and head of the American Arbitration Association—and Bob Lawler, from Dover, New Hampshire, who would become a physician, like his father.

Bob Coulson wore a leather jacket and drove a convertible with his sailboat upside down over the top. We took a picture of him in his leather jacket, needing a shave and looking completely disheveled, and ran him for the Class Council as a kind of a joke. He won in a landslide. During our senior year, he entered the Boston Marathon for the heck of it. We got together bets that he wouldn't be able to finish the race and had a pool of about $50. Then we thought, "What if he cheats?" We figured he would finish but take three days to do it. So we decided he had to finish before the judges went home. He actually finished the race in 4½ hours. The judges had gone home, but we gave Bob the $50 anyway.

My academic performance improved over my freshman year. I had taken some Spanish at the Merchant Marine Academy. I took first-year Spanish at Yale. I received a score of 100 on every exam that term and expected a final grade in the course of a perfect 100. When my grades came and I received a 95 in the course, I went to see the young Ph.D. candidate who had taught the course. "But I got everything perfect in the class," I objected. "Yes, you did," he said, "but I'm not allowed to give anyone a 100."

I majored in economics and I remember one particular professor I considered to be the brightest person I had come across up to that point in my life. I just *knew* that if he and I could run the country, we could do a better job than anyone else. It took my later experience in the Air Force, seeing a very large organization being inadequately managed, to realize that there are some institutions too large for human beings at the top to make all the decisions. That experience would turn me into an advocate of delegation and decentralization.

Later, when I got to Jewel, I would come to think of a store as the size of organization people could put their arms around and manage. Still, while I was at Yale, I admired the genius of this "new era" economist and thought William Buckley, who sat in the seat behind me in the class, was absurdly conservative when he objected to much of what the professor said. He really gave that professor a hard time. Buckley, in his college days, was every bit as articulate as he showed himself to be later in life.

At one point, while I was an officer of WYBC, the radio station at Yale, and Buckley was editor of the *Yale Daily News*, we held a debate over which was the most important medium for delivering the news. Buckley argued for print media; I argued for radio. It was a lively debate, although it all boiled down to whether you wanted news fast or whether you wanted it in depth.

I spent considerable time at WYBC, including as an announcer and disc jockey. When it came time for the election for president of the station, I was very disappointed when I lost. I had spent more time and accomplished more for the station than the person who was elected president, but as I found out from talking to others, it made a difference to be a member of a fraternity. He was; I was not.

I couldn't begin to afford to belong to a fraternity (a place to eat at Yale, not a residence), but I would sometimes go with my roommate, Ted, to his fraternity house to watch Milton Berle and the *Texaco Star Theater* on Tuesday nights. Still, losing that election to become president of the station and taking on the role of vice president of public relations instead was hard to take. I vowed that I would figure out a way in the future not to be excluded from a role where club membership was a factor in getting where I wanted to be.

Many of those at Yale in the late 1940s were there on the G.I. Bill. Those who had served in the Merchant Marine were not eligible for the G.I. Bill, but I wasn't concerned when I returned. I believed that Yale would continue to honor the scholarship I had had during my freshman year, which indeed they did. My scholarship was greater than the amount of my tuition, and I could actually go to the Bursar's Office to withdraw money! I also had a series of student jobs, called Bursar's jobs.

My first such job was in the library at Calhoun College. Other than a brief interruption every few hours when someone came in to study or to ask for a book, I could spend the time studying. My next job was in the Bursar's Office itself. Miss Hackett, the woman in the Bursar's Office who made all of the student job assignments, liked me, and I got first choice of the jobs that came through the office. I stayed around at Thanksgiving and spring vacation to work when most of the other students went home. I worked with the grounds crew washing squash courts one time, but the most lucrative of the Bursar's jobs was the coat check concession for proms. I attended the prom one year but otherwise I was there managing the checking of coats, not dancing.

Most summers, I went back to St. Louis to work. One summer, Sam Capen got me a job in the J. C. Penney warehouse in the long underwear section. On the résumé I prepared a few years later, my job title reads "Inventory Control." That's a fancy way of saying I was a stock boy. The reality was that I had to pick and pack store orders for long underwear, as stores ordered in late summer for their winter stock. I can still smell the awful wooly odor of all those pairs of long underwear.

Another summer, Sam tried to help me get a job at the local radio station, since I had become so involved with the station at Yale. When my announcer tryout was less than successful, Sam offered me a job cutting grass and building retaining walls on his estate overlooking the Missouri River. He even gave me the use of a car to get back and forth from Cabanne Avenue. I discovered something new about myself that summer when I got out of the city and started to cut grass. I had hay fever!

My need to earn money every summer, however, did not permit hay fever or other forms of discomfort to interfere. The summer after my junior year at Yale, a group of classmates talked about going to Wyoming to work as "roustabouts" in the oil fields. I thought it sounded great and decided to go with them. We arrived there without any firm job offers, but the Ohio Oil Company took all of us on. They sent three of our group to one oil field and me to another field thirty miles south of Cody, between Cody and Thermopolis.

I remember arriving there on a Friday. When they put me to work the next day, the sun was blazing down and it hadn't rained in God knows how long. The ground was hard. The men handed me a pick and shovel and said, "Dig a hole here." Several hours later when they came back, I hadn't dug much of a hole. The work was terribly hard, but the pay was twice what I could have earned back in St. Louis—$1.625 an hour. With scholarships, my summer jobs, and the Bursar's jobs during the school year, I was able to leave Yale only $1,500 in debt.

The oil field work didn't get any easier after that first day. Being a "college boy" earned me the same level of esteem awarded the prize drunk in the roustabout crew. The oil field crew decided that the drunk and I should deal with all of the oil leaks, the dirtiest job in the oil field. When an underground pipe leaked, which happened regularly, the black oil would start bubbling up to the top of the ground, mixing with the dirt. It was like trying to dig glue. It was very difficult to pull the shovel out once it was in the muck. But I eventually learned how to get the shovel out and how to patch a leak in an underground oil pipe.

Weekends provided a welcome respite from the exhausting oil field work. I learned that I could get to Yellowstone Park, despite the fact that it was a good 50 miles away. I always hitchhiked and never had a problem. I remember an Amish family picking me up once and giving me a ride. In the park was the Canyon Lodge, where lots of college girls worked. They could always feed and house me, and so I would go up there every weekend until I got to know Yellowstone Park pretty well. I saw Old Faithful so many times that I decided one time to show how unimpressed I was by the eruption of the geyser on its once-every-55-minute cycle. I stood around with the tourists reading a *Life* magazine. Everyone else "oohed" and "aahed" as Old Faithful went up, but I just kept reading.

I majored in economics at Yale because I thought it would help me get a job when I graduated. We were always talking about an economist named Schumpeter and his theories, which I am sure I have never had to refer to since. But I also took courses in statistics, which I dearly loved, and in marketing research and anything that leaned toward marketing and advertising.

During my senior year, I had the option of writing a thesis in place of two courses. I looked around and found some materials in the library related to advertising for Arrow shirts. I supplemented that information with first-hand reports I was able to obtain when I went to New York to visit Young and Rubicam, the ad agency that had created the campaign. My thesis, "The Use of Market Research in the Development of Advertising," included lots of exhibits that were more interesting than most of the things people were writing about in their theses; I earned the highest possible mark on it.

In June 1949, Yale awarded me an A.B. degree cum laude (why they used A.B. when most colleges award a B.A., I never figured out). My mother came to my graduation—on a bus— and that's how we went home. But it was a very proud time. I graduated with high orations—Yale's term for honors. My less-than-stellar performance during my freshman year prevented me from being elected to Phi Beta Kappa (daughter Betsy would be the first in the family to achieve that distinction).

My greatest Yale regret is that I didn't have the voice to participate in any of Yale's famous singing groups. I enjoyed listening to them and would have loved participating even more, but a Whiffenpoof I was not. Still, my academic achievement level had picked up, and I was hitting my stride as I looked forward to graduate school.

While I loved going to school and thought that graduate school would be the ideal next step, I did go on some job interviews as a college senior. I talked to the American Thread Company. I could have sold spools of thread ... if they had offered me a job. I was interviewed by the Vicks Company— an incredible interview. The interviewer held a product in his hand, tossed it at me, and barked out, "Here, catch this! How would you sell it?" That was the nature of the interview. No job offer came from Vicks, either.

I might have gone back to St. Louis with an introduction from my brother Bob to Southwestern Bell, but the fact of the matter was that I really enjoyed going to school. I looked around and tried to find a law school that would offer me the kind of scholarship I would need to be able to attend, investigating both Yale and Harvard. I didn't find anyone offering a scholarship for law school.

A squib in one Sunday *New York Times* that year produced another major turning point in my life. Not more than two inches long, it read, "Donald K. David, dean of the Harvard Business School, announces that anyone who is admitted will not be prohibited from attending for lack of finances." "Hey," I thought, "that's for me."

I hadn't really thought about business school before, but was intrigued by Harvard and started to think that it might be the place for someone who wasn't spectacularly good at any single thing, but reasonably good at a lot of things.

I went to Boston for my interviews that spring with my roommate Bob Coulson, when he ran in the Boston Marathon.

The dean of admissions interviewed me by silence. I would say something. He would nod his head and wait for me to say something else. It was a difficult interview, and I wasn't sure how I had done. The other interview was with a recent graduate and we hit if off, shot the breeze, and seemed very compatible. I later learned that the dean of admissions gave me a glowing report, and the recent graduate found me rather average.

As part of the interview, I asked the dean to tell me about scholarships. He said, "You don't understand. The problem here is getting in." My immediate response was, "Come on. The problem all my life hasn't been getting in—it's been how to pay for it!" He took that well, I guess. In fact, I was admitted to the Harvard Business School and granted a full scholarship, plus extra funds to cover personal expenses. It would prove to be exactly the kind of place for a person who was "reasonably good at a lot of things."

CHAPTER 3

GO GET ME SOME OF THEM

My initiation at the Harvard Business School proceeded more smoothly than my early days at Yale. I had a far better feel for the academic requirements, and understood the value of taking a clear, defensible position and avoiding meandering in class and written work. I took courses in marketing that reinforced my belief that I would probably pursue a career in advertising. Courses in management and organizational behavior were fun.

Soon after my classes started at the Business School, I realized that, for the first time in my life, I was in an academic environment where my judgment and ability to think were being tested, rather than my memory. It was a startling and delightful discovery. At the end of the first term, I went to the basement of Baker Library to retrieve my grades with less worry than I had had as a freshman at Yale, but was still shocked by what I saw.

Harvard had five grade alternatives: Fail, Low Pass, Pass, High Pass, and Distinction. Distinctions were few and far between; we had been soberly advised by professors and second-year students alike that receiving one in a term would be a matter of extraordinary pride, and that more than one or two was rare. I opened my grade report—five Distinctions and one High Pass!

I tried for as long as I could to avoid revealing my grades to my classmates, but eventually I gave in to the badgering of my roommates, and soon my record was the talk of the school.

In addition to impressing those around me, my academic record brought requests for tutoring from fellow students, despite the fact that tutoring wasn't technically allowed. I could earn $4 per hour tutoring—more than twice the highest wage I had ever been paid—for all the hours I could spare.

The first request came from a student who should rightfully have been in music school rather than business school. His father owned the Westinghouse distributorship in England, and had sent his son to the U.S. to prepare him to take over the business. Sadly, the son was completely uninterested and unqualified. I agreed to help him, starting with the financial control and accounting courses he was having such difficulty with.

I started with a lesson on how to use a slide rule, the business-student standard method of computation at the time. My tutee had a question as I began my explanation: "What are all those marks on there?" "Well," I said, "it's a lot like a regular ruler." "Oh," he said. "How does a regular ruler work?" Nevertheless, he developed to the point where he managed to eke out a Low Pass in that course. Ultimately, he flunked out. I can only hope he went on to a far more satisfying and successful career in music or some other endeavor free of rulers.

I took on another tutoring assignment during my second year when Dean of Students Les Rollins came to me and explained that there was someone in the class behind me who could use some help, and would be willing to pay for tutoring. Of course, I couldn't tell him that I was already tutoring, since I thought it was not allowed, so I said yes to tutoring Amory Houghton. It turned out that Amo didn't need tutoring as much as reassurance, and we became good friends. Twenty-one years later, Amo, by then the latest in several generations of Houghtons to become CEO of Corning Glass following family tradition, would invite me to join Corning's board of directors.

My scholarship at Harvard covered tuition and some additional money for expenses, but there was a need for more. My last "name" scholarship at Yale had been the Calvin K. Kazanjian scholarship (through a foundation overseen by the leaders of the Peter Paul Candy Company). I had gotten to know the staff at the foundation, and went out to the company's headquarters in Naugatuck, Connecticut, to thank them for their help at Yale. After thanking them, I then asked them for a scholarship to help me through business school. That was before I knew the amount of the scholarship I would receive from Harvard. While it was out-of-pattern for them, they very kindly gave me an additional $500 for each of my two years of business school.

I also continued to work hard during the school year. When I arrived at Harvard, I managed to get a job as the campus representative for one of the local laundries. I really worked the campus and developed a very profitable business; I also had the chance to meet virtually everyone in the process. By my second year, I had so many things going on, I wasn't sure I could manage to keep up with the laundry. I didn't want to lose the franchise, however, so I hired someone else to work for me as a salesman.

The classmate I hired to help me was the son of the general manager of the Cadillac division of General Motors. I was a long way from Blewett High School now.

One thing that followed me from Blewett High School days was my desire to do *everything*. I have never had a busier schedule than I had at Harvard. I ran for student government and was elected to represent my section, ending up serving as an officer of the council.

One of the most time-consuming activities was my involvement in the *Harbus News*, the school newspaper. I

suppose Bill Buckley might have told me that I had proved the
point he made in our debate at Yale, had he been at Harvard;
but I was too busy working my way up to president of the paper
to consider that. The newspaper actually made money, which
the officers then divided up. I may have gotten $1,000 or so
from the *Harbus News* in addition to the experience of running
an organization with a bottom line and a regular deadline.

The first issue of the *Harbus News* that appeared when I was
a student was issued on September 21, 1949. A Page 3 article
reported on "Regional Scholarships Awarded to 43 Men from
28 States," among them only one from Missouri: Donald S.
Perkins of 5601 Cabanne Avenue in St. Louis. The following
announcement also appeared:

> **All Welcome at 'Harbus' Callout Next Tuesday**
> The Harbus News, student newspaper of the Business School,
> invites all students interested in newspaper activities to attend
> its annual "Callout Party" in the Student Club on Tuesday,
> September 27 at 5 p.m. Practically unlimited supplies of beer,
> Cokes, and other refreshments will be supplied by the staff
> of the Harbus to all past, present, and future members of the
> fourth estate.

Of course, I was interested in more than the "practically
unlimited supplies of beer" when I showed up for the meeting
on that September Tuesday. During my years at Harvard,
according to the newspaper: Stanley Marcus revealed the
formula of his success; the *Harvard Business Review* published
an early issue ("144 pages of timely, challenging reading");
the Misses Littlefield offered their services as professional
typists; Barnard Gals offered a tongue-in-cheek response to the
B-School Men's "Call of the Wild" contest; the school received
gifts from R.H. Macy, Corning Glass, Rockefeller, the Cabot
family and Kresge; and, last but not least, the faculty predicted
that 1950 would be as good as 1949.

While there was a regular article in the *Harbus News* for "Business Wives," the May 2, 1951, issue also reported that the "Radcliffe Management Program Parallels Training at B-School." Women were not yet full-fledged students, but the idea was beginning to surface in some imaginations. It was only a matter of time.

The last issue of my second year is dated May 17, 1951. It looks forward to Commencement on June 21 of that year, a ceremony I would miss, but for a very good reason.

One of the people I met early in my time at the Business School was Arnie Berlin. Arnie, who had graduated the year before I started, was in charge of the report-writing course that first-year MBA students were required to take, Elements of Administration—General. I liked Arnie, and knew that he could help me understand the Harvard Business School culture—and, if there was one, the "school solution" (the key to being successful at Harvard). We became good friends.

Arnie also had a car, and I was very agreeable when he offered to get me a date. He was going out with a girl at Wellesley who had a friend named Phyllis Babb. That made things a little complicated, since I had dated another girl from Wellesley when I was a senior at Yale. I wasn't really interested in that girl, but I found out how quickly word could get around the Wellesley campus, especially when the young man in question had bragging rights to five Distinctions and a High Pass at the Business School.

In January 1950, Arnie and I drove to Wellesley to pick up our dates and then headed toward the South Shore of Boston. Arnie had been in the Navy and could go to the naval air station in Cohasset, where we could eat and drink inexpensively. Phyllis and I talked and danced that night. The band played a song I liked but had never heard before, so I asked her what it was called. When she told me it was called "Bewitched, Bothered and Bewildered," I didn't believe her. I thought nobody would give a song that name!

She talked about theater, about the theater group at Wellesley called Barnswallows, and about growing up on the North Shore of Chicago. I learned that her father, Jervis J. Babb, worked for Johnson Wax in Racine, Wisconsin. We had only been out on a couple of dates when I read in the lead article of the business section of the *New York Times* that Phyllis's father had been named president of Lever Brothers. More importantly, I thought she was pretty and shapely and smelled good!

Phyllis would come over to Harvard on Saturdays to help me type my reports. There wasn't time for much else before she had to return to Wellesley because of what were called parietal hours. Wellesley women had to be back in their dorms by 11 P.M. on weekends and by 10 on weeknights, and a man could never go above the first floor of their dormitories. I got to know Phyllis' friends and became an adopted part of that circle.

She and I were thoroughly enjoying each other during our time together between that first date and June, when Phyllis would graduate from Wellesley and I would go home to St. Louis for the summer. Phyllis planned to work in the summer theater program at Wellesley and spend time with her parents in New York, where they had just moved for her father's job at Lever Brothers. She would then travel to Evanston, Illinois, in the fall as she had been accepted in the theater program at Northwestern, while I would be returning to Harvard for my second year.

That summer, Sam Capen came through once again. Since he knew I was interested in advertising, he introduced me to the Gardner Advertising Agency in St. Louis. I saved my money all summer so that I could buy my one and only summer suit for $35. Every day I rode the Hodiamont streetcar to and from downtown St. Louis. One day, I caught the loose weave of my suit pants as I got on the street car and it made a small hole. From then on, I crossed my legs to hide it when I was sitting.

In addition to learning about advertising, I also got to know about absence making the heart grow fonder. Phyllis and I corresponded regularly—not quite a letter a day—but easily every other day, full of loving words and thoughts.

Phyllis and I had arranged that I would go back to Boston via New York at the end of the summer. I arrived in Manhattan and went to the Pierre Hotel where the Babbs were living while their apartment at River House was being renovated. I found Phyllis alone when I got there, one of the few times we were permitted to be together by ourselves. Or rather I should say that she was alone except for the window washer outside the window. If the window washer had been able to hear, he would have heard me say, in quick succession, "Hello. How are you? Give me a kiss. Will you marry me?"

I stayed at the YMCA on the west side of Central Park on that visit, and I would walk through the park since I couldn't afford taxis to go to the Pierre to see Phyllis, wiping my dusty shoes off on the back of my pants just before I arrived. The Babbs took us to dinner one night at the Pierre. At the end of dinner, I could see the bill—it was more than the cost of my $35 suit, which I had worked all summer to buy! Another evening, the Babbs arranged for us to go to the theater to see *South Pacific* with Mary Martin, my first Broadway show.

My future mother-in-law Ruth was concerned about my background early on; I didn't have the kind of pedigree she would have wanted for the husband of her only child. It took until sometime into our first few years of marriage for her to conclude that I was as able as Phyllis's father, and warmer. Jerry Babb, like my own father, never showed or expressed affection. He never hugged Phyllis, much less me. Sometimes she would kiss him on the cheek or the forehead. While her father's reserve could have made Phyllis draw closer to her mother, the opposite occurred. At critical times in Phyllis's early life, her mother had had to undergo electric shock treatment for psychiatric problems.

In contrast, Phyllis considered her father perfect. I saw Jerry Babb as strong, competitive, self-centered, tough to live with, and very tough to work for. I had the utmost respect for him, but there was only one way in which I wanted to be like him … to emulate his business achievements.

All too soon, my brief summer visit with Phyllis and her family in New York was over and I was on the train to Boston. Phyllis headed west to Chicago to enter the program at Northwestern. I don't think she was there more than three weeks before she concluded that she didn't like it at all. She came back to Boston, moved in with five other girls in a three-bedroom apartment on Beacon Street, and got a job at Wellesley.

Phyllis wanted to get married right away, but I was busier than I had ever been. Between running the *Harbus News*, tutoring, and making sure I kept up my own grade record, I knew I couldn't do justice to marriage as well. I had a head start on graduating first in my class and I wanted to finish that way. Needless to say, however, the route between Beacon Street and Harvard was well-traveled that year.

There was one more obstacle to overcome, however, before a wedding could be planned. I had to ask Jerry Babb for Phyllis's hand. We were spending the weekend with the Babbs in Duxbury, Massachusetts, at the home of Ed and Beth Ryer (Ruth and Beth were sisters). Every time I started to speak to Jerry Babb that weekend, someone would come into the room and interrupt. I felt like I had landed in a Marx Brothers comedy.

During our last evening, Phyllis and I were playing gin rummy with the Babbs and, as it got later, Phyllis's father yawned and announced that he was going to bed. Panicked that I might not accomplish what I had come to do that weekend, I asked, "Are you too tired to talk?" "Yes," he answered, further raising my anxiety in typical Jerry Babb fashion before adding, "but I'm not too tired to listen."

Phyllis and I waited until my classes and exams were over, but I attended my wedding on June 9, 1951, and missed my graduation from Harvard to go on our honeymoon. We were married in Duxbury at St. John's Episcopal Church, celebrated at a reception at the Ryers', and honeymooned in a cottage on the Bass River in South Yarmouth on Cape Cod that a Ryer family friend invited us to use.

In 2004, the wedding of Scotia Ryer, Ed and Beth Ryer's granddaughter, was an occasion for nostalgia that would be difficult to match. Ten days short of 53 years after I married Phyllis, Scotia was married … in St. John's Episcopal Church … with a reception at the old Ryer home at 245 Washington Street in Duxbury.

While I had expected to be launching my business career upon graduating from the Business School, world events began to interfere during my second year. In the winter of 1950, I wrote a piece for the *Harvard Business School Bulletin* with the following description of the changing tenor of conversations among my fellow students:

> It is really remarkable to observe the extent to which the Business School student body revolves around word-of-mouth communication. It is only necessary to sit in Cowie Hall or stand in Baker Library showing the least indication of being awake to attract some harbinger of "the" news of the moment, whether it be fact or rumor or some increasingly confused combination of the two. So it is relatively easy to feel the pulse of the student body; it requires no more than (1) being awake; and (2) listening.
>
> For the last few years, the pulse could most easily be described, content-wise, as a combination of studies and their variations, and women and their variations. The latter is true of the married and the single, for the conversations seem to turn just as easily to marital problems as to problems of trying to arrange to have marital problems.
>
> But with the advent of the Korean unpleasantness, the pattern has been changed. Although there may be some doubt whether it replaced studies or women as the leading topic of

conversation, there can be no question that the Korean war, and particularly its draft and reserve developments, is now on top.

The abundance of articles on the fighting, the draft, and the reserve call-ups has led to an uncommon amount of attention to the first pages of the *Times* and the *Tribune*, even among those who don't take Manufacturing. But since there isn't any necessary correlation between information and conversation, even when facts grow scarce, there is rumor to take over.

The Korean War was, needless to say, not just a rumor. The country was at war again and I was astounded to learn that my Merchant Marine Service, which had fulfilled my military service requirement in World War II, no longer provided an exemption under the Korean War draft law. I was so angry! I knew enough law to know that there isn't supposed to be such a thing as a retroactive law, and this was nothing if not retroactive as far as I was concerned.

Several of us who had served in the Merchant Marine in World War II wrote eloquent objections to members of Congress—on paper bags because we thought that would make them stand out from all the other mail the congressmen received. But the draft law Congress passed for the Korean War didn't provide the exemption for Merchant Marine service that the World War II law had. I would have to serve again.

There were numerous Army, Air Force, and Navy brass in my class at Harvard. Bob Northwood was a friend and a captain in the Navy at the time. After graduating from the Business School, Bob became an admiral and led the Naval Supply Corps. So I decided to try for the officer's program in the Navy. For some reason, the day I went for my physical exam, my blood pressure was too high and the Navy turned me down. I talked to another friend who was in the Air Force and he arranged for me to get a direct commission. My blood pressure was all right. I was going into the Air Force; I just didn't know when.

When we returned from our honeymoon, Phyllis and I moved in with her mother and father at River House in New York and I accepted an offer from McCann Erickson, a large Madison Avenue advertising firm, to be a trainee at a salary of $5,000 a year. "I'm going to have to go into the Air Force," I warned them. "Come for 30 days or 30 years," was their response. "We'll take you for as long as we can get you."

From June until November, my time at McCann Erickson was like a survey course in advertising, getting my hands dirty in each of the departments of the agency and being part of a group that was mentored by the senior people there. In fact, I later used that training program as a model for the one I developed at Jewel.

The most important thing I learned there, though, was that I didn't want to be in the advertising business. Much of my negative reaction was to the culture of an agency. The women who were account executives wore hats in the office to distinguish themselves from the women who had more menial jobs. Everyone went out to lunch and drank so they weren't worth a damn in the afternoon.

They were nice people, and I loved the creativity of the work, but the culture was uncomfortable and phony. They were communicating to the multitudes while feeling greatly superior to them. I also concluded that I would rather be at the mercy of a large group of consumers than the whim of one corporate advertising manager.

I recall being asked by a friend in New York at the time how it felt to be out of school and I replied that the biggest difference was that I now had cash in my pocket. At school, I could sign my name for anything except taking Phyllis out on a date. Even that didn't take much cash. We once spent an entire evening at Jake Wirth's in Boston spending $2—$1 for a serving of braunschweiger (the rye bread was free) and another $1 for two glasses of beer.

Living with the Babbs in New York, even temporarily, was a strain. It was then that I saw the evidence of the mental health problems from which my mother-in-law suffered. While we were sharing the River House apartment with them, she fell into one of her states where she simply stood by a window and refused to communicate with anyone. As he had done four times before, my father-in-law sent her to the hospital for electric shock therapy. She appeared to have recovered when she came back to River House, but Phyllis and I just wanted to get out of there.

Jerry Babb had a connection with the Metropolitan Life Insurance Company, owners of some relatively new buildings on the Lower East Side of Manhattan called Stuyvesant Town. We moved a couple of pieces of furniture into an apartment there, complementing them with orange-crate end tables and a bookcase I built out of bricks and planks of wood that I sawed and shellacked. I have to confess that I found the bricks at some building site, although I did buy the wood.

The week after we moved in, right at Thanksgiving time, my Air Force orders came. We put the bricks and wood boards in storage, along with anything else we couldn't fit into the Chevrolet Phyllis had been given in her senior year at Wellesley, and we headed for San Antonio, Texas, by way of St. Louis and a brief visit with my family.

We arrived at Lackland Air Force Base, near San Antonio, to find that my officer training group was somewhat unusual. The Air Force had closed down all its officer training programs, except for the women's training program, and I was one of 17 men attached to a group of 48 members of the Women Air Force. I was the only one of the group with any previous military experience, so I was appointed leader. I would march the group of men and women wherever we had to go around the base.

The Air Force didn't know what to do with the men during the physical training part of the program, so they told us we could go exercise however we wanted. There was a golf course on the base and Phyllis, with incredible luck, won me a set of golf clubs and a golf bag playing Bingo at the officers' club. So I played golf for my physical training in the Air Force.

Our "home" in San Antonio was the Victory Motel. Its chief attribute, as I recall, was an unpleasant and persistent infestation of cockroaches. It was only when we were moving out and pulled out a dresser drawer that we found, on the underside of a drawer, the nest of our unwanted company. We celebrated Christmas shortly after we arrived in Texas with great practicality. I gave Phyllis new tires for the Chevrolet, since we had ruined the old ones on the trip from New York. And she gave me a clock radio so we could get up in the morning. That was the extent of our Christmas presents that year.

According to my orders, we expected basic training at Lackland to be followed by an assignment in Waco, Texas. Suddenly, in its infinite wisdom, the Air Force changed its mind and several of us received new orders instructing us to report to Wright Patterson Air Force Base, in Ohio. The group of us who had been reassigned tried to figure out what had caused the change. We were all from the Harvard Business School, but not all of the Harvard graduates were going to Wright Patterson. It wasn't class ranking, it wasn't grades, it wasn't alphabetical or anything else we could figure out. But I was delighted.

Before we set of for Ohio, though, San Antonio had one hard lesson for us. When Phyllis miscarried what would have been our first child, a son, she and I were crushed. I had thought that having babies was automatic; it hadn't occurred to me that something could go wrong or that there could be difficulty in having children. We consoled ourselves with the doctors' reassurance that there was no reason for Phyllis not to get pregnant again right away, and we busied ourselves with the move to Ohio.

The mystery of the change in my orders was solved not long after we arrived at Wright Patterson. I went to a meeting of Harvard Business School alumni in Dayton, Ohio, and encountered one of my classmates, Colonel John Goodell. John was standing at the bar with General Rawlings, head of the Air Materiel Command headquartered at the base. (General Rawlings later left the Air Force and became the CEO of General Mills.) When I walked up to John, he turned to Rawlings and said, "General, this is Don Perkins. He's one of those guys I told you about."

Then the story came out. General Rawlings, like John, had gone to Harvard. When John had learned that a number of us whom he knew from Harvard were in the Air Force, he mentioned it to Rawlings. Rawlings's reaction was, "Well ... go get me some of them." John had gone through the list and checked off six people he knew. He had turned it in and the Air Force had rewritten our orders. It helped to be known at Harvard.

Phyllis's and my first home when we got to Ohio was a big old house in the town of Springfield; Wright Patterson was halfway between Springfield and Dayton, and either was a reasonable commute. The house was very cheap and run-down, but it was furnished. The highlight of those furnishings was a needlepoint moose in front of the fireplace. The moose invariably became the subject of conversation when our friends came over because it was cross-eyed.

But while the house had all the charms of the cross-eyed moose, it became obvious that it was not a suitable place for a family, and Phyllis was pregnant again. We managed to find an apartment in Dayton, at 1520 Gummer Street, took our furniture out of storage (including all those bricks and wooden planks that had become our traveling bookcase), and settled in to welcome Betsy (Elizabeth Baker Perkins), who was born January 10, 1953.

Life changes with a newborn, and our life was no exception. Ruth and Jerry Babb came to visit and I learned, as I told my friends, that having a baby lets you know where you stand. The grandparents would come to the door, walk right by me, and head for the baby.

As a second lieutenant, my Air Force assignment was in the Procurement Office, headed by Brigadier General Phillips Smith. General Smith had pulled together a group of senior consultants to review the procurement practices of the Air Force's major contractors. With cost-plus contracts, the Air Force had to live with the efficiency or the inefficiency of the military equipment contractors we worked with. Our office's motto was printed on the bottom of our letterhead: "More Air Force Per Dollar."

One of the Procurement Office consultants was Lewis Jones, former head of the National Association of Purchasing Agents (NAPA, later renamed the National Association of Purchasing Managers and now the Institute for Supply Management), a group probably best known for its regular economic outlook reports. Lew Jones loved that Procurement Office assignment. He had assembled a group of former NAPA presidents, so I worked with 20 or so different people who had been in procurement. I was responsible for organizing inspections of major contractors, going on the inspections, and then drafting the reports and the letters to the contractors, which would be signed by Lew Jones and General Smith.

Our inspections were essentially audits, and the contractors we audited—companies like General Electric, Pratt & Whitney, Curtis Wright, Boeing, and Western Electric—were required to respond. We could be very pointed in our recommendations and were undoubtedly a pain in the butt to those firms. Few companies we inspected had strong procurement departments and, in most cases, we would note the need to get better talent in the purchasing function.

We also invariably found that the companies were not doing much of a job inspecting the procurement practices of their sub-contractors because those costs were just a pass-through to the federal government. We even inspected some of the sub-contractors and asked direct contractors to put procurement monitoring programs of their own in place.

I enjoyed the travel and didn't mind being a pain to those big companies, but I was now 26. I was anxious to be done with the Air Force and to get on with my career and my life.

CHAPTER 4

THE LAST BUFFALO

I t was the summer of 1953. I knew I would be getting out of the Air Force in September, and it was time to apply the education and maturing experiences of two service stints to a business career. I had three criteria for deciding where I wanted to work.

First, I wanted to work in a consumer goods business, because that was what I thought was fun, and where my success would be based on attracting many customers. I was not interested in a business-to-business company which might be overly dependent on a single customer.

Second, I wanted to work in a company where I wouldn't get lost. I wanted experience at the point where the money came into the business, where I could really learn the business, but I didn't want to get forgotten in the process.

And third, I wanted to work in a well-managed business. I had confidence in my ability to think through problems and in what I had learned at Harvard, but I wanted to see what really good management looked like up close.

One of the obvious people for me to consult during my job search was my father-in-law, Jerry Babb. Phyllis and I were again visiting with her parents at the home of Ed and Beth Ryer in Duxbury, and my job hunt was a topic of conversation.

My father-in-law did me a great favor when he said, "First, I'm going to tell you something and then I'll be ready to answer your questions." His opening, in his usual brusque fashion, was, "There are three companies in the country you can't work for: Lever Brothers, because I won't hire you; and P&G and Colgate because, given our relationship, I don't think you should work for them. Now, what are your questions?"

As I explored a series of opportunities, I had attractive offers from Campbell Soup, General Foods (where I met the legendary Clarence Francis), General Mills, Scott Paper, and Pillsbury (where CEO Paul Gerot interviewed me). Campbell Soup offered me a job as assistant to the general manager of their Canadian affiliate, and gave me the highest salary offer of any that I received. Pillsbury offered me a territory in Iowa and said, "Of course, we'd watch you."

I received two rejection letters, both quite funny in retrospect. One was from the Wrigley Company. It said, "We've read your résumé and we're not sure you have the work ethic for our business." Ralston Purina wrote back and said, "Most of our successful people grew up on farms and we don't find that in your résumé."

While I was investigating consumer packaged goods manufacturers, another opportunity surfaced. At that time, Frank Lunding, effectively the chairman of the Jewel Tea Company although he didn't hold that specific title, was also a director and chairman of the executive committee at Lever Brothers. It is odd now to think that a grocer who originally came from North Dakota would end up as a director of Lever Brothers, especially when outside directors were so unusual at the time.

But there had been some major management missteps at Lever, precipitated by its CEO, Charles Luckman. Luckman's architectural taste in building Lever House on Park Avenue in New York City was admired. However, his imperial leadership, including designing the top floor of Lever House as his personal apartment, outweighed the good he had done. The Lever board had reacted by bringing in a crew of people with a Midwestern work ethic, including Jerry Babb as president and Frank Lunding as a board member.

There was a party in New York in connection with a Lever Brothers board meeting, which Frank Lunding naturally attended. At the party, Ruth Babb bragged about her son-in-law, who was looking for a job. She described me in such glowing terms that Frank Lunding said, "Oh, that's the kind of person I'm trying to get at Jewel." She had the perfect response: "You'll never get him."

Jewel Tea Company, as it was known at the time, had started as a home delivery service for coffee and tea, expanding its product line over time, but retaining the personal service and home delivery aspects of the business. The company had gone public in 1916, which had removed control from the founding family and ultimately created opportunity for people like me in the business. In 1932, Jewel Tea had acquired a group of stores in Chicago from Loblaw's (later the dominant grocery chain in Canada). So, there were two major parts to the business at the time—the routes and the food stores.

It turned out that Don Booz (son of Ed Booz, a founder of Booz Allen Hamilton), whom I had known at the Harvard Business School (where he had been a research professor and had been aware of my academic record), was head of human resources at Jewel. Don invited me to come to Chicago; I went to 135 South LaSalle Street where Frank Lunding had his office, apart from Jewel's day-to-day operations. The Home Shopping Service was headquartered in Barrington (a suburb about 40 miles northwest of Chicago), and the Jewel Food Stores were based at 3617 South Ashland in Chicago, where George Clements, president and chief operating officer, had his office.

I will always remember that first meeting with Lunding. I walked into his office knowing that Jewel was a coffee business.

When I was offered it, I said that I didn't drink coffee. So they served me tea. When I got back to Dayton, where we were living, a package arrived in the mail. In the package were a teapot, some Jewel tea bags, and a note that said, "We enjoyed your visit and hope you'll consider coming with Jewel." None of the other companies that were making me offers had shown quite that degree of personal attention.

Frank Lunding was a smart, highly principled lawyer from North Dakota by way of Georgetown Law School. He had been hired away from the Securities and Exchange Commission to be Jewel's general counsel, an unlikely beginning to a successful retail career. In 1944, Maurice Karker, who was CEO of Jewel, responded to the challenges of war-time retailing by throwing his hands up and moving to upstate New York to build a life-sustaining farm that would survive even if the rest of the world went to hell.

As Jewel's general counsel, Frank Lunding was one of those involved in a company meeting to decide how the business might survive, given war-time exigencies. Despite his lack of retail experience, Frank was the only one at that meeting anticipating Karker's retirement with any positive ideas about what to do—things like turning Jewel's manufacturing facilities over to war-time K-ration production and hiring women for the route sales force. Amidst his peers' pessimism, Lunding's positive approach won out, and, at the age of 37, he became Jewel's CEO.

Frank pushed Jewel in the constant search to improve operations to better serve customers—a characteristic that became the foundation for Jewel's way of doing business. He also had a dramatic influence on Jewel's approach to recruiting and keeping strong people. Frank attracted and supported good people, and understood how to organize a business around talents like George Clements's. When I met with Frank in 1953, he had delegated the running of the business to George to the point that he had moved his own office downtown and away from day-to-day operations.

Frank put Don Booz to work to get me to come to Jewel. When Don asked me what I would like to do, I started running through my criteria. "I would like to find out what happens in the business where the money comes in and not be lost in the process," I started. He said, "That's easy. We'll work out a program. You'll spend time working both in the route business and in the stores. And I'll stay in close touch with you all during that time."

Don then asked, "What did you earn in the Air Force?" As a first lieutenant, I was making $6,200 a year. He said, "Can you live on it?" I said, "Well, I've been living on it." And he said, "Good! That's what we'll pay you." It wasn't a bad wage at the time. I think the Campbell Soup offer was $300 higher, but that wasn't going to make the difference, as long as the job met my criteria.

Jewel was a consumer business; they'd proposed a plan to let me learn the business without getting lost, and I knew from Jerry Babb and from my own observations that it was a well-managed company. As Don Booz was describing Jewel, he told me, almost as an afterthought, that no one at Jewel owned any commercial real estate.

I did not appreciate the meaning of that remark until years later, when I watched competitors pick new store locations that "just happened" to be owned by company executives or their families. As Don Booz knew, however, this was an example of the integrity of Jewel's management. Furthermore, the founding families were out of the business soon after Jewel became a public company. By the time I joined Jewel, there had been over 30 years of professional management working for a diverse group of shareholders.

As Phyllis and I discussed it, we also liked the idea of being in Chicago, since the Babbs were in New York and my family was in St. Louis. We could see either one of them, but we weren't going to be neighbors. I accepted the offer to become a management trainee at Jewel.

Accepting the job at Jewel meant a move to the Chicago area for Phyllis, Betsy, and me. It was not easy to find a decent apartment right after the Korean War—there had been little building going on during the war years and even less building of apartments. Finally, we found an apartment on Tenth Street in Wilmette, but it wouldn't be available for several weeks. That meant I wouldn't be around for the move, something Phyllis didn't let me forget for a long time. In the interim, to save money, Phyllis and Betsy went to St. Louis to stay with my mother.

My first assignment as a Jewel trainee was to attend the school for route salesmen in Barrington. My record for that whole week of route salesman training was 99.9 percent. They gave me a card saying that this was the all-time record. With my MBA and a stellar record from route salesman training school in hand, I headed out to Oakland, California, to learn what the business was about and to see if I could prove myself. I would also have an opportunity to spend some time in the Houston branch following several weeks in Oakland.

Sending me to California had a purpose besides training. The routes were becoming a problem, although the California district was regarded as being among the best managed. While I was being trained and learning the business, I would also be reporting my observations and thoughts back to headquarters in a weekly letter to Don Booz. So, I left Phyllis and Betsy in St. Louis, knowing that it would be 10 weeks until I would see them, by which time they would have moved into our new apartment. I would be unfamiliar enough that Betsy greeted my return with screams—although we made up for it pretty fast.

As soon as I had arrived in California, Don started fulfilling his promise to keep in touch with me:

10/16/53—Don Booz to DSP—"Mort Summer had a discouraging collection of route men in for training today. We are making some progress toward the establishment of the new regional set-up… I will be looking forward to your first communiqué and I trust that the unshaded light bulb hanging from the center of your room is not too discouraging…"

They sent me to Oakland first, because it was one of the most profitable branches and the company's number-one salesman was there. He was doing almost three times as much business as the average route salesmen. I remember riding with him; he just had incredible energy. He would run and never wasted any time. He also had a good residential area north of San Jose.

My letters were full of my observations about all aspects of the business, including talent (which I found abundant in the Oakland district); the development and promotion of route men (I learned and was concerned by the fact that a promotion from route man to assistant manager reduced a person's earnings); paperwork; mail order; promotional programs; products; and many other topics.

10/17/53—DSP to Don Booz: "Tuna (Van Camp's) at 29¢ a can is selling like 5¢ dimes. The route men are fighting over the little Lee has left in stock…" "Graham crackers on the West coast should be called graham crumbs…. They are not making a good name for Jewel…" "You don't have to call on many homes to see that Gene Autry guns are not selling like they once did…"

Communicating my observations to Don Booz and feeling that at least I had an ear back in Barrington helped a lot during those lonely 10 weeks.

While the content of my reports seemed of great interest to him, I discovered early on that Don was having a hard time with my handwriting:

10/23/53—Don Booz to DSP: "One other suggestion I might make; if it is more convenient for you to find a public stenographer and dictate your weekly report, I hope you will feel free to do so and include it in your expense account."

10/31/53—DSP to Don Booz: "I have acquired a typewriter..."

With a typewriter and more observations, my letters could go into even more depth on some of the issues I encountered. And, according to Don, the letters were well received:

11/9/53—Don Booz to DSP: "We appreciated your note of November 2 very much and your longer observations on October 31, which were full of ideas that Frank Spreyer [vice president of the route business] is anxious to put into effect ... You might be interested to know that Mr. Clements has been added to the reading list of those who see your letters. They are wonderful. Keep them coming."

George Clements was particularly interested in my observations. The route business was in trouble. In fact, Clements had moved his office to Barrington for that very reason—to be nearer that part of the Jewel operation. I remember when I came back from my training in the field in Oakland and Houston, he wanted to spend time with me. We spent a couple of hours talking about the business. I brought a fresh view of the routes that he wouldn't otherwise have had.

One behind-the-scenes reader of my letters to Don Booz was Bob Updegraff, one of Jewel's directors. I didn't know it at the time, but he reviewed the file of our correspondence that Don Booz collected in December of that year. He had "been wanting to have someone do just what (Perkins) had done—get out in the field and Live the Route Job." He liked the approach I had taken in my observations, saying, "One of the things I like best about his reports is that they are troubled but not cynical... It is so important to realize that people are problems to themselves and need to be treated with understanding and compassion, even when they disappoint us. It seems to me that is Don Perkins's attitude."

Bob Updegraff would help me in many ways over the years, but perhaps one of the most enduring was his recommendation that I try to always have "a calm temperament expectant of good." I was so impressed with that thought that I had Jewel's advertising department put it on a placard that I have kept posted near my desk ever since. It was initially a recommendation rather than a description, but I would like to think it has also become the latter. (Author-daughter Betsy discovered where Bob Updegraff picked up the expression. Charles William Eliot, president of Harvard from 1869 to 1909, attributed his good health and strong mind at age 88 to "a calm temperament expectant of good.")

Lee Laughlin, the first branch manager I worked with, didn't think much of college boys; no trainee had ever been sent out to California to work the routes before. It wasn't easy to convince Lee that I was serious about working hard, but I did and was rewarded (if that is the proper term) with the chance to run a route on my own. Lee assigned me to take over the branch's poorest performing route for two weeks.

A week later, I was exhausted but full of my experiences and wiser about what the life of a route man was all about.

11/15/53—DSP to Don Booz: "Well, I've just finished my first full week as a route man. And I have lots of calluses, not much sleep, and about $750 to show for it. The same book two weeks ago brought in $606. That's some increase but not enough. I'm still liable to be last in the branch. I'll never doubt anyone when they say that it takes time to build a good route."

It was very hard to take over a route in a strange neighborhood with five books of accounts (five days' worth of calls) for the week—10 for the entire two-week call cycle. And then there were the back calls if a customer wasn't home the first time. Back calls went well into the evening, even interrupting dinners. When I was riding with someone else who knew the territory, the houses and where to go, I could just follow him.

On my own I had to figure it out. I remember sitting looking in the rear view mirror of the truck at 6:30 one night when I still had 10 more back calls to make, thinking, "What the hell am I doing here?" And when I had finished my calls, in the evenings and on the weekends, I would have time to think and write. I summed it up early in my training, "If the Routes Division of Jewel ever wants a motto, I am going to suggest, 'We work from sun-up to sun-up!'"

I had one respite from work during my stay in Oakland. Toward the end of my time there, the Babbs were coming to San Francisco to visit with Bob McGowan, CEO of Safeway. It was part business and part friendship, so they invited me to come to a cocktail party and dinner. I guess I did have a sport coat, but I got off my route and took public transportation over to San Francisco, trying to polish my shoes on the way over. Once at the party, I kept being struck by the contrast between this fancy party in this fancy apartment, and the average American homes I had just left in Oakland.

In 1953, Jewel's route business was operating in 40 states. In the course of running a route in those first few months and then managing that part of the business several years later, I did a lot of riding on routes. I once figured out that I have been in 5,000 homes in this country. There aren't many people in the consumer goods business who can say that!

I did draw some conclusions about the average American home during my time on the routes. I thought most could use brooms and vacuum cleaners—and the desire to clean. The homes with motorcycles parked in the living room certainly needed more than that. It also seemed to me that the "off" button on the television set was used infrequently. The set was turned on in the morning and turned off at night (at least, I assume it was), but the television set was on all day.

Two homes I called on while I was running the route on my own stand out in my mind. One day, I drove up to the next address on my list and pulled out my call book to look at the account and the order. At the top of the account order sheet was an instruction: "Carry Room Freshener." Well, I went in and I understood what the previous route man meant. Between the dirty cat litter and the spoiled food, it was just awful. I guessed that my predecessor's routine had been to go in there and say, "Here, let me demonstrate this new air freshener." The route man never sold the air freshener at that home, but that demonstration spray got him through the visit.

Another day, I went into a home and started going through my basket of merchandise, following the routine I had learned. We carried a basket of products to show on every call. When I looked up, I realized that there were several women, not just one, walking around in bathrobes. Then I saw a sailor coming down the hall. Finally I said something about Mrs. So-and-So. The woman to whom I was presenting said, "Oh, she lives downstairs." Before I could pack up and go downstairs to find Mrs. So-and-So, another of the girls came in, sat down at the table and said, "Oh, is that a fruitcake?" When I replied, "Yeah," she said, "Do you think I could mail one? I want to send one to my mother." I said, "Absolutely." Then three or four of the other girls thought that sounded like a good idea, too.

All in all it was a pretty good call, even though I had mistakenly gone to the second floor of Mrs. So-and-So's house when I was supposed to be downstairs. I don't know anyone else who can say they've sold fruitcakes in a house of ill repute!

After my training on the routes, I now had an understanding (at least a much better one) of what was going on where the money came into the business. I had also learned some of the lore of Jewel, including stories about Frank Lunding's predecessor, Maurice Karker. During the Depression years, Karker had decided that it would be a fine thing to populate the fields around the company's Barrington headquarters with buffalo.

Later during World War II, to Karker's consternation, the pilots, taking off and landing at Glenview Naval Air Station, discovered the entertainment value of buzzing the buffalo. Karker would call up the air base commander and demand an end to the harassment of the Jewel buffalo. If the pilots got the message, however, the chance to stampede a herd of buffalo was too attractive—and soon the planes would be low over the fields again.

By the time I arrived at Jewel, both Karker and the buffalo were gone, but the stories remained. The buffalo seemed to me an apt metaphor for what I had learned on the routes, and I wrote this story:

A Fable
SHUFFLE OFF THE BUFFALO

Once upon a time, there was a rather easily influenced buyer who was visited by a hell of a good buffalo salesman. The buffalo salesman could sell buffalo like nobody's business. With no more than a brief pitch about how every housewife really wanted a buffalo or two and about what nice pets they would make, he sold the buyer 144 buffalo. The buffalo were delivered and warehoused on the company's spacious lawn until a promotional program could be developed to help move them.

The promotional program was developed, tried, and failed. In spite of clever copy on the company's sales flyer, the buffalo simply would not move. In fact, throughout the promotion, only one buffalo was sold—this to a lonely inmate of a state institution for former buffalo trainers. Had it not been for the company's spacious lawns, the buffalo would really have been a problem.

Then entered onto the scene a shy, clear-eyed youth who could sell anything. And he did. He went to 1,000 customers and told them how his family had had a pet buffalo for years and about the satisfaction it had given him. Yes, he admitted, he didn't like cats, dogs, pigs, or giraffes, but he did like buffalo. And, lo and behold, he sold 142 of them in 1,000 calls. He was a hero and was given a gold ring, a promotion, and an appropriate cut in pay.

But alas, one buffalo remained. A year or so after his compatriots had departed, the buffalo was still there. Finally, the company managed to trade the buffalo to an interior-decorator-buffalo-fancier who was long on black tile. The black tile was used to beautify the lobby of the company's office building.

MORAL: You haven't made any money until the last buffalo is sold.

When I had finished my training period in the routes, I spent a month in each of four Jewel grocery stores and got to know all of them pretty well. For the most part, it was a lot of fun, although it got pretty cold in the winter trimming lettuce and cabbages in the back room. One manager wanted to show me how to do a better job trimming lettuce. He cut himself and we had to take him to the emergency room. That wasn't much of a lesson.

My favorite memory of the store experience is of the last one I worked in—the Wilmette Jewel, which was then located on Lake Avenue. I was building what I thought would be the world's biggest Easter candy display. I looked up as I was working and saw Phyllis and my mother walking into the store. I had had no idea my mother was coming to visit, but I realized immediately what was happening. It was the week of my birthday and it was obvious that Phyllis had arranged to surprise me by bringing my mother from St. Louis to visit. As they came into the store, I was at the end of the entry aisle with my white apron on, building that candy display.

And my mother, who always was smiling, looked up, saw me in my apron and lost the smile on her face. I could tell she was thinking, "Yale and the Harvard Business School, and this is the best he can do…." As she took the next step, her smile was back. I know she was thinking, "Well, if this is the best he can do, I love him anyway."

CHAPTER 5

NOT JUST YOUR
AVERAGE TEA COMPANY

Wearing a white apron and building Easter candy displays, I reassured my mother, was not the goal—it was just part of the plan. Getting experience at the point where the money came into the business without getting lost in the organization was the way I wanted to learn, and it was a significant part of the reason I had chosen Jewel. Over the next nine years, between my birthday week in 1954 and my mother's death in 1963, her unfailing support and belief that my career need not be limited by our early struggles would be rewarded.

As I was completing my training program, I hoped that I would be assigned to the Jewel Food Stores because that was the growth part of the business. I confess that I was disappointed when I was assigned to the route business instead. The "routes" were officially the Jewel Home Shopping Service—the original Jewel Tea Company, founded shortly before the start of the 20th century. Jewel Tea had addressed the problems of obtaining freshly roasted coffee before the advent of vacuum packing technology. The "route" format was to call on each home on the route every two weeks, delivering the order placed during the previous call—including that freshly roasted coffee—and taking the order for the next trip. Adding staple groceries to the line was a natural extension.

Many home shopping service businesses in the early 1900s had offered premiums of general merchandise, much like the Green Stamps craze of 50 years later. Over the years, the "tea companies" started offering general merchandise for sale. By the time I joined the business, the Home Shopping Service had semiannual catalogs of 100-plus pages, and had become much more than a coffee business.

The heyday of Jewel's Home Shopping Service was during the Great Depression. High unemployment meant that good salesmen were plentiful, and a good salesman could always locate a housewife who had money. It may seem surprising that the business—a relatively high-cost, high-price method of retail distribution—thrived when economic times were worst. But good salesmanship and giving a premium to the customer in advance of her purchase combined to make the Jewel Tea Company one of the most successful companies in U.S. retailing in the 1930s.

At the same time, the Depression era also fostered the seeds of the route business's decline. An ordinance was passed in Green River, Wyoming, which required an advance invitation to knock on the door of a home. The protective effect of the law for local stores was apparent. Concerned that this signaled the beginning of the end for the Home Shopping Service, Jewel Tea management acquired a chain of unprofitable food stores in Chicago from Loblaw's, the Canadian grocery store chain.

Jewel's leadership was correct in making that investment, even if they made it for the wrong reasons. As threatening as the Green River Ordinance was, the Home Shopping Service was threatened by a stronger and more far-reaching cultural shift—women joining the workforce. The effect was clear—if women were not at home, the Home Shopping Service could not call on them.

Perhaps the biggest surprise of my career at Jewel came during my second year in the route business, when the head of merchandising was hired away by Justin Dart at Rexall to be one in Dart's series of would-be successors, and I was made head of merchandising for the Home Shopping Service. I had never been a buyer, but there I was, with 10 buyers reporting to me. I took an approach that turned out to work well and would stand me in good stead in later experiences. I went to each of the buyers and said, "If you're surprised about this, let me tell you no one could be more surprised than I am. What would you try to accomplish if you had my job?"

A perennial challenge in the route business was how to get the attention of the route salesman. We had a catalog, but the point of sale was the route salesman's aluminum basket—a foot wide and three feet long. The contents of the basket guided what the salesman presented to the customer. So the challenge was how to get the items we were selling into the basket.

We came up with very creative displays, including one I especially remember—a pop-up dress display that the salesman would pull out of the basket, unfold, and stand on the floor to display an actual dress. It helped sell an incredible number of sweater dresses the first time we tried it. We also discovered the magic of the word "new." We introduced 26 "new" grocery items every year, one for each two-week sales cycle.

As I was finding my way in the route business, Phyllis and I were anticipating an addition to our family. This pregnancy was proving not to be an easy one; Phyllis was bedridden for most of the last two months. Betsy had been born routinely, if late, but it was hard not to remember the earlier miscarriage. On February 10, 1955, I raced home from Barrington when Phyllis called to say she was in labor, and we were at Evanston Hospital a few minutes later. By the time I had registered her, all I had to do was follow the trail of her clothes to find her and baby Jerry (Jervis Babb Perkins) who had been in such a rush to be born. Even had they allowed fathers to be present in the delivery room in those days, I would not have made it in time. Our small apartment in Wilmette was now even more crowded.

It was also in 1955 that Grandpa Meinert died. With all the help he had been to our family, he was also a "papa is all" German father. When I went to St. Louis for the wake and funeral, I was surprised to hear my grandmother chatting away with my mother. I told her I had never heard her talk so much before! She said, "Well, when Grandpa was alive, I didn't have to." Until then, I had taken Grandma for granted. Not long after that, while I was driving her to church, our conversation went something like this:

> Don: You must enjoy seeing your friends at church.
> Grandma: Oh, all of my friends are dead.
> Don: Aren't you proud to have outlived them?
> Grandma (with a reprimand in her voice): Donald, I never thank God for letting me live so long, but since He has, I thank Him for leaving me with a clear mind.

Grandma, called Minnie by Grandpa and her friends (and recorded as Elizabeth in the family Bible), spread her wings in other ways after Grandpa died. When she was 92, I arranged a trip for her to visit us while we were vacationing in Florida. Before that, she had never been more than a day's drive from her St. Louis home or her nearby Illinois birthplace; we were concerned about how she would handle the trip.

We needn't have been concerned. She liked the airplane because being up in the air made her "feel closer to God" and the palm trees in Florida reminded her of "the palm trees that grew in the Holy Land where Jesus lived."

Our other visitors that spring included a group of Jerry's friends from Williams College, who encouraged Grandma to talk about her life at their age. She described the failure of the small-town Illinois general store that Grandpa Meinert had owned, and their move to the big city: St. Louis. "Wasn't that a scary experience?" one of Jerry's friends asked. "Oh no," Grandma answered. "I was just proud to show off my two beautiful daughters to more people. And besides," she added, "I was too busy running the boarding house where Grandpa and I provided room and board for street car conductors Grandpa worked with on his first job in St. Louis."

For Grandma, wastefulness was a sin and cleanliness was next to godliness. On one visit to her home after Grandpa died, I remember that we arrived earlier than expected and found her on her hands and knees scrubbing the 20 or so steps that led up to her front door, so that they would be clean for us to walk on. And we enjoyed the peach pie that she made from the peach tree she treasured in her back yard.

Grandma showed her strength and independence when she decided to move from her daughter Elsie's house to live with my brother Bob and his family when she was in her 90s. It seems that Grandma had worn out her welcome at Elsie's, and the unpleasantness prompted her to ask Bob and Marilyn if she could move in with them and their seven children. Her influence on the family is something they still talk about. Grandma lived to be 100 days short of her 100th birthday.

The same year that Grandpa died, my mother read of my father's death in the newspaper. I had not seen him since that last conversation when he had told me, "I don't have to answer to the likes of you." My brother Bob and his wife Marilyn had visited him, though, and reported that he had a daughter from this third marriage who looked a lot like our sister Joan when she was young. He lived in Flint, Michigan, and worked for General Motors, but he had come back to St. Louis for reasons never explained. He was crossing the street near the airport when he was struck by a car and killed.

Hearing of my father's death reminded me of how angry I had been—angry mostly at what he had done to our family, especially my mother. I had been angry, too, that he never seemed to take any responsibility for his three children. After he left, he had never sent any money, nor acknowledged a birthday or any achievement, not even my going to Yale. My mother only learned that he was back in St. Louis and about his death because she happened to read about it in a newspaper.

But I put my father's failure to acknowledge family achievements behind me as I continued to thrive at Jewel. After running the merchandising group in the Home Shopping Service for a couple of years, I finally had my chance to move over to the food stores where I became chief of staff to the vice president of food store operations. I wrote his speeches for him, ran the safety department, ran store planning, and did a number of odd things that nobody else wanted to do. It was George Clements's way of getting me indoctrinated in the food store business after my initial exposure to the route business.

George Clements, then president of Jewel, was tall (six feet three inches) and lanky. With only one year of college, he was nonetheless extremely bright and strategic in his thinking. When I joined Jewel, he thought I was over-educated and he doubted my ability to influence people in such a down-to-earth business as Jewel. I had known from day one that winning his support would be the most difficult and the most important determinant of my career at Jewel. When he asked me, one day in the early 1960s, "How do we get some more talent like you into the business?" I knew I had succeeded in winning over a man I genuinely admired.

Phyllis and I welcomed our third child while I was in the midst of my indoctrination into the food store side of Jewel's business. Susan's arrival (Susan Sheldon Perkins) on April 11, 1958 occasioned a move to a new home a few miles from the apartment we had been living in—our first house at 2100 Drury

Lane in Northfield. We would live there until 1965 when the five Perkinses would move to Winnetka and the home I have enjoyed ever since.

Another surprise in my career at Jewel came in 1959, when I had been with the company for six years. Seemingly out of the blue, I was appointed to the board of Jewel's venture with Grand Bazaar (GB), a Belgian retailer based in Antwerp—Jewel's first international experience. It was particularly surprising because I was not an officer of Jewel.

The genesis of the Jewel-GB venture was a change in Belgium's retail laws in the 1950s. Traditionally, the laws had required separate stores for produce, meat, and dry groceries. Belgium then had one retail outlet for every 20 people in the country, making it "the land of shopkeepers." The only retail companies with general food experience in the country were the department stores, because they had been allowed to have full-fledged departmentalized food stores within their department stores. When the laws that protected small shopkeepers started to change, Maurice Cauwe, the CEO of GB and a thought leader in European retailing, sent one of his young staff, Freddie Bienfait, to the U.S. to look for potential partners with supermarket experience.

Freddie, who had an MBA from Columbia, visited the Harvard Business School among other contacts. The Harvard professors he met with suggested two companies they thought might be interested—Stop & Shop, a regional New England supermarket chain, and Jewel. These were the two supermarket chains that had been most active at Harvard. Jewel was indeed interested—Frank Lunding had been concerned about Jewel's being limited to the Chicago market—and Freddie Beinfait's inquiry led to Jewel's investment and ownership of about one third of Supermarché GB.

Jewel and GB each appointed six people to the board. I was one of the six from Jewel, although I had had nothing to do with the investigation or creation of the venture. When the board assembled, the six representatives were paired off, chairman with chairman and on down the line. The two "young kids"—Jacques Dopchie, a nephew of Cauwe and COO at the time, and I—were paired together. When Maurice Cauwe and Jacques would come to visit, Cauwe stayed with the Clementses and Jacques came to our home. That was the beginning of a warm and wonderful friendship. Jacques and I got a kick out of the fact that we shared the same March birthday. Our families exchanged visits and children for language and cultural experiences over the years.

GB and Jewel built supermarkets in Belgium; and then, later, hypermarkets, restaurants, and specialty stores. It gave me many opportunities to visit stores in Belgium and elsewhere in Europe, observing ideas that we could apply back in the U.S. I remember one trip there during which we visited every one of the GB stores that had been built at the time—about 20—in all parts of Belgium. Of course, it was the equivalent of visiting 20 stores in Rhode Island. Most U.S. supermarket operations thought their industry was so advanced that little was to be learned elsewhere. How wrong they were was brought home repeatedly over the years as I watched the changes and creativity of the European retail industry.

One Saturday in 1960, just about seven years after I had joined Jewel, George Clements asked me to meet him at his office. Fred Woerthwein, district manager for a group of food stores, including the Lake Avenue store where I had worked as a trainee, was also called in. I didn't know what to expect, being asked to come in on a Saturday, and I facetiously told Phyllis that I was probably going to be fired. George told Fred and me that we were both to become vice presidents; I was being named vice president of growth, planning and development; and Fred would be vice president of store operations.

In that Saturday meeting, George told me, "I want you to think about where the business should go, but there's one specific question I want you to have in the front of your mind. How can we sell more general merchandise without screwing up our food reputation?" Sales of general merchandise in the stores had been increasing at a very fast rate. Even so, other companies around the country were arguably doing a better job than we were at selling general merchandise.

One of our problems was that we had many 10,000 or 15,000-square-foot stores, and the more general merchandise we added, the more it interfered with our presentation of traditional food items. So I began to ponder the question and talked to a lot of people in and outside the business. One suggestion that surfaced was that we should be looking at drug stores.

As I explored the drug store business, one of the people I talked to was Bob Patrick, then the buyer for general merchandise and candy in the food stores. I asked him what he knew about drug store chains. "I don't know much about them," Bob said, "but there's one that I hear just 'chews up' merchandise. It's called Osco." That comment ultimately led to Jewel's acquisition of Osco. As I worked closely to bring the Jewel and Osco businesses together, the president of Osco, a wonderful man named Paul Stratton, started calling me "Mr. Josco"—a melding of Jewel and Osco—which I considered to be highly complimentary.

The leaders of the original Osco organization liked small town "country" stores. They would fill those Osco country stores full of merchandise, undersell everyone else, and pay the store manager a base yearly salary of $25,000. Many of those store managers, however, made six-figure bonuses which were calculated annually at inventory time. Inventories were the managers' focus, because they determined what the profit of the business had been and what the bonuses would be. That affinity for country stores meant that the traditional Osco management initially wanted no part of Chicago, so we started what we called "Chicago Osco" as a separate business, taking a handful of people out of the original Osco.

One of the things we observed as we started running both drug stores and grocery stores was a surprisingly common pattern of shopping. It seems obvious today, but it was far from conventional wisdom at the time. We realized we could build traffic by having the two stores, Jewel and Osco, together in one location. When the concept of connecting the two arose, everyone was so indoctrinated in the separation between Jewel and Osco that the initial stores maintained a physical separation. The first three Osco stores we opened in Chicago were what we referred to as "side-by-sides."

The first Jewel-Osco side-by-side on South Archer Avenue in Chicago was the site of my greatest market research experience. I was there with Max Harnden, who had succeeded Paul Stratton as president of Osco. Max, a very conservative man, resisted changing anything about the way Osco stores were run. He and I were visiting these new side-by-side Jewel and Osco stores as they were opening, when a heavyset bohemian woman came up to us and said, "Are you part of management?" "Yes," we said. "Well," she said, "these are two wonderful stores. But would you answer just one question for me?" We smiled and said, "We'll sure try." And she literally said, "Who put that fuckin' wall between these two stores?"

We had talked about doing something like combining food and drugs in a single store, but we had gotten all wound up in jurisdictional and operating problems. Jewel was unionized; Osco wasn't. Who would have the paper products? Who would have the baby products—departments that were common to both stores? And could anyone run a store that was a combination? There were lots of internal arguments, but that woman's reaction even got to Max Harnden. From then on, we built combination stores—the first one in Highland Park, one of Chicago's northern suburbs. Jewel really did pioneer the so-called combination store and it all started with George Clements asking the right question—how we could sell more general merchandise without screwing up food sales—and one honest if foul-mouthed shopper.

If my most memorable market research experience was somewhat informal, it didn't diminish the importance of more formal market research in the business. Jewel's market research was conducted by the firm started by Leo Shapiro, an outstanding talent. Leo and his firm developed an index for key consumer measures—our price reputation, our produce reputation, our meat reputation, etc. And then he added a wonderful question that summed it all up: "Which store appreciates you the most?"

Many of Jewel's innovations were driven by our sense of responsibility to our customers. As we expressed it in the 1971 Jewel annual report, "We will strive to fulfill our role as the purchasing agent for our customers, and we will continue to search for opportunities to help our customers make better buying decisions." That statement underscored our conviction that we were purchasing agents for our customers, not sales agents for our suppliers. Generic products, Miracle Prices, private label products, shops within a store, and home economists were Jewel innovations in our search for value for our customers. Opening stores on Sundays (not a popular action in all neighborhoods at the beginning) and fighting with the butcher's union to keep meat counters open on Sundays were ways we worked to be there whenever and wherever customers wanted to buy groceries or drugs.

Jewel pioneered generic products by being the first in the U.S. to put good-quality products in plain boxes with the generic word for the product in stencil-style black lettering on the front of the package. During the Carter presidency, inflation had reached double digits and escalating grocery prices were a major irritant to homemakers. A group within Jewel Food Stores created a whole new line of value-oriented products with less expensive packaging and no marketing expense. Grade A peas had to be the same size and color. Generic peas had the same nutritional value, but varied in size and color ... and cost much less. Planters peanuts were whole and consistent. Generic peanuts of the same nutritional quality, but with mostly broken pieces and a generic label, could be sold for just half the price. Detergent without perfume could be sold for less, as well.

In category after category, Jewel gave its customers a choice—familiar national or store-branded products or generic products with the same intrinsic quality, but without the frills and the cost. One of the best lessons I learned from Jewel's generic products program was the benefit of youth in the organization. As I reflected on the program's success, I realized that no one responsible for the program's creation or introduction had been as old as 40.

Later Tom Stemberg, who was a trainee at Star Markets (a Boston-based supermarket chain acquired by Jewel) after he graduated from Harvard Business School, would build on his experience implementing generic groceries at Star Markets to found Staples. I remember when he sent me the business plan for Staples, I read it and told him it was a fine plan but that I wouldn't encourage anyone to invest in it until he could tell who was going to operate the business. Tom was a brilliant visionary, but needed tough-minded operators around him. He has done that very successfully. When I went back to my 50th Harvard Business School reunion, Tom brought together 17 Staples people in the Boston area whom I had known from Star or Brigham's (the ice cream/candy store and restaurant business Jewel acquired along with Star Markets). One had even started in the route business! It was an incredible evening.

At times it took great fortitude and restraint to sustain our commitment to deliver real value to consumers. S&H Green Stamps had appeared in the late 1940s and Jewel was the only sizeable grocery chain in the nation that did not offer them or their equivalent. Many in the company thought we were missing the boat. We actually had stamps printed and a subsidiary company set up to distribute and process them, in case we needed to implement the program. But we were not going to offer savings stamps just because everyone else did—and we were growing without them. We realized that what consumers were really buying with trading stamps was 98¢ of groceries and 2¢ worth of as-yet-unselected general merchandise.

With that 2¢, we could do something that no one else could—reduce prices significantly. We determined that a 20 percent increase in business would allow us to significantly lower our prices. Intrigued, we tested a program we called "Miracle Prices" in Rockford, Illinois, a city about halfway between Chicago and the Mississippi River. When the program worked and we rolled it out, all the other chains were so dependent on trading stamps that they could not afford to match our lower prices. We achieved the volume increase we needed.

We thought discount department stores were another way to offer value to consumers, as shoppers throughout the country showed that they were ready for them. We started our own chain of discount stores, called Turn*Style, experimenting in the real marketplace from the ground up. We began with one store in Racine, Wisconsin, at a location that had been an outdoor movie theater. Outdoor movie theaters were going out of style, and the properties could accommodate a 100,000-square-foot store and four times that amount of space for parking.

When we brought the concept to Chicago, Turn*Style was a big hit. My biggest mistake was misjudging how many Turn*Styles could be put in Chicago. We thought the market would support a dozen or so. We could have put 50 of them in Chicago, but we didn't figure that out. Stupidly, we went out to Omaha and Indianapolis to expand instead. In the Chicago area, we put a Jewel store next to the Turn*Style to help build traffic.

It became clear that if we started Turn*Style-Jewel Food stores in a place where we didn't already have a strong food reputation, it didn't work nearly as well. Unfortunately, our failure to saturate the Chicago market drew other discount department stores into the area, including Venture and Kmart. Jewel would later sell the Turn*Style stores to Venture, which in turn would succumb to stronger competition from Target, Kmart, and eventually Wal-Mart.

One important aspect of selling the Turn*Style stores was that Venture didn't want to buy the dozen or so outlying stores—in places like the Quad Cities and Omaha and Indianapolis—and we had to close them. When we made that decision, we called in Joe Jannotta, Jewel's retired Human Resources leader. Joe, whose great grandfather was one of the founders of Jewel, had come to Jewel in 1954 when he was discharged from the Navy. He had worked on the routes for a while but ended up where he should have been—doing personnel work.

Joe was always a good listener, and when I became president and then chairman, he served as a true HR ombudsman for me. He would keep track of all the MBAs we hired in our corporate sponsorship program. He could tell me how they were feeling and who I needed to talk to; he would give me a heads-up if we were about to lose someone. Although Joe had left Jewel, we called him in to ask for his help with the Turn*Style situation. He took on the assignment as a consultant. We wanted everyone taken care of; we even wanted the part-timers to have help finding other jobs. Joe proceeded to do just that, in thorough fashion. Neither Wes Christopherson (by this time president of Jewel) nor I as chairman had even one call or letter from anyone saying that they were mistreated or weren't helped following those store closings.

Years later, Joe would take that experience to join Bud Bray in founding Jannotta-Bray, an outplacement firm based on the same human concern Joe had displayed in helping those Turn*Style employees. He and Bud would ask me to serve as an advisor to them.

Helping to get Osco and Turn*Style going was exciting, and I would have loved to run Turn*Style. Instead, I was asked to go back to the route business again, this time as its general manager. So back I went to "ride-withs" and route problems and to all the challenges of a declining business format. As general manager, I did everything I could think of to try to inject new enthusiasm and excitement into the business. We started a program to have every route salesman wear a white shirt, and we put them through a new sales training program. They were rewarded with a higher commission structure when they completed that program.

As a result, the business started to attract better people and provided better customer service. That program and other efforts also taught me a lot about communicating and reorienting a large organization. Introducing a new program to 2,000 moderately educated salesmen, spread over 40 states, took months of patience and simple words. It was good training.

I even championed an effort to try the catalogs that we used on the routes in several Jewel Food Stores. We developed displays and store-oriented catalogs; everything else, including the ordering system, was already in place. We got a little business, but not enough to warrant rolling out the program. I was always embarrassed that I lost the $50,000 that I spent to pilot the program, but I was also grateful to George Clements for letting me try it. I have had many occasions to remember in later years the importance of allowing young managers to try out their ideas, even when they fail and it costs the company in the process.

When I compared the routes to the stores, I realized that each needed different personality types to make them successful. The route business needed people who wouldn't accept "no" for an answer and who would remain enthusiastic even when the business was declining. The food stores operated in a team environment and, therefore, could operate with people who were mutually dependent. Because of these dynamics, the routes were the ideal place to train leaders, and many of Jewel's leaders came from that part of the business.

When I became general manager of the routes, we decided to promote one of Jewel's talented future leaders—Wes Christopherson—from his regional role in Binghamton, New York, to a headquarters role in the route business. At this point, I took the unusual approach of going to Ed Johnson, then vice president of sales, and asking him, "Would you mind training your next boss?" He did just that, and with enthusiasm. Not only would Wes become president of the Home Shopping Service, he would later become president of Osco and ultimately chairman of Jewel Companies.

The Home Shopping Service was still alive 20 years later when I retired from Jewel, but we knew it was on a declining trend. The Jewel route people kept what was becoming an anachronism alive much longer than anyone could have expected. It is a strange feeling to have lived and worked in an era in retailing when the customer-friendly Home Shopping Service declined and the more impersonal Home Shopping Network arose… when shopping moved from the streets to the Internet, and the computer replaced the truck. Efficiency has replaced the friendly salesman and his basket.

But what really has changed is the customer and the ways in which he or she chooses to shop. One of our Jewel Concepts stated that however we were satisfying customers today would prove to be inadequate 10 years from now. How true!

CHAPTER 6

FIRST ASSISTANT

At the time, I may have been disappointed to be asked to be general manager of the route business rather than to work in the growth part of Jewel. But, in retrospect, my years in the routes meant that, when George Clements started to consider succession, I was the one person who had worked in all parts of the company and its operations.

George told me that I was being made executive vice president of the corporation in 1963. He said that I had both impressed and surprised him.

Shortly after the announcement of my promotion, I visited my mother in St. Louis. She had terminal cancer, but learned before she died that all the education and hard work had paid off. I told her this promotion meant that I was likely to be president of Jewel some day.

Indeed, two years later, in 1965, I was named president of Jewel as George Clements became chairman of the board. I was 37—the same age Frank Lunding had been when he became president; George Clements had been president at 40. I had believed from the start that if it had happened to them, it could happen to me. It could and it did.

When I received word of being named president, Phyllis wasn't at home, so I called her at The North Shore Country

Day School, where she was in a parent-teacher conference with Susan's first grade teacher. We decided to share the news with the three children that evening before dinner. With an air of seriousness and collective involvement that normally accompanied such important announcements as the purchase of a new car or the description of a vacation plan, I explained to Betsy, Jerry, and Susan (then 11, 9, and 6) that I would soon be elected president of Jewel.

There were a few seconds of silence until Susan, who had little tolerance for silence and who wanted to make sure she wasn't missing the point, asked, "Is that good?" Yes, Susan, by any measure, it was good.

As a young president, I enjoyed being involved in Jewel's geographic expansion. That expansion included the acquisition of Star Markets in Boston, as well as Montana-based Buttrey Food Stores and, most importantly, the growth of Osco. Through the process of integrating Star, we came to know Steve and John Mugar (a last name shortened from the original Armenian surname Mugarian). Steve owned the business and John ran it. Everyone assumed that they were brothers, but they were actually cousins. Everyone also assumed that John owned a big piece of the business, but they were wrong about that too.

Steve had been looking for a way out of the business so he could give money away, as he did to Boston University. I remember visiting him once in Boca Raton as he was floating on his back in his swimming pool with his large stomach sticking out of the water. "I've been poor and I've been rich," he said, "and rich is better."

While John Mugar hadn't been an owner of the business, what he did have was great natural talent as a leader, and he would lead Star Markets until his retirement.

In addition to grocery stores in the Boston area, Star had two other interests—Brigham's, a small group of ice cream and candy stores, and SIAS, a supermarket venture in Italy that

Star had launched with an Italian confectionary firm (Motta). I joined the SIAS board in 1964. SIAS was far from a repeat of the positive experience Jewel had had in Belgium. It was a mess.

The Italian government was responsive to the anti-chainstore complaints of small shopkeepers, and found countless ways to harass SIAS. For example, we used the same type of plastic trays in both the meat and produce departments. The government required that the trays be separately marked for the two departments. The trays were the same and were never reused, but nonetheless we had to keep two separately marked supplies. The government also mandated that we provide chairs for the checkers at the check-out stands.

Ultimately, we became concerned about the slow sales growth and the lease liabilities of the business, and decided to sell our investment. It wasn't easy, but we managed it. I remember saying to Howard Wagner, Jewel's chief financial officer, on the plane ride home after the sale had been completed, "The next time I come back to Italy, I want it to be as a tourist."

In contrast to Italy, Jewel's positive experience in Belgium would be replayed with a very successful investment in Mexico. Several years earlier, when I was general manager of the route business, George Clements had received a message from Walter Rostow, an economic advisor in the Kennedy administration. Rostow had suggested to Mexican President Gustavo Diaz Ordaz that the reason Mexicans were poorly fed was that they didn't have access to the right retailers. Moreover, Rostow declared, he knew of a U.S. retailer—the Jewel Tea Company—that sold food door-to-door. Now wouldn't that be a wonderful thing for Mexico?

The hottest new retailer in Mexico at the time was Aurrera (Basque for "forward"), owned by Jerónimo (Jerry), Manuel (Manolo) and Plácido Arango, three brothers who had started a retail business in a corner of one of their father's textile factories and modeled it on U.S. warehouse-discount stores. Their business had become an instant success, thanks to their low prices and to investing in a new program on Mexican television, *The 64,000 Peso Question*.

President Diaz Ordaz asked Jerry Arango, the brother who managed Aurrera, to look into this U.S. business of "retailing by delivery truck." A meeting was arranged and Jerry came north to visit. It took Jerry and me all of a minute or so to observe the obvious—if people have money, retailers will show up... in buildings ... on wheels ... however. If one were going to bring a business to Mexico, it would be a no-frills warehouse-type business, not a high-cost, high-margin business like the Home Shopping Service.

Jerry and I started talking about what Aurrera was doing, which led George Clements and me to visit Mexico to see for ourselves. By that time, we had had a very good experience in Belgium and thought it made sense to bring supermarkets into developed or developing countries, where we could be among the first to offer self-service foods, drugs, and general merchandise, with ample parking for customers.

The major difficulty in figuring out a deal with Aurrera was the very high real estate value of their existing stores in Mexico. That obstacle was overcome when Jerry agreed to freeze the existing business and to use Jewel's investment for future endeavors. Jewel's initial investment in Aurrera was only $1 million.

When we entered into the agreement, George Clements put his deft touch on the spirit of the deal when he said to Jerry, "We'll get involved with you, but Jewel wants to be the fourth brother." We completed the deal, and it so happened that the next store they opened was just outside Mexico City. At that time, Mexico City's Federal District had strict rules limiting retail hours. The new Aurrera, a hypermarket, could be open 24 hours per day because it was outside the Federal District; it was an instant, incredible success.

The dynamics of the grocery business in Mexico were fascinating. Mexico had no equivalent to the Robinson-Patman law in the U.S., so the larger a retailer became, the more power it had. Because of Mexico's history of real estate inflation, retailers could rarely get anyone to finance real estate for them and needed capital for that. Suppliers essentially provided capital for inventory.

The contrast with the U.S. was striking. Mexican inventories were financed 125 percent through accounts payable versus perhaps 40 percent in the U.S. In fact, when Aurrera opened a new store, cash flow improved! On the other hand, borrowing for leasing and building stores was virtually unavailable in Mexico but plentiful in the U.S.

A year or so after we had made our original investment, Jerry decided that it was too difficult to operate Aurrera as two separate businesses. He offered either to give us $2 million for our original $1 million investment or to sell us 49 percent of the company for $20 million. When we asked why he would only consider 49 percent, he said that there would be a new law in Mexico within the next few years prohibiting a foreign company from owning more than 49 percent of a Mexican company. Mexico soon passed a law limiting foreign ownership of Mexican companies, just as Jerry had predicted.

It was a difficult time for a U.S. company to make a foreign investment. President Lyndon Johnson's advisors had persuaded him that the U.S. government should impose restrictions on U.S. dollar investment abroad. Jewel and Aurrera tried to figure out a way to do the deal with Jewel stock, but when we explained to Jerry all the restrictions involved in owning Jewel stock as a foreigner, it just didn't make any sense. The only way we could raise the capital was to sell Jewel stock. We could not borrow for the investment, but we could sell stock.

Jewel was willing to invest in Aurrera (subsequently named Cifra and later sold back to the Arangos and then to Wal-Mart after Jewel's acquisition by American Stores) and to help it in any way we could, but we never sent "gringos" to Mexico on a full-time basis. There was plenty of talent in the Aurrera business. We advised Jerry and his colleagues to treat Jewel like a library. "Like all libraries, if you don't use it, it's your loss. But it's here when you want help and you have the library card."

They tried many of the same promotions we used, often with great results. One promotion I recall involved giving away pictures and then selling picture frames. In a month-long promotion, Aurrera sold as many frames as had been sold in Mexico in the three preceding years!

We also helped them with a number of other projects. For example, we were critical of their meat quality. They told us that they couldn't get good meat in Mexico. So, we sent folks from our meat department to help them develop their program, starting on the farm. Eventually, the quality of the meat in Aurrera was as good as that in the U.S. Aurrera was such a successful investment that, during one year of a major price war in Chicago, Aurrera accounted for a third of Jewel's earnings.

The Aurrera involvement gave me the chance to work with and become friends with some wonderful people. Jerry Arango, of course, was key in our dealings, but Phyllis and I—and later Jane and I—also got to know the other brothers, particularly Plácido in Spain. Plácido later served on the board of the Metropolitan Museum of Art in New York as well as the Prado in Madrid.

We also became close friends with Hector de Uriarte, one of the professional general managers of Aurrera, and his wife Lilia. Henry Davis succeeded Hector at Aurrera; Henry and his wife Conchita also became very close friends of ours. As the Uriarte and Davis children came to the U.S. for educational experiences, including graduate business school for three Davis sons and one son-in-law, we've gotten to know them, too.

Meanwhile, back at Jewel, Frank Lunding and George Clements continued their pattern of making way for me, and I was elected chairman of the board of Jewel in 1970, at age 43. Their precedents and my own beliefs encouraged me to declare then that I planned to serve as chairman for 10 years.

The idea that businesses need renewal and new leadership after a number of years is one that my personal experience at Jewel and in dealing with the issues as an independent director of other companies has confirmed. I explained one aspect of the idea this way when I was interviewed in 1989 by *Directorship*, a monthly publication for corporate directors, in an article entitled, "Talking Succession with Your CEO":

> When you've been around for a decade or more, younger people in the business bring up questions that you probably thought about carefully and answered ten or fifteen years before.... Sometimes experience can get in the way of rethinking what needs to be done. Sometimes a new approach and new answers are needed.

My conviction that 10 years was the right amount of time for me in the CEO role at Jewel led to an unusual pact with Larry Fouraker, who became dean of Harvard Business School the same year I became chairman of Jewel. I had stayed involved at the Business School, serving on the Harvard Business School Visiting Committee (overseeing the conduct of the school) for eight years and then the Harvard Business School Associates (counseling the deans) for another 20-plus years.

Larry and I discussed our belief that 10 years was the right amount of time for someone to spend in each of our jobs. Recognizing that this idea that made such great sense to us at the beginning of our decade-long journeys might not seem as appealing at the end, we promised to jog each other's memory if needed. We both lived up to our pact.

The 10 years of the 1970s were to be busy and challenging times for Jewel, including our geographical expansion in Europe, Mexico, and within the U.S, as well as a number of ventures into alternative retail formats. One of the more successful ventures at that time was Jewel's entry into the convenience store business. Jewel was interested in convenience stores as another way we could be available when our customers were buying food.

In the early 1970s, Bob Patrick, the candy buyer who had come up with the Osco suggestion, came to me and said he had been observing the convenience store business. He asked if Jewel would back him in building some convenience stores. Building them was not terribly expensive to do, so we opened our first convenience store. That store was run by Bob Robertson, a Jewel butcher who would end up as CEO of the convenience store business.

Starting a chain of convenience stores from scratch required us to come up with a store name. Names are hard to come by, and don't mean anything anyway until the operation gives them some meaning. Many in the business had disliked the name Osco, but it had come to have a very positive meaning for drug store customers.

We cast around for ideas for another name that we could imbue with positive meaning for convenience store customers. At the time, Jewel owned the White Hen Egg Farm with hundreds of thousands of hens laying eggs, and it occurred to us to use the White Hen name, particularly because the egg farms had been such a success. So Jewel's convenience stores were to be known as White Hen Pantries.

It was fascinating to learn the demographics and develop the strategy for White Hen. Sixty percent of the customers in convenience stores were men—a great contrast with shoppers in supermarkets. Men generally stopped at convenience stores because they had been asked to bring something home after work, so the ideal locations were somewhere on the way home from the Loop (downtown Chicago).

It also fascinated me to watch this business in which, like the routes, convenience was more important than price. Jewel ended up with more than 100 White Hen Pantries in metropolitan Chicago and Boston; it was only seven years before White Hen profits paid back our cumulative investment in it.

Jewel was also a pioneer in bringing banking into supermarkets, taking advantage of a unique set of circumstances in Illinois. Illinois law prior to about 1980 severely restricted the operation of branch banks. This kept large banks from serving a broad metropolitan area. (It is also one of the reasons—probably the principal reason—that Chicago doesn't have a strong national position in banking today. The large banks were prevented from acquiring other banks and therefore were unable to build presence. When large banks in other parts of the country started to merge, Chicago and Illinois were left behind.)

As a result, Jewel became the check-casher for our customers. At one time, Jewel cashed 11 times as many checks as the then-largest bank in Illinois—Continental Bank. The checks we cashed totaled over 100 percent of our sales—we brought money and food into our stores and took checks out!

As the challenge of managing so many checks increased, we worked out an arrangement with a bank in the basement of the Merchandise Mart. We delivered to them all the checks that had been cashed at our stores by mid-afternoon. The checks were processed overnight so that the funds were in our bank account the next morning.

There was one problem—at first, our customers didn't know that we had changed our system. They were in the habit of writing a check on Thursday even though they wouldn't get paid until Friday. About 15 percent of the checks would bounce on the first pass. We deposited them again the next day and the bounce rate would go down to a fraction of a percent. When the Illinois Constitution was amended to allow for branch banking, and because Jewel was handling all that money, we were delighted to welcome banks into the stores.

During my 10 years as chairman, Jewel was not always in acquisition and growth mode; at times we had to be defensive, as well. In 1974, Phyllis and I were taking daughter Susan on a tour of New England colleges. On a Sunday morning, while we were staying with friends near New Haven, I received a call from Chicago. The day before—a Saturday—a bread truck driver had told one of our store managers that National Tea was changing a considerable number of prices in a nearby store.

The manager went to see for himself, decided it was significant, and called his district manager. Within hours, Jewel people had visited National's stores across the Chicago area and the pattern became clear ... a new lower food price structure was being installed.

Guessing that National would make a major announcement on Monday morning, senior Jewel Food Store executives met most of Sunday, dusted off and polished up an experimental discount program which we had been evaluating in stores in our test market of Rockford. They started groups working on store communication, new ads, and even pro forma income statements. Our share of market had taken years to build. Regardless of the cost, we were determined to maintain that market share.

On Monday, National made its announcement. On Tuesday, Jewel held a press conference. By the next weekend, not many Chicago consumers knew who had started what would turn into a major price war.

Overnight, the profits of Jewel Food Stores dropped 70 percent and the stress on Jewel people mounted. At one point, I thought everyone in the business looked haggard. So I went to a meeting of the Jewel Food Stores leaders and said to them, among other things, "I am worried that you are trying to make up in hours for what the market won't let you change. I am going to say something to you that I mean from the bottom of my heart. Take care of yourself. Your health and your family are more important than Jewel."

I wasn't much into rhetoric, but I repeated the last sentence for emphasis. I don't know for sure that anyone did anything differently, but many people who were at that meeting remember my statement, and I have recommended the approach to other corporate leaders in similar stressful situations over the years.

One memorable health-related experience from my years as chairman of Jewel started with reaching down to flush a toilet the afternoon before an annual meeting. As I reached down, I had a muscle spasm in my back. It wasn't the first time it had happened—and it wouldn't be the last. I knew that I should stay in bed, but I was determined to chair the annual meeting the next day.

My doctor gave me shots and muscle relaxants to try to get me in shape for the meeting. The next morning, it took me a full 45 minutes to get out of bed and into the corset that would enable me to stand up. I realized that I had to choose between taking a lot of painkillers (and sounding dumb) and hurting. I chose the latter.

The newspaper coverage of that year's annual meeting reported that the meeting surfaced no problems as great as the problem in my back! Because I stubbornly persisted in running the meeting, it took me a week—twice as long as it typically did—to recover.

Jewel weathered the price war, at least far better than National, but the bottom-line impact was substantial. During my time as executive vice president, president, and chairman—a span of 17 years—there were only two in which the company did not have record earnings. One of those was during that price war. National fared even worse, becoming the victim of its own strategy.

All in all, Jewel had come a long way since I had joined
the company. We were now Jewel Companies, a group of
decentralized, independently managed businesses, including
the Home Shopping Service, Jewel Food Stores, Osco Drug,
Eisner (a small central-Illinois grocery chain acquired by Jewel
about the time I joined the company), Buttrey Food Stores,
Star Markets, Brigham's, and White Hen Pantries. We had
investments in Belgium and Mexico. The route business, which
had accounted for 15 percent of Jewel's sales in 1960, had grown
modestly, but in 1980 accounted for only 2 percent of Jewel's
sales. In addition, we had become more vertically integrated,
thanks to our manufacturing operations.

When I joined Jewel in 1953, Jewel lagged both A&P and
National in Chicago. By the time I retired, National and A&P
had both left the market, and Jewel had an unprecedented 35
percent market share in Chicago. The company's ratio of debt
to total debt and equity was the same in 1980 as it had been in
1960 (22 percent). Shareholder value had grown five-fold. And
the company was well-positioned for continued growth.

As admirable as those accomplishments are, they are not the
only measures of a successful retail business. In 1974, I gave a
speech at Stanford University. In my remarks, I said:

> A successful retail business starts with dedicated and talented
> people ... who develop a philosophy of value and service ...
> and who work with that philosophy to earn a reputation, the
> strength of which determines their future.

That was not just a prescription, it was a capsule description
of Jewel over many years. Building its reputation and
developing its people are my greatest sources of pride in what
Jewel accomplished.

Jewel's emphasis on people meant that we had to have more
concern about others than ourselves, and more concern about

families and health than Jewel. We needed to support innovative people who made mistakes as they grew. We had to have the patience to turn around a problem or build a new business from scratch. As I described it, we put audits of human attitudes on a par with financial audits, and we considered recruiting and development expenses a long-term investment.

Perhaps the most fundamental element of Jewel's management style and philosophy was what we called the upside-down organization chart. We visualized an organization with the customer at the top and the CEO at the bottom. Management acted as "first assistants" to those above them on the upside-down chart. As managers, we didn't run anything, we emphasized—our job was to help and assist. Prestige would come from what we helped others accomplish.

With my Harvard Business School cynicism, I had rolled my eyes when I started at Jewel and first heard about the upside-down organization chart. "How corny!" I thought. But as I saw it work, I was converted from cynic to evangelist. The youthful cynicism I had brought with me to Jewel in 1953 was washed away and replaced with the conviction that being a first assistant rather than a boss really made the difference in an organization and in how people felt about themselves, about each other, and about their commitment to the business.

After a few years at Jewel, I would find myself starting each day by thinking about who needed help instead of what orders I would be giving. And I referred to the upside-down organization chart constantly, sometimes tongue-in-cheek, as in the following limerick I wrote for a company meeting in 1979:

Just imagine our founder, Frank Ross,
In his wagon, he says to his hoss,
"Will you please watch the time?
I'll relax because I'm
First assistant and you are the boss."

I didn't appreciate at first that Jewel's focus on people and their development was so unusual. In a way, I was rationalizing my own decision to come to Jewel by persuading others to do the same. Now I can take great satisfaction in seeing the results of our people programs in the post-Jewel achievements of many outstanding Jewel talents, including:

Wes Christopherson.............Chairman, Northern Trust Bank
                              (deceased)
Tom Stemberg ....Founder of Staples
Sam Parker.........................Founder of PETsMART
Philip Francis.....................Parker's successor, Chairman &
                              CEO of PETsMART
Robert Nakasone ....Chairman & CEO of
                              Toys "R" Us
Dick George ....Founder of Ulta 3
Walter Elisha.......................Chairman & CEO of
                              Springs Industries
Dick Cline ....Chairman & CEO of Nicor,
                              Chairman of Hussman
                              Refrigeration
Ron Floto ....CEO of Dairy Farm Group
                              (southeast Asian and
                              Australian retailer)
John Shields........................Chairman of Wild Oats, CEO
                              of First National Supermarkets
Larry Howe ....President of The Commercial Club
Bill Bennett..........................Founder of Yoplait, with
                              Joe Jannotta
Peter Cook..........................White House Fellow
Joe Jannotta ....Founder of Yoplait, Founder of
                              Jannotta Bray

Although I could tell interesting stories about all of those Jewel executives and many others, four examples of unusual talent are on my mind:

WALTER ELISHA

My relationship with Walter started in 1965, shortly after I became president of Jewel, with what I think of as the "brother-in-law letter." Frank Lunding sent me a memo saying that his brother-in-law, the editor of a newspaper in Gary, Indiana, had told him about a young man graduating from the Harvard Business School whom we should meet. So, I dutifully went to Harvard to meet Walter, who was then 32 years old. After his father's death, Walter had sold the family rug and carpet business and moved his wife and three children to Boston so he could go to Harvard. Boy, was I impressed! I knew he was a Baker Scholar and was graduating near the top of his class. But what I realized as I got to know him was that Walter had grown up in retailing and was great with people. I wanted to recruit him for Jewel. "What would it take to get you to come to Jewel?" I asked. When Walter said, "$15,000," I said, "Fine. What else do you want to talk about?" Despite competition from Cummins Engine, McKinsey, and Harvard (who wanted him to teach after he graduated), Walter came to Jewel and stayed until after I retired as chairman.

Within a year of his coming to Jewel, we asked Walter to run Brigham's, the ice cream and candy business that was included when we acquired Star Markets in Boston. Because of his age and previous retail experience, Walter was somewhat unusual as a trainee, but then our program was never designed to operate the same way for everyone. After he had successfully managed Brigham's, we moved him to Barrington to run the Home Shopping Service at the time Wes Christopherson became president and I became chairman. Later, he became president of Jewel Food Stores.

I never doubted that Walter's solution to any problem would be the one that considered what was best for the people involved, as well as what was the right thing to do. Typical of his people-sensitive style, when Walter became president of Jewel Food Stores, he visited every store in the company—all 200 or so of them. More impressive, after each visit, he sent a personal note to the manager of the store, referring to some incident that had occurred or person that he had met during his visit.

I was terribly disappointed when Walter left Jewel to become CEO of Springs Industries not long after I retired as chairman. For a time, I resented what seemed to me a lack of loyalty, but I had to acknowledge that my successor's view of Walter did not match mine. I also have to acknowledge that Springs turned out to be a great opportunity for him. And, it is likely that Walter would have left with the other Jewel executives anyway following American Stores' hostile takeover of the company four years later. As CEO of Springs, Walter asked me to join his board and I accepted with great pleasure the opportunity to work again with this eminently able executive.

DICK CLINE

Dick came to Jewel after editing a veterinary magazine owned by one of his relatives. When he finished his training year in the Jewel corporate sponsorship program, he joined Osco. Wes Christopherson was overseeing both Osco and the routes at the time, which gave him ample opportunity to watch Dick grow. Wes was an advocate for making him president of Osco when it came time for new leadership in Jewel's pharmacy business.

If Dick had done nothing more than develop and implement the immensely popular Osco program that took the mystery out of prescription drug prices (Chapter 9), he would have been a success. But he did much more. He built an Osco business in Chicago that grew from no stores to a market-share tie with Walgreens in a span of 18 years.

Dick had a second career following the American Stores acquisition, straightening out a complicated mess at Nicor, a

Chicago area natural gas utility company. He also spent some time as non-executive chairman at Hussman Refrigeration, where he mentored a new CEO. Later, at my encouragement, Dick joined the Kmart board, an encouragement that subsequently made me feel guilty. It was all work and no reward as Kmart ended up in bankruptcy.

One distinctive aspect of Dick's life was that, in his later years, he would receive a liver transplant. As one of his doctors told me, no lay person she had ever encountered knew more about liver transplants than Dick.

BOB NAKASONE

Bob came from a family that was confined to an internment camp for Japanese-Americans during World War II. When he graduated from the University of Chicago Business School and interviewed at Jewel, he told me his brother had advised him that no Japanese-American could succeed at a large U.S. company. He asked me, "Is that true?" I answered, "We haven't yet had a chance to prove him right or wrong. Why don't you give us that chance?"

Bob had a wonderful career at Jewel and left only after the American Stores takeover. He then became president of Toys R Us. Not long after he took on that role, Jane and I saw him at a Booz Allen Hamilton conference for new CEOs. He described his board as filled with directors chosen by his predecessors, and it was easy for me to predict a future conflict. The conflict took shape and Bob was pushed out.

Bob gained my admiration again when he confronted a difficult situation with the leadership and board of a company where he served as an independent director. With characteristic class, he shared his serious concerns with the rest of the board. When it became clear that he could change neither the leaders nor their ways, he resigned.

BETTY McFADDEN

Sadly, I cannot speak of the illustrious career Betty might have
had in a business life after Jewel, since she died in 1983, the year
that I retired from the Jewel board.

I can only speak of what she accomplished at Jewel, as I did at
her memorial service. I met Betty shortly after I joined Jewel. In
a sense, we traveled through our business careers together. She
was then the buyer of children's wear for the Home Shopping
Service. In the mid-1960s, she was made a vice president of the
company. Her reaction—"It's about time"—was exactly right.

Jewel may have been early in elevating women to management,
but we weren't too early for such an able executive as Betty. My
most cherished memories of Betty are from the late 1960s, when
she found herself in a personal tug-of-war between her roles as
new mother and accomplished executive. When she returned
to work after the birth of her daughter, I noted the change from
her usual smiling face. Betty admitted that she felt she should
be spending more time at home with her "marvelous Mindy."

I asked her how she would design her life, if she could.
"Oh," she said, as though relieved finally to be asked, "I'd take
twelve weeks off each year to be with Mindy." That's what
we arranged. We modified her job, and, I'm embarrassed to
remember, we cut her pay. A year later Mindy taught Betty that
she didn't need her mother all day, and the sad look returned
to Betty's face. "I should either come back full time or leave,"
Betty told us. We welcomed her back, increased her pay, and
she set out on the road to becoming president of the Jewel
Home Shopping Service.

Betty was a pioneer among successful women who earned
their way to the top in business. Yet she never made it seem
that she was blazing trails. Whatever she did seemed to be
done naturally, with femininity, with wonderful good common
sense, and with a true concern for the well-being of all with

whom she worked. Betty was one of the finest executives with whom I have worked. Though the word executive, especially in the 1960s and 70s often implied the male gender, anyone who worked with Betty knew differently.

As my retirement date neared, I asked a special committee of the Jewel board, chaired by Harvard Business School dean Larry Fouraker, to pick my successor. Because Wes Christopherson had been president for the 10 years that I had been chairman, he was my logical successor, but I was anxious for the board to own the decision.

Wes was smart, straight-laced, unselfishly devoted to Jewel, and an excellent speaker. I kiddingly referred to him as the "Reverend Doctor" Christopherson in acknowledgment of his oratorical prowess. Although I worked with him, often closely, during my 30 years at Jewel, some of Wes's actions when he succeeded me as chairman and CEO surprised me. For instance, he decided that Jewel should have its own airplane. I had always said that we could build two stores for the cost of one airplane, and the profit potential of an airplane was nil. It was so unlike his previously hair-shirt approach to cost control for our retail businesses.

And in 1984, when Jewel received the offer from American Stores, Sam Skaggs's business, Wes called me and said, "I don't want to make you an insider so I am not going to involve you in any of our efforts to fight off this unfriendly offer." The strategy he and his team developed to fend off the unsolicited and unfriendly takeover bid failed to deter it. Mistakes were made during those critical times. I cannot be certain that I could have helped prevent what Wes referred to as "certainly not the way anyone would want to end a career," but I would have liked to try.

The result of the takeover was that Jewel people were now being led by Sam Skaggs, who, I had learned from our previous dealings, might be described as a Utah redneck, and, oddly enough, someone still trying to prove his worth to his father ... years after his father's death. The other result was that a management team of the highest quality and integrity was scattered to the winds. Wes went on to a successful career as chairman of the Northern Trust. From everything I heard, he did an outstanding job there. The other Jewel executives did likewise in their post-Jewel careers. My pride was mixed with nostalgia. As I said in a *Chicago Tribune* interview in 1986,

> I feel terribly out of phase with the business world in one respect. I always thought the way to make a contribution to a company was to build its talent. If you check, I think you'll see Jewel has as good a reputation as any company in that respect. Now the business world seems to reward good portfolio managers. I feel I'm looking back on Camelot.

In 1980, as my self-imposed 10 years of tenure as chairman and my 30-year career at Jewel were coming to an end, however, there was no time for nostalgia. I felt confident that I was leaving Jewel in the hands of the strongest possible management team, and I had developed a set of new professional involvements that I would find both challenging and rewarding—as a director of a number of public companies and not-for-profit institutions, and through involvement in Chicago civic activities.

Of course, the fact that I had stated my intention in advance to limit my tenure in the chairman's role at Jewel to 10 years did not prevent people from asking, when the time came, why I would retire so young. When I ended my term as chairman of the board's executive committee and any official role at Jewel in mid-1983, I summarized the reasons for doing so at a retirement celebration with the Jewel management team:

Because I got the top job so young;

Because, unlike the first time, I just can't get as excited about it the tenth time I see an annual budget;

Because it is human to think through the answers to problems early in one's career and difficult to rethink them later, even when circumstances may have changed;

Because more companies are hurt by people staying in charge too long than too short a time;

And, because I wasn't really retiring ... just being "repotted."

CHAPTER 7

THE JEWEL CONCEPTS

Jewel's philosophy extended beyond the upside-down organization chart. In 1972, early in my time as chairman, we articulated the elements of our philosophy in a document called "The Jewel Concepts." Our purpose was to capture our business philosophies, building on the principles that started with Frank Lunding's book, *The Sharing of a Business.* Those principles had evolved under George Clements and incorporated my insights. The Jewel Concepts were a recruiting tool as well as an everyday reminder of what was important to Jewel people.

MERCHANTS OF EMPATHY

It is not groceries or merchandise we sell as much as solutions to needs, problems, and the well-being of our customer.

Considering ourselves to be the purchasing agent for consumers rather than the selling agent for suppliers was an example of being merchants of empathy. Empathy required treating each customer as we would like to be treated ourselves.

RESTLESS UNSATISFACTION

In a rapidly changing world, with quickly shifting consumer needs and expectations, we dare not be too satisfied with anything we are doing. We dare not assume what we are doing is all we might do.

The concept of "unsatisfaction" meant, for example, that if our facilities were to become obsolete, we should be the ones to obsolete them, not our competitors, even if that was an expensive decision.

WATCHING THE HORIZON

Leadership requires going out to meet the future with courageous new ideas.

Yes, it's corny. It's also true. Osco's going public with prescription drug prices is a good illustration.

REPUTATION FOR INTEGRITY AND FAIRNESS

The most important long-term concern of the people in our business must be the reputation they are making for themselves and their successors.

A retail business is not a cold economic entity; it is people dealing with people, and the reputation that evolves from that relationship.

MEETING OUR SOCIAL RESPONSIBILITY

It is important to be a good corporate citizen of each community or neighborhood in which we operate.

I found I could convey the concept succinctly in a one-liner: If Chicago isn't healthy, Jewel isn't healthy.

SHARING THE BUSINESS

Management, by sharing the successes and the problems of the business with its people, helps to blend the goals of both groups.

The concept of sharing the business was originally developed and instilled in the company by Frank Lunding as he described the upside-down organization chart. The philosophy crystallized twin objectives—making Jewel "a better place to work" as well as "a better place to trade." The goal of sharing was that everyone involved in the business would share fairly in both monetary and non-monetary rewards, which would follow from a culture of service.

THE SPIRIT OF WANTING TO

Setting inspiring goals beyond the mere selling of goods develops a crusading spirit.

Organizations can function based on one of two primary theories about people—one that centers on discipline, orders, and obedience; or one that recognizes a desire for individual accomplishment and fulfillment. We acknowledged that it is more difficult to be a boss who encourages cooperation, initiative, and resourcefulness than to give orders. But that was the expectation we had of Jewel's managers.

RECRUITING PROMISING PEOPLE

Our progress 10 years from now is being determined by the quality of people we recruit today.

We emphasized that everyone should be a recruiter of talent, ranging from high school part-timers to MBAs.

DEVELOPING PEOPLE FULLY

We give our time, talent, and attention to maintain a challenging work environment which promotes growth and encourages Jewel people to fully develop their talents.

The emphasis Jewel placed on developing people was underscored by the fact that George Clements, who never spent money needlessly, supported the training programs and the money we invested in them. This commitment made Jewel highly unusual among supermarket retailers.

MOTIVATING PEOPLE

Jewel recognizes that the individual spirit is motivated by human considerations as well as by monetary rewards.

One key word was "sharing" ... sharing profits, sharing opportunities, sharing problems, sharing our business philosophy.

ORGANIZING AROUND PEOPLE

Our philosophy of organization starts with people—not boxes on an organization chart.

George Clements was always very bothered by formal organization charts. Early in my career at Jewel, Booz Allen Hamilton conducted a study (one that helped to identify me as a future leader) in which they recommended the creation of a formal organization chart, so that people could visualize their career path. George never liked that. He said, "I start with a blank sheet of paper and figure out what jobs there are to be done. Then I list the talents we have or need. And then I put the two together in boxes on an organization chart." I was really impressed by that, and continued to approach the organization that way in my own thinking. That way, we were not constrained by a previous organizational design. The boxes fit the talent, not the other way around.

MAKING AN OPPORTUNITY OF ADVERSITY

Problems can often be turned into opportunities, and mistakes into progress.

Jewel's vernacular for this was "making lemonade out of lemons."

DECENTRALIZATION FOR HUMAN REASONS

Most people want jobs that challenge their abilities and an evaluation system that records their progress.

A store was the ideal organizational element in retailing. It was one that a manager could figuratively put his or her arms around and say, "I am responsible for and want to be measured by what happens here."

AN ASSOCIATION OF AUTONOMOUS COMPANIES

It is cooperation among our companies on behalf of the consumer and the shareholder that helps guarantee the high degree of autonomy desired by Jewel people.

There is no way that a single person can be involved in every decision at a company the size of Jewel, with 50,000 employees. We created an organization with strong, autonomous presidents. This was balanced with the concept of sharing. Our sharing goal, difficult as it might have been, was that these independent managers would wear their corporate hats when the interests of an individual company or division or store conflicted with the overall interests of the corporation. The corporate management team acted as first assistants, providing special talents as they were needed, and accepting the ultimate responsibility for the success of each separate company without usurping the daily operating authority of individual company management.

The presidents of the operating companies represented an extraordinary collection of retail executive talent. My way of appraising them was to spend time in their businesses, with the people at the next level or two down from the top. I could always get a feel for how the leader of an operating company was doing by spending time with a middle manager. It provided excellent listening time.

It also seemed to me that we could develop a stronger Jewel spirit within the operating companies if we got the presidents together once a year. We called it the Presidents Conference; only four or five people from corporate would attend. At one such conference that included spouses, I looked over the audience and spontaneously observed that each member of the couples present was still married to their first spouse. I suggested that these marriages illustrated a wholesome family atmosphere at Jewel.

Of course, I was more premature than prescient. Within a few years, there were several divorces within the group. On reflection, the phenomenon may have been a better illustration of the youth than the marital constancy of the management group.

The Jewel Concepts guided our strategic and day-to-day actions. I added one other concept whenever I was faced with a difficult decision. Whereas some suggest as a rule of thumb that a difficult decision should be made as though it will appear on the front page of a newspaper the next day, my yardstick for probity has been, "Would I be comfortable explaining this to my children?"

CHAPTER 8

A FATHER AND A POET

O ur first house, on Drury Lane, had not a stick of furniture in the living room for the first couple of years we lived there. The "landscaping" consisted of a newly seeded "lawn" which Phyllis (pregnant with Susan), Betsy, Jerry, and I would go water every evening as the house was being finished. We would picnic on the bare concrete floor of the porch while I moved the sprinklers around. We managed the down payment on the house thanks to what we had saved, plus a special Christmas gift of $5,000 from Phyllis's parents that year.

Another do-it-yourself project was putting a fence around the back yard—a necessity because ours was one of four houses around a one-acre pond. I am not a natural handyman, but I bought a rustic picket fence and rented a post-hole digger.

In addition to kids and toys and a swing set, the fenced-in back yard was also the purview of Pollyanna, a poorly-trained basset hound who ate everything in sight.

Once she got at a package of frozen spinach thawing on the counter. She ate it, carton and all, and got sick all over the kitchen. When she wasn't in the yard, she was usually in the mud room/breakfast room where she would chew the wrought iron legs of a table as if they were vertical bones.

The pond provided much family entertainment when the children were young—fishing in the summer and ice skating in the winter. Each child started off on skates with double runners. One of the secrets we learned about teaching friends to skate—and many adults as well as children learned to skate on that pond—was a wooden kitchen chair. The chair would slide on the ice but provided enough support to limit the spills. Hot chocolate and visits from friends were plentiful in the winter.

We didn't take many vacations in those early years, but a visit with "Grandmère" and "Grandpère," as the children were asked to call Phyllis's parents, in Duxbury, where they now had a second home, became an annual event. The first time, we made the two-day trip by car, when Susan was just a few months old.

I remember getting a kick out of spending the night in Bedford, Pennsylvania, because we had a Ford station wagon and thus were able to put the Ford (and ourselves) to bed in Bedford. That was one of the few things to get a kick out of during that car trip—before Route 128 was built, getting to Duxbury meant driving through the heat and congestion of Boston. After that first trip, I flew to Boston for our summer visits, although Phyllis, whenever she had a choice, preferred the train.

Duxbury was a wonderful, relaxing place to vacation. We would play golf, picnic, or go to the beach. The children all played their first golf at the Duxbury Yacht Club golf course. On rainy days, the children played in the attic adjacent to the bedroom that Jerry used when we were there. There they read hundreds of comic books and played restaurant or some variation on the theme with a well-used set of plastic dishes and utensils. A favorite family story recounts how the three were playing airline flight with Susan as the stewardess (as they were still called then).

Susan made a slight modification of the standard question: "Coffee, tea, or milk?" She asked Jerry whether he would like

"Coffee, tea, or whiskey—?!" The three came downstairs in such hysterics, it was awhile before they caught their breath and could tell us what was so funny. Soon, children and adults alike were in stitches.

As the children got older and we could afford it, we took a number of other trips as a family—to Disneyland; Washington, DC; Mexico; Bermuda; and to historic sites in Illinois. One year we went to Yellowstone Park, the five Perkinses along with Annic and Myriam Dopchie, daughters of our close friends in Belgium, Jacques and Jacqueline. That trip also included a stay at a dude ranch in Wyoming, where Susan would get up at the crack of dawn to go out with the wranglers to bring in the horses; the rest of us slept in.

Each trip evokes memories. Most have a family story that any of us could tell you—like the time shy Betsy got up on stage when she was four at Florida's Lauderdale Beach Hotel and sang "Love and Marriage" during a visit with Grandmère and Grandpère … or Jerry's sunburn from waterskiing in Acapulco, which required a visit from a doctor … or the Blue Fox Restaurant in San Francisco, where Susan lost her prized frog pin.

Whether at home or on vacation, card games were always a part of Perkins family life, especially gin rummy and cribbage. I never thought there was any benefit to letting the children (or later my grandchildren) win when I played with them. They knew that I was competing with them as I would with an adult. So whenever they were "lucky" winners, there was great glee and cheering. Jerry became so proficient at gin rummy that he regularly beat his kindergarten teacher when they played during rest period.

Many of our activities centered on The North Shore Country Day School. I had originally resisted the idea of a private school, not wanting my children to be like the white-shoe crowd that I encountered at Yale. Phyllis had had a different experience, however. She promoted the idea, at first with the argument that junior kindergarten at North Shore wasn't much more expensive than any nursery school. I was persuaded to have Betsy start there.

I went to a parents' meeting and heard about the school's Gillingham reading program. When I learned the term dyslexia, I realized that was what my brother had suffered from. I also learned that dyslexia was inherited. It seemed there was a good chance that one of my own children would need the kind of program that North Shore offered.

We stayed, and all three children ended up graduating from North Shore—without ever needing the reading program. While there may have been some snobbish people who attended the school, elitism wasn't an attitude that the school nurtured. Anyone who doubts my change of heart need only consider that I paid 42 years of tuition for my children, before they even went to college! I also stayed involved with the school through its board and foundation.

When I think of my children's growing-up years, I think of going to innumerable performances of Gilbert & Sullivan operettas, dance programs, go-to-school nights, plays, and athletic events. Jerry was always an athlete, so that attending games was a way to relate even in those years when we couldn't communicate about much else. I remember once returning from a meeting in Belgium, getting off the plane, going directly to North Shore for a basketball game, and arriving just in time for the tip-off. Nobody could have come much farther to see that game, I thought!

Susan was also an excellent athlete, as were other members of her class. Her senior-year field hockey and basketball teams were undefeated in their league.

As North Shore increasingly became a focus of our activities, we moved to Winnetka. We were now just under a mile from school in a beautiful house I still call home.

A few years after we moved in, it was our good fortune that Jack and Jeannie Cardwell moved next door. Jack would leave a successful career at consulting firm McKinsey & Company to become president of Consolidated Foods (now Sara Lee), and a potential successor to John Bryan. When that succession didn't work out, Jack then worked with The Bessemer Group, the private equity management firm, until his untimely death from lung cancer. We went back and forth between the houses, which was handy since Jack and I shared a fondness for red Bordeaux. When Jack and Jeannie put a swimming pool in their back yard and had to fence it in, they added a gate between their yard and ours so that the Perkins family would always feel welcome.

Susan and Betsy were pretty easy to raise, but Jerry was much tougher. His years between 14 and 18 presented the biggest human relationship challenge I have ever had. I knew that Jerry was only trying to do what I had been doing at the same age—establish his independence from his father—but it was still difficult. Jerry emphasized his desire for independence from the family by moving into the separate servants' quarters in our house, above the garage, and posting a "KEEP OUT" sign on the entrance.

And like that of many young men during the 1970s, his shoulder-length hair was a symbol of rebellion. I said to Jerry, "You know that I don't like the length of your hair, but if we're going to have a confrontation on some subject, it should be a subject a lot more important than the length of your hair."

The one place I found where we could communicate was on the golf course. He loved to play golf and would always come out to play a round with me. But other than that, the type of communication that I wished we could have didn't happen until those teenage years were behind us.

One concern I had as my children were growing up was how they might handle money. As each started high school, we discussed what his/her allowance should be on a weekly basis. We agreed to a dollar amount, multiplied by 52 (weeks per year), which I then rounded up. At the beginning of the year, the annual amount was put into a bank account. If it wasn't spent, the money still belonged to him or her. They also added their earnings from summer jobs to their accounts. Phyllis and I paid directly for school expenses and clothing, but each child budgeted and paid for his or her entertainment and incidental expenses.

The allowance program continued through college; each child was frugal enough to graduate with enough left in his or her bank account for something special. Betsy was able to pay for a trip to Europe and Russia with her "leftover" funds. I would take the same approach later with Frank and Elizabeth after Jane and I were married. I think that all of my children do a better job of managing money because they were challenged to manage a yearly allowance from high school on.

When we talked about college, I told each of my children that they could go to any school they could get into, as long as it was at least 500 miles away from home. Betsy claims that she was only six when I first told her this, but by the time she was ready to go, she thought it was a very good idea indeed.

Phyllis and I both enjoyed going on college visits. Phyllis and her friend Gwen Gilbert accompanied Betsy and Jerry Arango's daughter, Marisa, who wanted to look at colleges in the U.S. Jerry Perkins and I went with his classmate Bill Hines and Bill's father Harold (president first of Marsh & McLennan and then of Aon, both insurance companies).

We had so much fun on those trips that both Phyllis and I went with Susan on her tour of colleges. I encouraged all three children to look at Yale; both Jerry and Susan were admitted, but Jerry chose Williams and Susan picked Dartmouth over Yale. Betsy, who had decided that Wellesley was the place for her, didn't apply to Yale.

Birthdays were always important events in the Perkins household. We would take the birthday child and a few friends

My mother, Edna Ann Meinert, in 1923.

My father, Arthur Sheldon Perkins—or Al, as he liked to be called—circa 1926.

My parents' wedding picture in 1926.

As a baby in 1928. I haven't worn a dress since.

My father with my brother Bob and me in front of our home on Wallace Avenue in 1931. My father would leave our family the following year shortly after my sister's birth.

I was 10, and Bob and Joan were 7 and 5, respectively.

Right: As a Boy Scout, in 1939.

Below: My father came back to the family when we lived at 6417 S. Kingshighway in 1939.

With my mother, brother Bob, and sister Joan, in 1941.

My senior yearbook portrait and capsule from June, 1944.

Donald Perkins

"Work and acquire and thou hast chained the wheel of chance."

Brochure Editor-in-Chief, Senior Play, President Student Council, Vice President City-Wide Student Council, Principal's Cabinet, Honor Student, Griffin Reporter, Senior-New Senior Party, Ring and Pin Committee, Victory Corps, Bowling, Scroll and Gavel, Usher, Track Team, Poetry, Saddle Spur, American Legion Oratorical Contest.

Above: A candid picture of the yearbook editor.

Right: The Merchant Marine Cadet in 1945.

My graduation from Yale in 1949 was a very proud time, and my mother and sister came to New Haven for the occasion.

As a Baker Scholar at the Harvard Business School in 1950.

I attended my wedding rather than my graduation from the Business School in June 1951.

In my air force uniform, with Betsy as a baby, at our home near Wright Patterson Air Force base—January 1953.

My mother with baby Betsy in November of 1953. She still lived in the house on Cabanne Avenue.

Right: Grandpa Meinert as he looked in 1953, two years before his death.

Below: Jerry as a baby in February 1955.

Phyllis with our children, Susan as a baby, in 1958.

On a family vacation in Florida in 1964. All three children learned to play golf at a young age.

A 1966 family vacation took us to Washington, D.C., where we were greeted by Don Rumsfeld, then a young Congressman.

A picture of me with Frank Lunding that appeared in a 1967 issue of the Harvard Business School Bulletin.

JANUARY 1968

chain store age

Supermarket Executives Edition • Issued in 2 Sections
1 and 2 Bound Together • Three Dollars a Year (10¢...)

Jewel's Don Perkins:
His '68 projection—more
growth via diversification
—but with other execs, he
sees expenses, prices up

Contents P. 4

January 1968 cover of Chain Store Age, *a retail industry publication.*

In 1967, Jewel was negotiating a covenant with Operation Breadbasket, represented here by Revs. Strom Freeman, Martin Luther King, and Jesse Jackson.

Jacques Dopchie and I visit a Supermarché GB in Belgium in August 1967.

George Clements, my mentor and role model at Jewel, and I flank Edward Brooke, then U.S. Senator from Massachusetts. We are joined by John Mugar, president of Star Markets.

Businessmen still wore hats in the early 1970s.

*The children in a
more formal setting in
late 1970.*

Phyllis and I enjoy Parents Weekend with Jerry at Williams College in the mid-1970s.

Top: Phyllis' parents, Ruth and Jerry Babb, in 1974.

Left: Grandma Meisnert (Minnie to her friends) with daughter Betsy in 1972.

to a special event—Betsy usually wanted to see a ballet or musical—for Jerry it was always a sports event, usually hockey, given his February birthday—for Susan, something that involved music. For Betsy's 14th birthday, we went to see the Tijuana Brass at McCormick Place. I remember looking around the theater, noticing how few exits there were, and wondering how to get our group out if there was an emergency.

We left there around 10 P.M. when the performance ended, and woke up the next morning to learn that a fire had broken out at 2 A.M. and burned McCormick Place to the ground. We had missed the fire by four hours.

A desire to memorialize and celebrate family events, especially birthdays, was what originally led to my calling as a poet. If I wrote any poems before the age of 35, I don't remember them, and they have gone unrecorded. My inspiration in January 1963 was the fact that I was visiting Jewel routes in Decatur, Georgia and was therefore not at home for Betsy's 10th birthday. I would produce many more poems over the next several years.

Sharing some of these efforts requires a caveat. Most of my poems borrow their meter from Clement Clark Moore's *A Visit from St. Nicholas ('Twas the Night before Christmas)*—and even at that, the rhythm was not always quite on track. For a change, I would throw in a limerick or two along the way. The typical poem would be 15 or 20 verses. If they aren't great artistic works, they do foster nostalgia.

It started with a birthday poem for Betsy, as a way to make my happy birthday wish seem special, even if I couldn't deliver it in person. It started,

Ten years ago I remember bragging
That other newborn babes were lagging.
The most they put in their mouth was a thumb;
You managed four fingers and then some.

Remembering back to infancy and reflecting on how much change had occurred in how seemingly short a time were favorite themes. On Jerry's 21st birthday, I reminisced about his arrival:

> Flash back twenty-one years from today and you'll see
> In Wilmette it is snowing, the streets quite slippery.
> Just returning from work, I was set to relax.
> "There's no time to sit down," Phyl said. "Start making
>   tracks!"
> "Leave our Betsy with neighbors and grab my suitcase.
> Drive as fast as you can or we might lose this race."
> With abandon, I skidded down Sheridan Road,
> As Phyl worked to contain her unborn squirming load.
> In the time that it took me to register Phyl,
> Doctor Burge quickly earned his obstetrical bill.
> Though at Evanston rushing his hospital story,
> Not once since has our Jer been in such a big hurry.

I suppose the rhyme wasn't always perfect either... Susan's 29th birthday caused me to remember her arrival and her initials—SSP—which prompted Grandpère at the time to observe that it made her sound like a steamship—the SS Perkins:

> With prophetic foresight, Grandpère, showing his mirth
> Nicknamed Susan "Miss Steam Ship" the day of her birth.
> While she cried like all babies beginning life's trip,
> Not a one of us knew we were launching a ship.
> Has the good Steam Ship Perkins lived up to her name,
> As she plows through stage waters in seeking her fame?
> Our unsinkable Steam Ship's left waves in her wake,
> Charming both of our coastlines and one large Great Lake!

The poems mark the usual progress through grade school accomplishments and driver's licenses, foreseen in an early conversation with Betsy and recollected in the poem I wrote for her 12th birthday. The conversation I retold herein was a real one.

> After only four years of her being alive,
> Betsy questioned me, "Daddy, now when will I drive?"
> My answer was, "When you are sixteen or so."
> "That's nice," Betsy said, "but then where will I go?"

The intervening 12 years solved that problem for Betsy; soon Jerry, too, would take his place behind the wheel. Jerry's car, a hand-me-down Buick station wagon, led to this verse:

> Of course, Jer now has wheels ... some might call it a car.
> It looks kind of sad ... but it needn't go far.
> Every morning with Susan, he drives it to school
> Several minutes too late, as a general rule.

While not memorialized as a poem, one of my favorite car-related conversations took place many years later with my grandson Jeremy when he was five or so. While the two of us were sitting in my car, he noticed some paint or putty on the seat belt. "Why is that there?" he asked. I said, "Oh, someone made a mistake when they made the car." He then asked, "Did they have to go to jail?" I smiled and answered, "No, for something like that you wouldn't have to go to jail." He thought about it a bit and followed up, "Didn't he at least have to go to his room?"

The poems capture both the special events and the personalities of each child, as well as my parental pride, nostalgia, wonder and, on occasion, bemusement. Some gentle teasing accompanied the accolades for accomplishments. For Betsy, while most of the poems take note of her scholarship and love of books and school, there was a lot else going on, too, as I kidded her on her 15th birthday:

Once her glove was for nothing except playing catch,
Once her pants were of rubber, but now they just stretch.
Once her hair was just something on top of her head;
It's now to hold curlers, when she goes to bed.
Once shoes were just something that covered her feet;
Now they come in the colors that she thinks are neat.
And dresses, which once covered down to the knee,
Today are so short they leave plenty to see.
Oh come, Daddy, wake up, you certainly see
Fifteen years have now led to some changes in me!

The natural subject to tease Jerry about when I wrote poems
for his birthdays was his hair—first at 17:

Now some might describe Jerry's hair style as bold
And it's certain his hair keeps his ears from the cold,
While in Jerry, it's true, generosity harbors,
Except fighting the hunger of poor starving barbers.

Then at 20:

Over twenty fun years as our Perkins named Jerry
Has developed his humor … becoming quite merry;
He will laugh at himself, though that's ever so rare!
(Almost all he won't smile at's the length of his hair.)

I was able to note modest progress at age 23 when Jerry had
spent the summer between his two years in Northwestern's
Kellogg MBA program working at Foote, Cone & Belding
(F, C & B in the poem), a leading Chicago advertising
agency:

And last summer's event, which we'll always recall,
Was of F, C & B … advertising and all.
Mister Jervis commuted with definite flair,
Sporting new three-piece suits and his somewhat-trimmed
    hair.

Fortunately for our relationship, I found other things to write about, his athletic accomplishments chief among them, including the following account of three seasons of varsity sports as a high school junior:

> In football, his offense gave North Shore its score,
> He's a Gordon, an Alworth, a Warfield, and more.
> On defense he's Pettibone, Taylor, or Green.
> Number 10's interceptions are great to be seen!
> This year's basketball team had just one single loss
> While their twenty-one wins showed their league who was boss …
> Now sooner than soon, baseball's season is here,
> And Jerry the shortstop will soon reappear.

But Jerry would go from visions of a college football career to a harsher dose of reality as a senior in the next year's birthday poem:

> But sad is the tale of this past senior year
> When a Morgan Park back hung up Jer's football gear …
> When an elbow was hit and the bone just let slip
> From its socket, that ended his fun ego trip!

The Susan of the birthday poems goes from energetic 12-year-old …

> She's a student, an athlete, and horses she loves.
> She's a dancer, musician, and friend of the Gov's.
> She's a leader and camper, a tumbler, and more,
> She's the jigsaw speed champion south and North Shore.

To musical theater talent at 18, with references to the George M. Cohan and Gilbert & Sullivan shows she appeared in …

> George M. Cohan's been sung by a million or more
> Lovely girls who auditioned for parts with his score.
> But no "Mary" has better praised "Broadway's" bright lights
> "Yankee doodling" with cane and straw hat and black tights!

Yes the eighteenth year ended and closed with a bang.
This year Psyche had fun as she acted and sang,
While in Gilbert and Sullivan's women's lib tale,
Princess Ida ran Adamant Castle like jail.

The children's college choices and experiences also figure
prominently in the poems, starting with Betsy at Wellesley,
where I recounted her academic achievements and then was
unable to resist a not-so-subtle reference to the fact that Phyllis
was at Wellesley when I met her.

'Twas a year full of study, with results of all A's.
One would think that just books kept her busy all days.
That may be the case ... but though winds keep up kites,
Neither books nor the winds kept her up all those nights.
In the hills west of Boston, not far from Route 9,
There the girls are all smart and at work to refine
Both themselves and the world ... yet as everyone knows,
Wellesley girls can attract some incredible beaux!

The reference to beaux referred to Betsy's flourishing
romance with Dave Hill, a pre-med student at Dartmouth,
and the increasing frequency of travel between Hanover, New
Hampshire, and Wellesley which turned into marriage plans as
graduation approached:

Although thanks go to Wellesley for building her brain
And for teaching Bets how to come in from the rain,
Her strong thanks go to Wellesley for being quite brave
To accept male exchanges ... which let her find Dave.

There's a trace of a tear as the Wellesley years end...
No more trips up to Dartmouth to cook for a friend.
No more freezing your tail off in weather that's "fine."
No more toaster-type oven meals served with cheap wine.

Dartmouth would also welcome Susan as a student, although she ended up spending a great deal of her four years at other schools. Determined to pursue her love of musical theater, Susan would end up graduating from Dartmouth having spent the minimum amount of time possible there, as her 20th birthday poem reflects:

She's admitted to schools as are ships to world ports
(Application submission's now one of her sports).
With SC and blue Yale and now Dartmouth she's vexed,
As she sails into Boston Conservat'ry next.

Yet, despite her absence from campus, another Dartmouth romance blossomed and Susan's future husband, Joel Getzendanner, entered the poems on her 21st birthday:

Oh, her twentieth year is the one to recall;
The key scene is a football game late in the fall.
As our Joel and Sue fell in love without doubt
No one knew whether Dartmouth or Harvard won out.
As we now start the year when Sue seeks twenty-two,
It's one year from the age when at some August do
She has plans to make Dartmouth again prove of course
Its monopoly claim as our son-in-law source.

Jerry's college career did not produce a lasting romance, but did cause me to wonder from time to time how he spent those cold winters in Williamstown, Massachusetts:

After four years at Williams some questions appear …
Did you soak up more knowledge or pitchers of beer?
Did you major in Am. Civ. [American Civilization] or having
    a lark?
Did you sleep more in daylight than when it was dark?
Did you win more at cards than the cost of your books?
Did you spend more on pizza than food Williams cooks?
And of greatest importance, just where'd you learn more –
In a class or bull session on Hopkins' top floor?

In contrast to Betsy and Susan, who married just out of college, Jerry's single life persisted until I found myself commenting on the fact on the occasion of his 27th birthday,

This year weddings of friends were occurring quite often,
And while Jerry attended, he never did soften.
For although at a party he's fun and a mingler,
With each year passing Jerry grows older and singler.

And, just when I was beginning to worry, Pat Mayland came into Jerry's life and his 30th birthday poem:

I've been scratching my head. Can it be? Is it true?
Can procrastinate Jer change to Mister Will Do?
As he's switched from his bachelorhood, Jerry says that
"Plan ahead" is his motto when plans include Pat.
Should we worry when commoners wed royalty…
When a grocery brand manager weds a V.P.?
No, all stories like this enjoy endings immutable;
Cinderella types blossom and turn out to be suitable.

In due course, my grandchildren start to appear in the poems, as well, beginning with the birth of Jeremy Jefferis Hill, recalled on Betsy's 27th birthday:

The excitement that came before November 8
Was to pale into nothing compared to that date.
For 'twas then that the newest came out of a Hill …
Now the twosome's a threesome and, oh, what a thrill!
Not too many would go to the Loop on the morn
Of the day when her son would decide to be born.
Since for Betsy efficiency's more than a quirk,
She had Jeremy Hill on her way home from work.

Zachary Richardson Hill's arrival was duly documented in Betsy's 29th:

For our Betsy last year was sure short on sound slumber,
Eighty-two was the year with the two the key number.
Second Master's degree, number two in that pack
While the best number two came in nine pounds of Zach!

And that of Andrew Nicholas Hill in the poem written for her 32nd birthday:

And the baby is Andrew, our newest arrival
Who must fend off both brothers, an act of survival.
He's a cuddler, a smiler, and coos with such charm,
With a fist in his mouth almost up to his arm.

For Betsy, motherhood was balanced with career endeavors. As a young wife and mother, she added to her Wellesley accomplishments with an MAT (Master of Arts in Teaching) and an MBA from Northwestern's Kellogg School. Her MBA was particularly distinctive as she was raising a two-year old (Jeremy) and gave birth to Zachary in May of her second year. Betsy took one exam at home, another at school, and squeezed in a final presentation to finish her degree with only two B's and second in her class.

Despite her academic performance, however, she graduated without a job offer. Being pregnant during job-hunting time, she found more than one interviewer staring at her stomach and asking one way or another if she was seriously interested in full-time employment. The chauvinism made Jerry and me both so angry!

One day, I telephoned John Robson, president of G.D. Searle & Co. I asked him if he would be interested in a Wellesley Phi Beta Kappa who graduated second in her class at Northwestern's business school. He said, "Of course!" I then asked if it would bother him that I was talking about my daughter. He laughed and said, "Send her in to see me." Betsy started at Searle not long after aspartame had been approved by the FDA, was the fourth employee of Searle's newly created NutraSweet division, and would enjoy and master a variety of challenges there over the next 14 years.

Betsy and Dave were divorced a year and a half after Andrew was born. Dave moved to Battle Creek, Michigan, to practice neurology, where he met and married Dell. A few years later, Dave and Dell moved to Mt. Vernon, Illinois, where they welcomed his three sons for visits each summer and assorted other vacations. Sadly, Dave died of a brain tumor at the age of 47. Typical of Betsy, Dell is now a friend and joins our family for holidays and graduations.

While Dave's death affected each of his sons deeply, I was proud of their resilience as well as their unique talents. At Columbia College and then at the University of Florida for a graduate degree, Jeremy's mastery of the science and art of sound production and architectural acoustics impressed even someone who grew up before rock 'n roll. Jeremy's tragic death in a motorcycle acccident in February 2007 left a hole in our family that can never be filled.

Watching Zach's quick intelligence and charm, we often say that we know he'll run something someday—we just don't know what yet. At Willamette University, he has also developed into an accomplished poet. Andrew's Boston University career seems to indicate a continued interest in writing, as well as business—and I often think of a wonderful piece he wrote in high school, in which he interviewed me and wrote about my early life. I hope he finds the rest of the story as interesting!

Since NutraSweet, Betsy has honed her management and marketing skills in dot-com companies whose declines would have made it wiser for her to take more compensation in cash and less in stock options. She is building on those experiences as chief operating officer at Learning Enhancement Corporation, a promising young company, and an instructor at Lake Forest Graduate School of Management. Betsy's calm demeanor, her self-control, her self-confidence, and her combination of ability and wisdom make her someone others turn to for advice and help. She should inherit my "couch" when I am gone.

Susan soon followed in Betsy's steps along the motherhood path when she delivered Shelley Babb Getzendanner nine months after Andrew was born. The poem I wrote for Susan's 29th birthday recalls some of the challenges motherhood presented to her:

Shelley's mother is challenged to keep up with her,
As that two-year-old's movements resemble a blur.
She can look oh so innocent, quiet and all,
While she's drawing a picture in ink on the wall.

A few years later, I would turn to limericks as the style for Susan's 30th birthday poem and accurately predicted the athletic talents of Jessa Catharine Getzendanner who rounded out the Getzendanner family:

"Tennis clothes are not pregnancy smocks,"
Says Sue, grabbing her racquet and socks.
　　Now we're all taking bets
　　That the new baby Getz
Will join Mom, Dad, and Shelley as jocks.

When Susan graduated from Dartmouth, she established what may have been a record for getting a Dartmouth degree having spent the minimum amount of time in Hanover, New Hampshire. She developed her singing and performing abilities at the Eugene O'Neill Theater and Boston Conservatory, and we arranged visits around her shows whenever we could. After college, she continued to perform professionally for a few years, becoming a member of the Actors' Equity Association.

Susan had started performing long before college, however, working in the song and dance revue at Six Flags Great America

Park in Gurnee, Illinois, when it first opened; and traveling to San Jose, California, the next year to be a cast member there. It was in San Jose that Phyllis and I first met Joel Getzendanner; he had managed a summer visit there between semesters at Dartmouth. Joel and Susan would be married shortly after graduation.

When they were married, Joel's plan was to enter the ministry; he attended the Lutheran Seminary at the University of Chicago. He then switched from the seminary to the University of Chicago's business school, much to my surprise. After he received his MBA, Susan moved with Joel to Elyria, Ohio, where he worked for Borg Warner and where Shelley was born.

A few years later, back in Chicago, Joel entered the not-for-profit world in which he would focus his career, beginning at the Joyce Foundation. Jessa was born when they lived in Arlington Heights, a Chicago suburb. Then the Heron Foundation took them to New York City (with a home in Chappaqua) for a few years, and later not-for-profit consulting attracted them to Olympia, Washington.

As her girls are older and as the end of her marriage necessitated, Susan has reentered the work force. She now works with her special friend David McKenzie producing motion picture documentaries.

When Shelley was getting ready to submit applications to college, one of her teachers described her as a "Renaissance Girl." There is little she can't do, so that the description is perfect. At Carleton College, she is a scholar athlete, making the varsity tennis team as a freshman and serving as team co-captain as a senior as she completes her art major.

Jessa lights up our lives in much the same way her mother did when she was young. Her energy, love, and creativity are visible in everything she does. They will serve her well as she launches her collegiate career at Whitworth College in

Spokane, Washington, as they have in the work she has done with fortunate groups of young people in Olympia's children's museum.

In between Shelley and Jessa, we welcomed Christine Mayland Perkins. The limerick I wrote Jerry when he turned 30 foretold what would be many years of proud moments for Jerry and Pat:

> There's a new local camera man,
> Who has learned both to zoom and to pan.
> > Father Jerry gets misty
> > While filming his Christie,
> For Mom Pat who's the number-one fan!

Jerry went to school for 20 consecutive years (North Shore Country Day, Williams, and Northwestern's Kellogg Business School), a feat in and of itself. More remarkably, he did so without changing school colors—purple it was, three schools in a row. During summers he ran a Jewel route, and worked in a Jewel produce department and in the salvage area in one of the warehouses (where, he reported to me, the "f" word was used between syllables).

Quaker Oats gave him his first full-time job. His success there included winning a national award for Promotion of the Year for the disappearance of Cap'n Crunch from his cereal boxes—a promotion that had college students eating the cereal in record amounts.

Jerry met Pat when she was working on Quaker business at Foote, Cone & Belding. Their daughter Christine has kept them both running—to American Girl theater performances where she was a cast member through hundreds of shows. She has also performed in the children's chorus at the Lyric Opera in Chicago, and continued to enjoy acting and singing in every high school performance she could cram into her schedule.

Those experiences were steps in a path that have led to freshman year at the School of Music at Northwestern University.

After 16 successful years, Jerry was downsized and moved from Quaker to Brunswick, where CEOs and corporate strategy subsequently changed. Quaker and Brunswick's loss became Johnson Outdoors' gain when Jerry became the company's chief operating officer and subsequently president.

Of course, turnabout is fair play, and from time to time my children turned the poetry tables on me, especially Betsy, who mimicked my first poem in an "Ode to Jolly Don in Florida" for my 54th birthday. I was proud that Jolly Don was the nickname my children's friends bestowed on me.

> Ten years ago I remember bragging
> That other people's Dads were lagging.
> They seemed so old and worn and tired,
> But none of them as yet retired!

Even my grandchildren would get into the game, starting to show promise on my 75th birthday, when Zach (at the age of 18) crafted the following:

> I was told to write something for you,
> And I thought that a lim'rick would do,
>   But they're actually quite hard,
>   And, alas, I'm no bard,
> But I'm gonna force out at least two.

> Or maybe I'll stretch out for three,
> One for each quarter century,
>   This meter won't work,
>   But due to some quirk,
> You're still as happy as can be.

I know that these were kinda lame,
A sure source of my future shame.
> But take it from me,
> When your digits reach three,
I'll write more that will gain my name fame.

While many friends know of my poem-writing penchant and fondness for limericks, my career as a poet may be summed up in the following stanza from a poem written for Susan's 28th birthday, called "Ode to Shelley's Mom."

Odes are written for urns manufactured in Greece,
Odes make ref'rence to war, though more often it's peace.
As a poet it's shameful to have to unload
And confess this exhausts my whole knowledge of ode.

CHAPTER 9

THE RIGHT THINGS TO DO

During my years as president and chairman of Jewel, I was involved in two trade associations: the National Association of Food Chains and the Super Market Institute (the two later merged to become the present-day Food Marketing Institute). Neither impressed me with its accomplishments—in fact, I described them both as representing the lowest common denominator of their memberships.

One experience stands out, however. At a time when 19 percent of the U.S. family budget was being spent on food, the industry wanted to start a public relations campaign called "Only 19" to promote the fact. As they were wont to do with most programs, the retailers were pushing for manufacturers to pay for the campaign. I was glad when Paul Austin, then CEO of Coca-Cola, put an end to the discussion with his statement that, in his experience, "good public relations is being caught in the act of doing something worthwhile." I have always remembered that comment and hoped that, when Jewel did the right things, we would sometimes be "caught in the act."

I became president of Jewel in 1965 during a time of considerable activism in the U.S. Consumer groups, civil rights activists, anti-war protesters, inflation, and Watergate introduced a series of external challenges, some of which turned out to be actual opportunities for Jewel. Others were a drain and a distraction. We learned from both. Perhaps because of Jewel's obvious respect for and responsiveness to the consumer; or perhaps because I was the "new young president"; or perhaps simply because, as had occurred in the Air Force, I happened to be on someone's list of people they knew—Jewel and I were drawn into a number of these issues.

Preceding the 1972 election, President Richard Nixon and his staff were looking for ideas to get consumer advocates off his back. The idea they concocted was the National Council for Consumer Affairs. Establishing the Council allowed Nixon to say that he was helping consumers, although he created it without any fundamental commitment to its mission. I had gotten a lot of publicity as the youthful and recently appointed president of Jewel and, in 1971, Tom Brooker, then CEO of Montgomery Ward, and I each received phone calls from Nixon's staff, asking us to co-chair the National Council for Consumer Affairs.

When I discussed the invitation with George Clements and Frank Lunding, they thought I should do it. So, I accepted the appointment and started making trips to Washington, DC. Brooker and I divided Consumer Affairs into categories and worked very diligently on the effort.

Despite the administration's lack of commitment, the National Council for Consumer Affairs provided many lessons that subsequently helped Jewel. In part because of that experience, Jewel became a real leader in trying to give consumers useful information. Consumer information, I became convinced, was a win-win situation. It probably helped that I hadn't been steeped early in the grocery business, and that the route business had conditioned me to be innovative in satisfying customers.

As part of Jewel's commitment to consumers, we appointed Jane Armstrong as our consumer ombudswoman. I could always count on Janie to give me a straight answer on what would make a positive impression on the consumer. Among our consumer information initiatives, we introduced unit pricing (typically price per ounce) to enable consumers to compare prices more easily; and we went back to calling cuts of meat by their common names (as opposed to "party steaks" or "barbeque chops"). Open dating was another initiative driven by our desire to give consumers information. Prior to open dating, all perishable products had date codes that were cryptic and required a book of codes to decipher.

One day, I said to Fred Woerthwein, vice president of store operations, "Fred, why do we have these codes? Why don't we let the consumer look at actual dates?" He replied, "That's a good question. I spend so much time trying to get our people in the field to rotate stock, and it takes so much time for them to do it. It would make much more sense if we just let the customer do it." The codes were cryptic simply because that was the way it always had been done. Open dating made it easier for us and better for the consumer—a prime example of win-win.

The consumer information initiative for which Jewel may be best known—posting prescription drug prices—was managed by Dick Cline, then president of Osco. The old guard in the drug store business would never have challenged the status quo in this way, because advertising drug prices was felt to be unethical. "Lawyers don't talk about prices. Doctors don't talk about prices. Would you want us to be unethical? After all our training as pharmacists, and when we're responsible for protecting the health and welfare of the consumer, we should not be talking about prices!" is what we would hear.

But we felt it was the right thing to do. When it was time to replace the original Osco management, Wes Christopherson and I agreed that Dick Cline was the leader who could change the business. The program Dick came up with entailed posting prices of the 100 most-prescribed drugs in the store, taking a picture of the poster, and using the picture in Osco ads. I remember we were going to launch the program on a Monday, and we didn't know for sure whether any Osco pharmacists would show up for work that day. That's how dramatic the situation was. As it turned out, only one pharmacist quit, and Osco got tremendous publicity from posting drug prices.

While there was little backlash from the pharmacists who worked for Osco, the state pharmacy boards, who were made up of independent pharmacy owners, were another story—they were up in arms! The board in South Dakota told us they were sending a sheriff over to take down the sign in one of our stores because it was against the pharmacy rules of the state. We arranged to have television cameras in the store when the sheriff arrived. We announced how sorry we were that we had to take the sign down; local media took pictures of the sign being removed. What we were trying to do for the consumer was so right that our business boomed as a result, and the pharmacy board in South Dakota eventually backed down.

The pharmacy board in Massachusetts, the toughest we ever encountered, expressed their regulatory displeasure in a different way. In the mid-1970s, the rule in Massachusetts was that a drug store had to be fully stocked and ready to open before the board would come in to inspect it and decide whether or not to issue a pharmacy license. Although the inspection was normally a formality, it was not so for Osco. Our first store in the Boston area was fully stocked and ready to open for more than a year before we finally got a court ruling that directed the pharmacy board to issue the license and allow us to open. When it did, Osco became the first drug chain with a store in Massachusetts.

My participation in the National Council for Consumer Affairs had taught me about the value of consumer information, and the experience benefited Jewel. I cannot say the same for another Washington, DC involvement—the Food Distribution and Retailing Panel of the White House Conference on Food,

Nutrition and Health in 1969. Headed by Dr. Jean Mayer, who later became president of Tufts University, the conference was a boondoggle for advocates for various causes who enjoyed a few days in a Washington hotel at the government's expense. I gave a speech at the University of Notre Dame in March 1970 and described the experience as follows:

> It was a case study in social action and mob psychology. It was an advertising man's nightmare of sloganeering. It contained more closed minds and idealistic people than I have ever seen in one place before in my life. Delegates marched and demonstrated in the halls of a large convention hotel and demanded, "Bread Now."

At the same time, I recognized the value of having my eyes opened and being challenged to think through issues to which I might otherwise have given less attention. As I said,

> I was taken from the protection of my normal corporate activity and challenged by several individuals who apparently believed I was a robber baron. I was pulled back in time to my own college ideas by students who felt sure that given the chance they could plan a utopian economy…. But, most importantly, I was forced to think through some problems which previously I had just thought about in the most general terms.

One of the outcomes of the conference was the food stamp program. I was enough of an advocate for the poor that I supported food stamps at the time. Later, I came to understand that food stamps were actually a second form of currency, and that the costs of such a system are very high. I wished afterwards that I had been an advocate of something more like a negative income tax or a direct cash benefit, as opposed to a substitute currency, which is what food stamps are. But there were those who wanted to make sure that the subsidy wasn't spent on liquor or other non-food items. The government, in its paternalistic "wisdom," decided on the alternate currency of food stamps.

If consumer information and food stamps were controversial political issues, then inflation in the 1970s became even more so. In 1973 and 1974, the nation had reached a then historically high inflation level of 4.5 percent. Many in the country were demanding that the government do something about it. John Connally, the former governor of Texas who was then a domestic policy advisor to President Nixon, was an advocate of "doing something" and that something was price controls. That position held sway at least for a time and Nixon, in fact, froze both wages and prices.

I remember hearing the news in the car when we were on a family vacation in the Rocky Mountains. As well-intended as wage and price controls may have been, the approach was misguided; those price controls contributed directly to the double-digit inflation in the Carter administration 10 years later. The saga of wage and price controls was to eat up a significant amount of my time and turn into some of the most frustrating experiences of my business life.

Don Rumsfeld (best known for his role as Secretary of Defense during the Iraq War), prior to an appointment to NATO, headed the domestic Office of Wages and Prices. He was charged with trying to control wages and prices—essentially, to "do something" about inflation. I had known Don from his first run for Congress when he was barely 30 years old. When the Office of Price Controls was created, Dr. John Dunlop, a Harvard economist, came to Washington to head it.

Rumsfeld advised Dunlop that there were two areas of price control in which Washington would need experienced advice. One area was food pricing; the other was drug pricing. Rumsfeld and Dunlop put together advisory boards on those two issues and, because he knew me, Rumsfeld recommended that I be invited to chair the Food Advisory Committee of the Cost of

Living Council. In 1974, I made 20 trips to Washington, DC to work on Cost of Living Council issues.

The Cost of Living Council and the Food Advisory Committee tried to help the U.S. government formulate rules that had some control elements, but that would not excessively distort the production and distribution of food. For instance, we argued for controlling gross margins rather than controlling prices. That would allow the cost of raw materials to vary based on what was happening on the farm, but still provide some element of control on food companies' ability to raise prices. We succeeded in making our case through the early months of the price control program, but political pressures would soon challenge our attempts at logical persuasion.

The most discouraging development came about as the pressure on Nixon from the Watergate scandal was heating up. I was enjoying an infrequent vacation around the time of my birthday with my family in Naples, Florida, when a call came. George Schultz, then Secretary of the Treasury, and John Dunlop summoned me to engage in a "serious discussion on freezing meat prices." I had to drive across the state of Florida to get a plane from Miami to Washington, DC in response to Schultz's summons.

It is one thing to freeze margins. It is another thing to freeze prices and interfere with the basic ebb and flow of product supply. If prices were too low, the farmer just would not sell his product—after all, he could simply keep feeding his cattle for another year if necessary. The meat packers wouldn't buy product because they couldn't make ends meet with prices controlled. The only thing that a price freeze could do was dry up the retail supply of meat. Those were the thoughts on my mind as I traveled to Washington instead of celebrating my birthday with my family.

John Dunlop and George Schultz were present for the discussion, as were representatives of the cattle producers and processors. Reaction to the idea was heated. The industry was unanimous in declaring that the plan would devastate the entire meat industry.

I was somewhat comforted when George Schultz made it very clear that he thought the price freeze was a terrible idea. He even went so far as to declare, "If they do this, I'm going to seriously consider resigning as Secretary of the Treasury." I returned to my family, thinking that we had communicated our arguments as strongly as we could and that the administration, in the person of George Schultz, had gotten the message and was sympathetic.

The arguments all proved to be in vain, however, and Nixon froze meat prices the following week. I threw up my hands at the waste of time and effort I had been through. The final blow, however, came years later when I read the transcript of the infamous Nixon Watergate tapes. The transcript revealed that, the week after my birthday and my urgent trip to Washington in the midst of the family vacation, Bob Haldeman met with Nixon in the White House. Haldeman's news was that Jeb Magruder was about to blow the top off the Watergate conspiracy with his testimony to Congress. Unable to stop Magruder, Nixon and Haldeman discussed the need for a distraction—and the distraction they settled on was … freezing meat prices.

This story would not be complete without some background on Jeb Magruder and the irony of his role, albeit unknowing, in triggering the freezing of meat prices. I met Jeb in the summer of 1962, at the recommendation of Jim Allen, of Booz Allen Hamilton. I was vice president and general manager of the Home Shopping Service at the time, and had just established the Jewel corporate sponsorship program, our training program for MBAs. We invited Jeb to come to Jewel as a management trainee, one of the first group of three to go through the program. The other two were Dick George (Dick would go on to be president and CEO of Osco and later to found Ulta 3

Cosmetics & Salon) and Bill Bennett (Bill would found Yoplait in the U.S. with Joe Jannotta when he left Jewel).

Jeb had received his MBA at the University of Chicago and had worked at Booz Allen Hamilton before joining Jewel. As he describes in his book, *An American Life*, several years later, Jeb "proceeded to make the worst possible decision." He left Jewel. I tried to talk him out of leaving. I remember that in the process of trying to "save" him for Jewel, I asked Jeb and his wife Gail to visit with me at my home. In the discussion, I asked Jeb why he was leaving. "I have become too involved in local politics," he said, "and Gail and I have decided that the move to the west coast, where we can be near her parents, would help us save our marriage." I asked Gail if she saw the move as saving their marriage. She said she did. I told them, "That is the one reason for Jeb's leaving that I will not question. Good luck on your move." Not surprisingly, while the marriage survived Jewel, it would not survive Watergate and Jeb's time in prison.

When I read the section of the Watergate transcripts in which Nixon and Haldeman made the decision to freeze meat prices, I looked back on my young, idealistic self, leaving my family on my birthday and making the journey to Washington to debate and defend the merits of the issue, only to fall victim to Nixon's need to "take people's minds off Watergate." In fact, all of the meat industry's predictions about the effects of freezing prices were accurate. Jewel buyers actually had to go to the farms and ranches, buy meat on the hoof, and have cattle custom-slaughtered and delivered to us in order to have meat in our stores.

Not all of Jewel's activist challenges originated in Washington. During one of the most difficult and sensitive political situations we faced, I was especially glad to have thoughtful and independent directors on Jewel's board, such as Father Raymond Baumhart, one of my favorite directors. In 1972, when Ray joined the Jewel board, I could claim that I had a director with an MBA *and* a doctorate from the Harvard Business School (where he wrote his thesis on ethics in business), who ran one of the largest institutions in the state of Illinois (Loyola University), but whom no one had ever invited to be a director of a public company ... because he was a Jesuit priest.

When I called on Ray to ask him to join the board, he said he wasn't sure he had the time, as the president of Loyola. I said, "Well, you'll see how another large organization is run, which might be useful to you. And besides, we pay a director's fee." He shrugged his shoulders. I said, "It's $10,000 a year." "Oh," he said. "If it's that much, I'll have to consult with my religious superior." I said, "If there's any problem, I suppose we could make the check out to Loyola University instead of you." "Oh no," he replied. "If I'm going to do it, I'd want you to make the check out to me, because you can't imagine how poor the retirement program is for Jesuit priests."

Ray was on the board when Jewel was targeted by Cesar Chavez, the union leader who became active in promoting improved working and living conditions for migrant farm workers in California by urging food stores to stop selling grapes and lettuce. In fact, just as Jewel was community-concerned and consumer-concerned, we had already addressed the issue of farm worker conditions seriously. We took trips out to the farms in California and elsewhere to make sure that the farms from which we bought produce were indeed providing acceptable working and living conditions.

So, when Chavez started raising the issue, Jewel continued to sell lettuce and grapes. We reasoned that our customers expected to be able to find those products in our stores. Furthermore, we had approached the issue of working conditions for the migrant workers in what we thought was a responsible way. But once Chavez discovered that Jewel was sympathetic to the issues he was raising, he zeroed in on us. Unless we stopped selling grapes and lettuce in our stores, he and his followers would single out Jewel's stores for picketing. Our reward for being concerned was that we became the retail focus of his attention!

Chavez's followers had little trouble stirring up Loyola University students and they expended considerable energy protesting to Father Baumhart as the university's president because he was a director of Jewel. Ray consistently responded to the students' protests with the message that he could be of more help by staying involved with Jewel than by not being involved. At one board meeting as I was reporting on the situation, it suddenly occurred to me to ask Ray a question. If I had thought about it beforehand, I would have told him in advance, but I just asked, "Ray, given your concern about ethics and your religious background and concern for people, if you had my job, what would you do differently in dealing with the farm workers?" Boy, that stopped the board! He paused for 30 or 45 seconds, maybe even a minute. When he answered, he said, "Don, I wouldn't do anything differently than you're doing, but I would keep talking to them." Here was a man who was beyond reproach as an ethicist and as a human being. We were being accused of being anti-farm worker. Ray understood all aspects of the situation. I found Ray's advice very supportive. Jewel kept talking with the protesters, but continued to sell grapes and lettuce and other produce in our stores. Most growers eventually recognized the union.

Perhaps the most memorable and most productive encounter for Jewel with activists was my work with the Reverend Jesse Jackson, Sr. When I became president of Jewel in 1965, I received hundreds of letters. One was from the Reverend Jackson, who represented what was then Operation Breadbasket in Chicago. Operation Breadbasket had succeeded in signing "covenants"— the word that Jesse and Dr. Martin Luther King used—or agreements, with milk companies, soft drink companies, and ice cream companies in the Chicago area to hire more black employees. The gist of Jesse's letter was that Jewel was next on his list. I invited him to visit with me.

I had taken over George Clements's office, which was about the size of a large living room, when I became president of Jewel. I asked Lee Smith, a Jewel vice president, to sit in on the meeting with me as my witness. I was sure Jesse would bring his own witnesses and, indeed, he arrived with more than 40 associates. We scrambled to assemble enough chairs and everyone sat down. I let Jesse talk and timed it; he spoke for 45 minutes. His people were getting fidgety, but I continued to sit there, taking notes and listening. Finally, he stopped and asked, "Aren't you going to say anything?" And I answered, "I wanted to make sure I heard you out."

He had accused me of inheriting my position as opposed to earning it. I said, "You've got to understand me so you know who you're dealing with. I grew up in a poor neighborhood on the wrong side of the tracks. We didn't know enough to call it a ghetto. Anything that has happened to me has been the result of education and work. That's why I'm here. I didn't inherit anything, except perhaps the results of the hard work of Jewel people over the years."

But I thought that what he wanted to accomplish was right and I told him so, "I happen to agree with you that we need to do more in the black community." This was before "African American" became the preferred term and "black" was the word we both used. "But let me tell you something," I continued. "I will ask the Jewel organization how many black employees we can add. I will probably discount their projections by 15 percent because that is how much I discount the budgets they hand me." Jesse didn't like that. "But the most important thing I want to say to you," I went on, "is that I'm genuinely going to try to figure out what we ought to be doing. That will be it. If you don't agree, I would rather have you picket Jewel today for not promising enough than to picket us a year from now for not doing what we promised. You will find that Jewel will enter into the spirit of what you want to get done, but we will not promise something that we are not very sure we can do."

Jewel and Operation Breadbasket spent a year negotiating. I don't think anyone took this more seriously than I did—not the soft drink and ice cream companies—not even many of the people at Jewel. Lee Smith worked with Operation Breadbasket staff, although Jesse would only talk to me. There was a list of things they wanted besides increasing the number of black employees at Jewel. They wanted us to put money in black banks. "Fine," we said, "we'll do it." They wanted to know how much. I said, "No, any banker who would share that information isn't a bank we want to have money in. We'll put in something to service the account, and we'll keep additional funds there in order to be helpful to the community."

In addition, Operation Breadbasket wanted us to put black-made products on our store shelves. I said, "The problem isn't getting them <u>on</u> the shelves, it's getting them <u>off</u> the shelves—getting them sold. We'll help in two ways. Number one, we'll use our laboratory at Barrington [where we had a manufacturing facility] to test any product that is brought to us. And number two, we'll establish relationships between your black manufacturers and our buyers. Our buyers will give your manufacturers advice on how to promote and move the products off the shelves. We're not doing that for any other group, but, in the spirit of trying to be helpful, we're offering to do this for you."

It turned out that the first product they sent to the Barrington lab to be tested was a toilet bowl cleaner that was pure lye. We didn't put it on the shelves, of course, and we told Operation Breadbasket why. We did work with them on other products, though, including, as I recall, brooms.

Of course, Jesse's greatest interest was in seeing us add black employees in our stores. In order to do that, we would need to open more stores in the inner city. Doing so turned out to be one of the best things we ever did, because we ended up with a very profitable business in Chicago's inner city. But the environment in which we were going to open them was in a state of change and, consequently, fraught with tension.

Many Chicago neighborhoods were experiencing changes as their populations changed from predominantly white to predominantly black. The human reaction to the changes was anger. Whites were angry at blacks and vice versa. Sales volume dropped in all the stores in those transitioning neighborhoods. Many stores closed, and the remaining stores did not receive additional investment or updating.

Moreover, many of our black customers who worked as domestic servants in suburban homes knew about Jewel stores there. Based on the deteriorating appearance of our city stores, those customers incorrectly assumed that older Jewel stores in the city must have lower-quality food. Accusations were also leveled that supermarkets in the inner city raised prices at the beginning of each month when welfare checks arrived in the mail. Of course, that was absurd.

Neither the allegations of lower quality food nor those that we manipulated prices were true, but the net result was damaging. We concluded that the only answer to serving the inner city was to invest in first-class new stores, and to bring the high-quality appearance of the suburbs to black customers in the city.

Despite problems with insurance, theft, and shrink expenses (product that disappears and cannot be accounted for), the black community had somewhat more limited ways to spend their money, at least then, and more of the family budget was therefore spent on food. The business was there, but opening new and refurbished inner-city stores and staffing them with black employees required us to develop a flow of blacks applying for the jobs. In order to accomplish that objective, we opened a hiring center on the near south side of Chicago.

The hiring center had been open for a month when we gathered there to sign our covenant with Operation Breadbasket. The signing of the covenant was a memorable occasion. During the year of our negotiations, I had personally gone to Operation Breadbasket offices on several occasions—something that surprised them. Jesse was a negotiator, not a businessman, and whatever we said we could do, he would want more. Finally we had to say, "This is it. Take it or leave it."

Dr. Martin Luther King joined Jesse Jackson to sign the covenant with me. The fact that they arrived 45 minutes late did not diminish the sense of accomplishment of that day. I have seen Jesse a number of times since. He remembers me, he remembers Jewel, and he remembers that Jewel did what we said we would do.

As we started to hire through that south side office, we realized that to successfully employ what was then referred to as the hard-core unemployed, we had to take a new approach, so we created a coaching program. We would hire a coach for every 10 new "hard-core" employees.

The coach's job was to get his 10 employees up in the morning, and make sure they showered, combed their hair, dressed appropriately, and arrived at the store on time. There were plenty of failures in that program, since selling drugs on the street was more lucrative than working hard in a Jewel store (and didn't require getting up early in the morning). But there were also successes and, combined with all the other efforts, the coaching program helped to expand Jewel's base of African-American employees.

One of the great people we hired in the coaching program illustrates how deeply the program and the hiring of blacks changed the culture at Jewel. Sam Hill, a hard-working, attractive young black man, had been a street worker for the YMCA before he came to Jewel. When he had been a Jewel coach for a while, he came to me and said, "I'm not in the mainstream of the business. I like Jewel and I would really like to be able to grow as a manager." We offered to place him in the meat department, since we thought that would be one of the toughest departments in the stores for blacks to crack.

Sam subsequently trained in half a dozen meat markets, the last of which had an Italian market manager, typical of many in the business. If someone had told me that friends of that meat market manager were among those throwing rocks at Dr. Martin Luther King in Marquette Park, it wouldn't have surprised me. This manager observed to Sam at the end of his stint there, "You know, Sam. I didn't really want you in my store—but I have to admit that you're a good worker and probably have a future with the company ... despite the fact that you're a college graduate." It was a new experience for Sam to experience discrimination based on education rather than color. Sam went on to work in the store operations management of Jewel Food Stores.

There were some hard lessons to learn, as well, in expanding Jewel's base of black employees. When we built a store at 39th and Vincennes in Chicago, a very low income area, the front of the store was mostly brick instead of glass to avoid problems with vandals. The community and Operation Breadbasket protested; they also insisted we hire a black manager. We made the mistake of rushing someone into the store manager position who wasn't ready for the challenge. He failed. I decided then to stand up to that kind of pressure—to do what was right for the business and for people. We weren't willing to foul up any more careers by putting people in jobs they weren't ready for ... despite activist pressures.

The covenant was signed in 1966, and Martin Luther King was assassinated within a year.

Following the assassination, many fires were set in Chicago, but no Jewel store was burned. In one case, on West Madison Street, the fires burned right up to the railroad tracks near us, but never went beyond them. There were stories of incredible heroism. One situation I remember involved a store on the south side with mostly black employees and a small number of white employees. The black employees accompanied the white employees out of the store, got them in their cars, and escorted them off the property to make sure they were safe. I don't know how long they had been working together, but there was enough good feeling within that Jewel store that blacks and whites cared about each other.

As a postscript, I have to tell about the cultural change that accompanied Jewel's acquisition by American Stores after I retired. For a time in the late 1970s, a number of years before the eventual hostile takeover, we were trying to reach an amicable merger agreement with American Stores (subsequently sold to Albertson's, which was in turn acquired by SuperValu). Walter Elisha, then president of Jewel Food Stores, was driving Sam Skaggs, American Stores' CEO, around the city. "Oh, there's a black," said Skaggs during the tour. "Yes," said Walter, "do you have a problem with that?" Skaggs explained, "Well, our policy is if we drive around a neighborhood and there's one black, then we are on our guard. If there are two blacks, we don't put a store there."

There were a million blacks in the Chicago area, but for a number of years after the acquisition, American Stores refused to approve a new inner-city store. This has since changed, but Dominick's, Jewel's main Chicago competitor, probably has several locations today that Jewel should have had.

At Jewel, we found that we could and did serve the black community in Chicago, well and profitably. Like striving to be the leader in consumer information, it was good business, and it was the right thing to do.

Chapter 10

Not-for-Profit Challenges

The title of this chapter is intentionally ambiguous. It can be read as referring to the challenges I encountered while serving on the boards of not-for-profit organizations or to the challenges I presented while I served on them. Both meanings apply.

My first invitations to serve on not-for-profit boards came from local institutions. In 1961, when I was vice president and general manager of the Home Shopping Service at Jewel, I was invited to become a trustee of Evanston Hospital (the hospital where Jerry and Susan had been born, which is now part of Evanston Northwestern Healthcare). About the same time, I was also invited to be a trustee of The North Shore Country Day School (where Betsy and Jerry already went to school, and where Susan would soon enroll). Both were respected institutions; the offers seemed like good ways to expand my horizons beyond Jewel and to get more involved in the community.

I served as an Evanston Hospital trustee from 1961 through 1970. After nine years, trustees were required to leave the board for at least a year, although they could be and often were later reelected. I was a diligent board member, but became unhappy toward the end of my nine-year tenure. It seemed to me that the hospital was being run much more in the doctors' interests than it was in the interests of the patients and the community.

One illustration was found in the emergency room, which operated on a fee-for-service (for-profit) basis. Doctors were neither recruited for nor specifically assigned to the emergency room; they got paid individually for their work there. As a result, staffing was an issue, but the doctors resisted changes that would help the institution. On the whole, the doctors were a very conservative group. Some thought that managing the emergency room as a service arm at the hospital would lead to socialized medicine. I made it clear what I thought of the situation, but little changed.

When I completed my term, I didn't regret having to leave the board. I was invited back later, but by then I had other areas of involvement I found more satisfying. Eventually, the hospital's approach to emergency room staffing changed.

My interaction with The North Shore Country Day School lasted longer and had a more positive tone. Much of that had to do, of course, with the joys of watching my children grow up and their wonderful experiences there. I joined the board in 1963 and was elected president in 1968 for a two-year term, following which I left the board to serve as a trustee of the school's foundation. I served on the foundation board for over 25 years. The foundation was modest but helpful as all income was paid out to the school. Not long after I left the board, Phyllis was asked to become a trustee and also served as president, the only woman ever to have held that position. Betsy also later served as a trustee of the school.

Another Chicago-based not-for-profit board opportunity came my way in 1967—an invitation to join the board of the Museum of Science and Industry. The museum, an important educational center in Chicago and great fun for kids, is known for its German U-boat submarine (captured in World War II and preserved) and its experiential "real" coal mine. I served on the board for five years, including as secretary, until one event turned me off.

The board was responsible for managing the museum's endowment, in which the number-one holding at the time was stock in Sears, Roebuck & Co. Julius Rosenwald, a founder of Sears, had established the museum; a good deal of the stock then in the museum's portfolio had come from him. Because it seemed imprudent to have the endowment so reliant on a single stock, I asked if we should have so many eggs in one basket. Gordon Metcalf, chairman of Sears at the time and a fellow museum trustee, was indignant that "after all Sears had done for the museum, a trustee would have the temerity to ask a question like that." As if the past had anything to do with how the board should handle the endowment in the future!

I thought that attitude inexcusable. The next time my term came up, I said I had too many other things to do.

One of my major not-for-profit board roles began shortly after I became chairman of Jewel in 1970. At almost the same time, I received invitations to go on the boards of the University of Chicago and Northwestern University. The commute to Northwestern in Evanston was more manageable than traveling to the University of Chicago in Hyde Park, and I liked Northwestern's emphasis on undergraduates, so I accepted the invitation to join the Northwestern board.

I soon learned that even the board of a major university of Northwestern's caliber could have a lot to learn about governance. At my first meeting, Jack Searle, chairman of G. D. Searle & Co. and chairman of the Northwestern board, stood in front of the board with the only book of board materials. Nothing had been sent out ahead of time, and no materials were distributed to the board members during the meeting. Jack said, "I've got the minutes here. Does anyone want me to read them?" Everyone said, "Aw, no, they're approved." Then he said, "I've got a list of changes in faculty here. Do you want me to go through the list?" That produced a similar reaction.

Not long after that, Jack Searle retired as chairman and I started pressing for changes—first, to get materials, including agendas and background information, distributed to all of the board members in advance of each meeting. More important was the creation of an executive committee of the board, which could go into greater depth on issues than was possible during a full board meeting. Twice in recent years, we have had experienced university leaders from outside Northwestern review the board's activity and make suggestions for improvement of our governance processes. By the time I moved from being a Charter Trustee to a Life Trustee in 2003, Northwestern's governance had come a long way.

Another dramatic change since my first Northwestern board meeting is the composition of the board. Early in my involvement, a report came from the nominating committee on candidates for trustee positions. It bothered me that we did not have a single African-American trustee and that the nominating committee's recommendation didn't include any, either. Evanston is a well-integrated community and Northwestern had the highest percentage of African Americans of any Big Ten university student body.

"Shouldn't we have a more diverse board?" I challenged the nominating committee. The next time the committee brought nominations to the board, once again there were no African-American candidates. The candidates this time were Dean Swift, the president of Sears; and Blaine Yarrington, one of the top officers of the company then called Standard Oil of Indiana, later to be known as Amoco. Both were highly qualified and both were good friends of mine, as I told the rest of the board. "But," I said, "I'm going to vote against them, and then I'm going to call each one tomorrow and tell them why I voted against them. It is time to elect a black trustee."

Graham Morgan, then head of U.S. Gypsum and chairman of the nominating committee, said, "We just don't have any room." I replied, "I will resign tonight if you will replace me with an African American."

They wouldn't take me up on my challenge, but as would happen in similar situations on other boards, I would soon be moved from the "back bench" to chair the nominating committee. As chair of this committee, I took great pride in the board we put together for the university. George Johnson of Johnson Products and Daryl Grisham of Parker House Sausage were the first two African-American members of the board. The board is much more diverse today than it was, to the credit and advantage of the entire university.

I have had the rewarding experience of serving on the search committees for two outstanding Northwestern presidents, Arnold Weber and Henry Bienen. In each case we hired a search firm to do the background research and develop our list of candidates. However, all contacts were made and negotiations conducted by members of the committee.

We said to the search committee, "The quality of the person we get will be directly related to our ability to keep our efforts confidential." No sitting university president wants it known that he or she might be considering a new job. The 1985 Northwestern search committee had 30 members, including students; but we managed to keep our decision to hire Arnie Weber quiet for 10 days until he finished a series of speeches throughout Colorado, where he headed the state university system.

When we interviewed Arnie, I asked him, "Why would you want to leave that big system out in Colorado and come to a smaller place like Northwestern?" Arnie replied, "Because I'm tired of being a lobbyist; I'd like to be an educator again."

Arnie brought fiscal stability to Northwestern and instituted a program review process that is still very important to the university. As part of this process, each activity of the university is reviewed by a committee of Northwestern individuals independent of that activity, joined by outsiders independent of the university.

When Arnie finished 10 years as president and decided to step down, another search committee was formed. Two good candidates from Princeton were suggested to us, so I called Jim Henderson. I knew Jim from serving on the board of Cummins Engine, where he had been president and then chairman, and I knew that he had been chairman of Princeton's board. According to Jim, Henry Bienen, then the leader of the Woodrow Wilson School at Princeton, was the one we should focus on. I called Henry to invite him for an interview. Those of us on that search committee recall that Henry was the only one of our candidates who said that he enjoyed fund-raising. That turned out to be an understatement!

Northwestern has been extraordinarily lucky to have the leadership of Arnie Weber and Henry Bienen. They are very different, but each in his turn enhanced the status of the university. Bob Strotz, Arnie's predecessor, had a number of successful years, but in his last three years created successive deficits of $1 million, $3 million, and $9 million. Arnie turned the deficits around quickly by agreeing on a budget with deans and officers. Those who could not meet their budgets were replaced. Arnie also brought considerable talent to the university as he continued to emphasize undergraduate education. And, as a master of the English language as well as the one-liner, Arnie is the most laugh-producing CEO I have ever worked with.

I can't resist sharing a few of my favorite "Arnieisms":

On his financial achievements in eliminating deficits at the university and keeping tuition increases below Northwestern's peers:

I don't want to be known as the best accountant ever to serve as president of Northwestern…. I have nothing against accountants. In fact, I hope my son, who is a professional musician, marries one.

On the maldistribution of university funds:

The Chair of the Department of Medicine sits there with four million dollars, but the Chair of Modern Languages is lucky to have four million footnotes.

On the subject of many universities:

We have reached the point where the best students fight to get into institutions because of the high quality of the faculty they will never see.
   (Northwestern was and is an exception in that regard.)

Henry Bienen, as Arnie's successor, has maintained the surpluses that the university experienced under Arnie's leadership with his excellent financial management. And his ability to attract talent and money assures that Northwestern will be one of the leading U.S. universities when he decides to retire. The increase in the university's endowment for research, faculty chairs, scholarships, and buildings, both academic and residential, will certainly mark the Bienen legacy.

During the years since I became a trustee of Northwestern, the university and the board have come face to face with some extremely controversial and emotional issues. During the Vietnam War era, students protested everywhere, including at Northwestern. They demanded that the Northwestern board stop the war, seemingly convinced that we were hugely influential and could accomplish that, if we would just try. Protests were frequent, the most memorable being one in early 1970, when students erected barricades that closed Sheridan Road in Evanston to traffic for several days.

Another emotionally-charged issue was the university's response to apartheid and investment in companies doing business in South Africa. Students and faculty were so angry that they were unrealistic about what made sense as a policy for the university, and what the policy's impact would be. They wanted us to divest the stock of any company that was still doing business in South Africa. "You've got to show these multinational companies that they have to get out of South Africa!" they would demand of the board.

I chaired a committee to recommend what the board should do, an assignment I received because of my previous experience with the issue through another not-for-profit organization—the Ford Foundation—whose board I added to my list of involvements in 1977.

The Ford Foundation board discussed the issue of investments in companies doing business in South Africa extensively. We based our policy decision on the approach developed by a study group in which Frank Thomas, first a board member and then president of the foundation, and J. Irwin Miller, a foundation board member and former CEO of Cummins Engine, were very active.

The study group, sponsored in part by the Ford Foundation, recommended a balanced approach to investments in South Africa, noting that it was unlikely you could really help people by taking away the source of many jobs. With that background, I was strengthened in my feeling that Northwestern's policy should also be carefully balanced. The policy we developed involved looking at how each company was acting in South Africa, and not divesting its stock as long as it was following the Sullivan principles. (Rev. Sullivan was a director of General Motors who had put together principles to guide the actions of companies operating in South Africa.)

While the ultimate policy adopted by the university was thoughtful and balanced, the experience of arriving at the policy and the reactions of the most vocal in the university community were not. For a long time, it didn't matter what we said about the balanced approach. People were angry, and anger got in the way of understanding that the impact of U.S. companies pulling out of South Africa would be to cut back on jobs for people of color. It was a nasty, confrontational, name-calling experience.

Far more positive, although an even greater and more extensive commitment of time and energy, has been my experience chairing Northwestern's multi-year capital campaign. When we kicked off Campaign Northwestern, it was the thirteenth U.S. university campaign with a goal of $1 billion or more. Since then, the number of campaigns of that magnitude has more than doubled.

When it was clear that we would make our original goal of $1 billion, I invited fellow trustee Tom Hayward, a partner in the law firm of Bell, Boyd & Lloyd in Chicago, to join me as co-chair of the campaign. Though other Northwestern graduates have given time and effort on behalf of the university, no one has exceeded Tom's, either before, during, or after Campaign Northwestern. We reached the $1 billion goal 30 months before the end of the five-year campaign and raised our goal to $1.4 billion.

Our final result, announced in 2003, was $1.55 billion. At the time, that placed Northwestern third behind Harvard and Yale in university-only campaign fund-raising results (those not also raising money for affiliated hospitals). It was a pleasure to speak on behalf of the campaign and to observe that we were raising money to enhance the quality of the university, not to cover deficits.

When asked for the reason the Northwestern campaign was so successful, I have offered three reasons: Henry Bienen, Henry Bienen, and Henry Bienen. His energy, his salesmanship, and the pleasure he takes in raising money to enhance the excellence of the university have been nothing less than extraordinary.

One story stands out. Early in the campaign, Henry went to upstate New York to visit an alumnus who it was thought might make a seven-figure gift. Henry spent the night there and learned that the alumnus, Leonard Thompson, former general counsel of Pfizer, had an ill wife and no children. He had had no meaningful involvement with Northwestern since he had graduated. Henry was not very hopeful that his trip would have a positive outcome.

Before the end of his visit, his host said that, because of Henry's visit, he would give some Pfizer stock he owned to the university. The stock was worth $56 million—the campaign's largest single gift.

When he returned from the trip, Henry proclaimed, "I was lucky."

"No, Henry," I told him. "That wasn't luck. You were there."

Of course, I had to make my own gift. My own college and graduate education was made possible by scholarships. Without the scholarship award that came with my acceptance letter from Yale, I would not have been able to attend. Neither would I have been able to attend the Harvard Business School without financial aid. I saw endowing a scholarship at Northwestern as a way of doing for others what the scholarship at Yale, particularly, had done for me. I could not thank all the people who gave the money that helped me at Yale, but I could help someone else attend college who didn't otherwise have the resources. I established the Donald S. Perkins Scholarship to be awarded to exceptional students who would not otherwise be able to attend Northwestern, and who preferably had been raised in a single-parent household with an income in the lower brackets. I had previously set up a similar scholarship at Yale.

I looked forward to meeting the first recipient of the Northwestern scholarship I had established—Nicole Mash— and I couldn't believe the connections and common ground between Nicki's background and mine. An African American, she had been raised by a single parent as I had been. She had gone to The North Shore Country Day School (on a scholarship). Perhaps the most striking coincidence was that her mother worked at Jewel as a checker!

If one side of philanthropy is raising money, the other side is giving it away. I started learning about that with the Chicago Community Trust, whose executive committee I joined in 1971. The committee would meet in the Marsh McLennan offices of Herman Dunlap Smith (brother of Perry Dunlap Smith, the founder of The North Shore Country Day School), who headed the trust. The trust was not yet sizable, but the experience enabled me to learn about Chicago and philanthropy. In awarding grants, the Community Trust adhered to a philosophy of finding ways to help people help themselves—teaching them how to fish, as we referred to it, rather than giving them fish.

In addition to participating in the evaluation of funding proposals, I also pressed for greater fiscal responsibility, especially related to administrative expenses. I pushed back against the constant requests to add staff, taking the position that I have reiterated in many similar situations: "We existed last year with x percent of our budget spent on staff. My vote is that we maintain that same percentage. If the endowment grows, then staff can grow." I resigned from the Community Trust when I joined the Ford Foundation board and broadened my attentions to philanthropy on a global scale.

The Ford Foundation is yet another of the many involvements I can trace back to education and volunteering—in this case, to Yale alumni and fundraising activities. Through those Yale alumni activities, I had gotten to know Irwin Miller, who invited me to join the board at Cummins Engine while he was CEO. I had served on the Cummins board for a number of years with Irwin and Frank Thomas, who were both trustees of the Ford Foundation as well, when Irwin proposed that I be invited to join the Ford Foundation board.

In scope and geography, the Ford Foundation far exceeded the Chicago Community Trust, but its need for discipline, governance, and oversight was not so different. Some Ford Foundation challenges became immediately obvious—among them the fact that the foundation was spending 1½ times its income annually and that overhead was a high percentage of the annual budget—it was expensive to operate offices around the world. The foundation's endowment had actually decreased from a high of $4 billion to $1.7 billion. The board had been inconsistent, voting to have the foundation exist in perpetuity, but spending money as if there were no such policy in place. It also bothered me that there was more emphasis on the theoretical than the practical, which I described as "scholars supporting scholars."

When Frank Thomas was asked by other foundation board members what kind of addition I would be, I am told he said, "He will give you fits!" And it might be fair to say that fits are exactly what I gave McGeorge (Mac) Bundy, president of the Ford Foundation at the time I joined the board. Mac Bundy, former national security advisor to President Kennedy and one of those David Halberstam described in his book, *The Best and the Brightest*, sometimes ran the foundation as if it were his own personal fiefdom. While board-supervised budgets were set for most policy areas, an exception was a function called Program Related Investment. Program Related Investment operated at the discretion of foundation staff and was not accountable for its spending, except to Mac Bundy.

Mac had the idea that the country would be better off if the foundation could help to create a number of black millionaires through Program Related Investment. I believed that the country would be better off if we taught a whole lot more kids to read. There were ample opportunities to invest in non-profit programs that offered some promise of repaying and thus allowing us to recycle the investment to finance other ideas.

I joined the Ford Foundation board immediately following the retirement of Henry Ford II after his 33 years of service. In a letter to Alex Heard, then chairman of the foundation's board and chancellor of Vanderbilt University, Ford expressed mixed feelings about the future of the foundation. He acknowledged that, while "the foundation has been a source of pride for me in many ways, it also, on occasion, has been a cause of frustration and sometimes plain irritation." As I saw the foundation in operation, I could appreciate both sentiments.

Ford also credited the "caliber of those who have served on this board" for the strength of the institution and its future prospects. It was a strong board and became even stronger. At various times, Ed Spencer, president and CEO of Honeywell; Barbara Scott Preiskel, whom I brought to the board, having gotten to appreciate her capabilities on the Jewel board; and Wally Haas, CEO of Levi Strauss, were also trustees.

Others included Henry Schacht, CEO of Cummins Engine; Ralph Dahrendorf, president of the London School of Economics; Bill Donaldson, founder of Donaldson, Lufkin & Jenrette and later SEC chairman; Rodrigo Botero, who designed the tax laws for his native Columbia; and Olusegun Obasanjo, president of Nigeria. It became increasingly clear to a number of us that the foundation needed a president who would be more responsive to the board when, in due course, Mac Bundy decided to retire.

We initiated the search for a new chief executive. During the course of the search, Irwin Miller and I were sitting in the Calcutta airport on a Ford Foundation trip, waiting for a long-delayed flight. We started talking about who we thought should lead the foundation. At one point, we each said to the other, "I've got my candidate." It turned out that we each had the same candidate: Frank Thomas.

Frank had led the rejuvenation of the Bedford-Stuyvesant area of Brooklyn in exemplary fashion and with tremendous positive publicity. He had also served on a number of boards—Cummins, Alcoa, Citibank, and the Ford Foundation, among them.

The choice seemed obvious to Irwin and me, but we wanted to make sure that our enthusiasm didn't have a negative impact. All the trustees were very involved in the months-long process and, in the end, Frank was the choice.

The first time that the subject of race ever came up during the search process was after Frank was formally elected by the board. As we were discussing the matter of publicizing the appointment, Ralph Dahrendorf commented, "By the way, doesn't it help that he's black?" It did, but I was most pleased with the fact that race had never been an issue—it had never even been mentioned—during the search process.

During Frank's tenure, we brought in Professor Jay Light, who later became dean of the Harvard Business School, to advise us about the foundation's spending pattern. He concluded that if we had a portfolio of 60 percent stocks and 40 percent bonds, and spent an average of 4½ percent of the average of the last three years' endowment, we would have a very high likelihood of maintaining the endowment's real (after inflation) value. We put this approach into effect. I have since been told that the foundation has continued to adhere to Professor Light's strategy since I retired from the board. In 2005, the endowment exceeded $11 billion.

Frank also brought Program Related Investment under control and worked with the board to establish clear controls and accountability. I had the pleasure of chairing the board's Program Related Investment Committee. Frank used the board very effectively in handling questions such as whether or not the foundation should have offices across the U.S., as we did around the world. I believed it was an unnecessary expense and that we should work with and through local Community Trust organizations, which were already in place and needed help, as I knew from my experience with the Chicago Community Trust. Many other board members reached the same conclusion, and that's how the foundation went forward.

When Frank took over as president of the foundation, every senior staff person was a man. He initiated a study of women and their role in the foundation. Susan Beresford, a junior program officer at the time, headed the study. She did an outstanding job and became much more visible in the process.

I gave Susan a hard time about the disarray in her office. She was very bright and personable, but her office always looked like a tornado had gone through it. I would tell her that she should be out spending her time working with people not paper and thinking about the strategy of the foundation. Today, not only is her desk cleaner, she succeeded Frank Thomas as the Ford Foundation's president, and has done a wonderful job as its leader.

One of the richest, most extraordinary aspects of my involvement on the Ford Foundation board was the opportunity I had to see how the Foundation's money was being spent around the world. It was worth the journey to see the excitement in the eyes of people who benefited from foundation-sponsored programs.

When I think about those beneficiaries, I cannot help remembering these people: the young white South African university professor who could let only one of our group into his office at a time to avoid violating the apartheid restrictions of his "banning"; the unmarried teenage mother in Harlem who explained that she told her sister not to believe any man's promises to take care of her if she had a baby; the monthly baby-weighing ceremonies attended by the women in the hills of Bali as part of a program to identify and help infants at risk; and many others. As much deprivation as we saw, I was just as impressed by the strength, the resourcefulness, and the everlasting hope of the human spirit.

Upon completion of my 12-year term on the board, I wrote a letter expressing my feelings. I wrote the letter because I expected not to be able to attend my retirement dinner from the foundation board. When the flight I had planned to take to Monaco for a TBG (Chapter 13) board meeting was cancelled, however, I was able to convey my feelings in person by reading the letter myself, including the following:

I came to the Ford Foundation with an absolute faith in what educated, motivated people could achieve, working together in a healthy and supportive environment of freedom. I graduate with an absolute faith in what the least-educated, most deprived people can achieve, working together with a modest amount of help, even in an unhealthy, non-supportive environment of oppression. The spark of hope that remains in so many long-suffering humans is truly remarkable to witness. The Ford Foundation is at its best when it fans that spark, helping people in need help themselves find solutions to the improvement of their lives.

My travels for the Ford Foundation provided the chance to meet and talk with some truly remarkable people—some famous, some not; some powerful, some oppressed—and some just altogether memorable. Chapter 19 recalls some of those encounters.

CHAPTER 11

AN EARLY OUTSIDER

Inland Steel 1967-1997
Ryerson Tull....................1996-2000
Kodak............................1970-1978
Corning Glass..................1972-1987
Cummins Engine.............1974-1999

I declined my first invitation to join a corporate board as an outside director when Dan Searle asked me if I would join the board of G. D. Searle & Co. in 1966. I had been president of Jewel for only a year or so, and when George Clements and I discussed the invitation, we decided that I would not have the time. George also thought that being on the board of a family-owned business might not be the most positive experience. Fifteen years later, Dan and Don Rumsfeld would present me with a new invitation to join the board of the now-public G. D. Searle & Co., an invitation I would accept. In the 20 years following that board invitation in 1966, I received 86 more invitations to join corporate boards as an independent director. The offers didn't stop in 1987, but I did stop keeping track at that point. Obviously I have had to be selective about the boards I agreed to join. The quality of the company's management was always a key consideration in my decision, and—particularly while I was at Jewel—the frequency of meetings and need for travel also had to be taken into account. I restricted my involvement to those boards whose meetings fell in a triangle formed by Boston, Chicago, and Florida.

Board service, first as an adjunct to my Jewel career and later as a career in and of itself, has exposed me to a fascinating array of businesses and business leaders. It has provided challenges and great satisfactions, as well as many lessons about the role of a board and what makes for effective board membership. When I first started receiving invitations to join boards other than Jewel, outside directors were much rarer than they are today.

As of 2006, my experience as an independent director amounted cumulatively to more than 350 years over a span of more than four decades. In light of the variety and extent of my board service, I am frequently asked for my insights. The following are those that have been most important for me:

- When I serve on a board, I put my reputation in the hands of the CEO. If that ever makes me uncomfortable, one of us should go.
- Outside directors must be independent and in the majority. Each director must have the respect of the others in the boardroom. Each must be willing to be a critic on some occasions and a helpful counselor to management on others. And each must earn the acceptance of fellow board members in both roles. The purpose of directors is not to serve as the CEO's fan club or rubber stamp. Directors must be focused on what is good for the company, not what is good for the CEO.
- The need for directors to be watchdogs does not lessen the importance of board involvement in strategy, management evaluation and compensation, and the monitoring of operating results.

- CEOs are employees of their companies. They are elected, not anointed. Imperial CEOs are dangerous to themselves and to everyone around them, regardless of their record. Too much power serves no one well.
- The external audit firm works for the audit committee. The independence of the audit committee can be enhanced if the selection of the audit partner is made independently by the committee, and not by the audit firm or by management.
- Except in rare circumstances, CEOs should retire from the board when they retire from their management role. It is difficult enough for a successor to make changes without having to explain them in front of his or her predecessor.
- It is intellectually dishonest to determine a CEO's compensation without first evaluating qualitative and quantitative achievements measured against pre-determined goals.
- A good way to maintain reasonable CEO compensation is to develop successor talent internally. It can be outrageously expensive to bring in a leader from outside the company.
- It is intellectually dishonest to re-slate an existing director for shareholder election without that director being evaluated by his or her peers on the board.
- And two one-liners which serve an independent director well: Trust but verify, and When in doubt, disclose.

These lessons were acquired directly from personal experience—from doing—because, in the 1960s and 70s, doing was the only way to learn. I hope that recounting some of my experiences as an independent director, in this and subsequent chapters, will bring the lessons to life.

I have been fortunate to work with some of the outstanding corporate leaders and directors of my time during the course of my years of board service. I want to acknowledge the pleasure and privilege of their friendship. I have also been in some difficult situations, in which I experienced some of the negative consequences of my independence. There are important lessons in those experiences, as well.

In general, I hope to convey the satisfaction I have enjoyed in seeing the companies and organizations on whose boards I have served through some remarkable challenges and achievements. There are many memorable moments.

• • •

INLAND STEEL

While I turned down the first non-Jewel board invitation I received, I did say yes in 1967 to the second—from Chicago-based Inland Steel, one of the largest U.S. producers of steel. The invitation came about because Inland executives knew me through my volunteer work with the United Way (Chapter 17). Joe and Phil Block (chairman and chairman-designate of Inland, respectively, and members of the family that had founded the company) called on me to extend the invitation to join the board as one of a minority of outside directors. I was 40 years old at the time. I would serve on the Inland Steel board for 30 years, working with the last seven CEOs of the company.

My 30 years on Inland's board gave me an opportunity to observe the development of more efficient steel manufacturing processes, the intensification of foreign competition, and the rise of alternatives to steel. As the "Steel Belt" became the "Rust Belt," U.S. steel companies such as Inland were increasingly challenged to find ways to stay competitive. One of those challenges took the form of steel mini-mills.

Memorable Ways Not to Invest $1 Billion: As mini-mill producers of steel were starting to make inroads against integrated steel mills, Inland board members questioned management about Inland's long-term prospects. We were continually assured that Inland's operations were world-class. We were further assured that mini-mills, which produced their steel from scrap, could never produce the quality of steel required for the automotive and appliance industries which were Inland's primary customers. And besides, management rationalized, if mini-mills succeeded, the price of scrap would go up and make their position untenable.

This reasoning reminded me of Jerry Babb's story about Lever Brothers' reluctance to enter the detergent business when detergents started to challenge the company's traditional soap products. As detergents caught on, went the thinking of Lever's management, the price of tallow used to make soap would go down, enabling soap to greatly under-price detergents. Detergents and mini-mills both won out.

At one point in the 1970s, Inland's response to competition from mini-mills was to present a $1 billion modernization plan to the board. The board asked if the higher-quality steel the modernized plant would produce could command a higher price to pay for the investment. Inland's management genuinely believed that the answer was yes, an answer that would later be proved wrong.

During the discussion, I became the "skunk at the picnic" when I asked, "Are you telling me that if you had $1 billion sitting over in the corner of the room, you would choose to invest it in the steel business?" Joe Block was astounded by such heresy and responded, "We have to keep our business up-to-date!" The best I could do at that meeting was to break down the proposal into two parts. We approved $500 million for one-half of the modernization program. The second $500 million was never spent.

The competitive challenges of the steel business prompted Inland to explore diversification, a strategy adopted by many other companies at the time. Shortly after I joined the board and

Phil Block became chairman, Inland acquired a manufactured home business, a construction business, and a steel fabricator. Despite Phil's able management team, all three of those businesses failed to meet expectations and were later sold at a loss. That experience led me to question the assumptions then commonly used to rationalize conglomerates, especially the assumption that a good management team can manage any business.

In time, as the reins of Inland Steel's management passed from the Block family, I attended a board meeting which included a tour of Inland's Indiana Harbor steel plant. Each director was assigned to a member of management. As a relatively new director at the time, I was paired with Bob Darnall, an up-and-coming personnel manager at the Harbor. Bob impressed me then as being an unusual steel company executive.

He confirmed my early impression of him later when he became Inland's CEO. Unlike many in the industry, Bob recognized the globally competitive nature of the steel business. And, rather than wishing it weren't so and letting Inland become dependent on steel import tariffs, he initiated a series of international involvements. One initiative resulted in a partnership with Mexican steel producers for Inland's Ryerson Tull subsidiary. Another initiative was an attempt to purchase a Venezuelan state-owned steel company going through privatization.

While Inland's bid to purchase the Venezuelan company failed, Bob encountered Ispat in the process. Ispat was an Indian company that would eventually buy Inland's steel operations. The sale of the steel company to Ispat was controversial, including among members of the Block family. From my perspective, it was a stunning accomplishment. The extraordinary difficulty of his achievement may be best characterized by the phone call Bob received, shortly after the announcement of Inland's sale, from the head of LTV, another

U.S. steel company. "You lucky SOB," he said to Bob. "You found the only person in the world who would buy a U.S. steel business. And you completed the deal!" Ispat is now one of the largest steel companies in the world.

Memorable Difficult Board Role: A particularly interesting experience at Inland emerged from a difficult contract negotiation with the United Steelworkers of America. Among many other demands was one to have a union representative on the Inland board of directors.

I joined Bob Darnall in a meeting with the union president in which we succeeded in negotiating a compromise. Under the compromise arrangement, we would select one director who would have the approval of the union. We thought Arnie Weber, who was already an Inland director, might receive the union's approval, but that failed.

With Arnie's help, however, we did get union approval of Bob McKersie, a labor relations professor from the Massachusetts Institute of Technology. Bob's role became a very difficult one. The union expected him to keep them informed about board discussions and decisions. The board, on the other hand, expected its discussions to be confidential and its decisions publicized only when appropriate.

Bob discussed his dilemma with me frequently and I was consistent in telling him that I felt his board responsibility for confidentiality was overriding in relation to the union's expectations.

Prior to the time Bob Darnall became chairman, there had been no CEO evaluation process—either formal or informal—at Inland Steel. Bob and I wanted to change things so that, as he described it in *Director's Alert* (now *Board Alert*) in 1999, we would have "open lines of communication" about his performance. Each year, Bob would come up with his set of goals, which could include financial, organizational, and operational objectives. The board would suggest changes, and

Bob's performance would be measured against these revised goals at year's end.

At evaluation time, as the senior director, I would make notes of the board's assessments and give Bob verbal feedback, which would be followed by a written evaluation. The process was very effective as a basis for determining compensation and communicating any concern or need for improvement, and it is a process I have consistently encouraged companies to adopt.

Bob retired as CEO of Inland when Ispat purchased the steel company. When I think about Bob, I cannot help wondering how different his success might have looked had he started his career in a growth industry rather than one in seemingly irreversible decline.

• • •

RYERSON TULL

Ryerson Tull had been a wholly owned subsidiary of Inland Steel, but had been partially spun off, and was 13 percent publicly owned at the time Inland agreed to sell its core steel business to Ispat. The Inland board determined that Ryerson Tull would be separated and would operate as an independent company following the Ispat deal. In the process, it was necessary to recognize the rights of the minority Ryerson Tull shareholders. I chaired the committee of the company's independent directors charged with representing the minority shareholders in the negotiation.

The committee of independent directors was keenly aware of the likelihood that whatever we negotiated with Inland might lead to a shareholder lawsuit. Dick Cline, Jerry Pearlman (former CEO of Zenith), and Ron Thompson (CEO of Midwest Stamping) served on the committee with me. Over a five-month period, we negotiated successfully to keep the minority shareholders whole in the percentage ownership of the surviving Inland Steel Industries (ISI) after the Ispat purchase of the steel assets. With great care for independence in our negotiation and for documenting each step of the process, we were able to avoid any subsequent litigation. After the transaction, ISI became Ryerson Tull and the other businesses in the post-Ispat company were divested.

The Ryerson Tull spin-off also created the unusual opportunity to start from scratch in creating the company's board. Although a few directors were carried over from the Inland board, an equal number were added as new independent directors. Neil Novich, a former Bain & Co. consultant, had been hired several years previously to be the CEO of Ryerson Tull while it was still a subsidiary. Neil became president and CEO of the company, and Bob Darnall was named chairman.

Eventually, Bob's conflicts (because of the consulting he did for Ispat at the time) forced him to step aside, and Neil added the chairman's title. Ryerson Tull performed better than its integrated steel company parent had. However, Joe Block and his family would probably have been better off if Inland Steel had not spent "to keep our business up to date."

• • •

KODAK

Three years after I joined the Inland Steel board, another board invitation arrived completely out of the blue—one that I found intriguing. I didn't know anyone at Kodak, but they were looking for a specific kind of director—a young person who knew the consumer goods business. Their advertising agency did some research and came up with my name.

Dr. Louis Eilers, chairman of Kodak, telephoned and came to Chicago to meet me. During lunch at the Chicago Club, he invited me to join the Kodak board. The composition of the Kodak board at the time is revealed by the fact that I replaced an

80-year-old director, reducing the average age of the 15-member board by almost three years!

I wasn't smart enough in 1970 when I agreed to serve on the Kodak board to fully understand the important changes in corporate governance that would emerge over the next couple of decades, though I would champion and welcome them as they did. They certainly hadn't arrived at Kodak yet. The board was composed of 10 members of management and five "outsiders," one of whom, Allen Wallis, was president of the University of Rochester. Kodak was the major corporate contributor to the University of Rochester each year. Some outsider! There were really only two of us—Bob Hatfield, CEO of Continental Can, and I—who asked the kinds of questions that the company's management was not asking.

Asking a question, however, was like interrupting a Kodak management meeting. Some of the issues seemed pretty simple to Bob and me, such as where the company held its annual meeting. They had been holding it at a little high school in New Jersey, which made attendance difficult for everyone; directors did not even attend. "What have we got to hide?" we asked. Finally, the board voted to accept a shareholder resolution to hold the annual meeting in Rochester, New York, instead. Normally, directors do not welcome resolutions from shareholders, but in this case the resolution helped us accomplish a change we knew was needed.

Another aspect of Kodak's management philosophy with which I disagreed was their sizeable cash holding; the company had $1 billion in cash on its balance sheet. While management pointed with pride to that $1 billion, they never really provided a good answer when I asked how its earnings would positively impact shareholders.

Dividends were also a sensitive issue. Management's bonuses were based in part on the amount of dividends the company paid to shareholders, so management was always eager to pay dividends. The attempt to align the interests of management and the shareholders worked well in the short term, but not in the long term. As capital was paid out in dividends, it might better have been spent developing new technologies, such as digital photography which would challenge Kodak's film business.

Even before digital photography emerged as a threat, other competitive pressures appeared. When Kodak developed an instant camera, for example, we recognized the threat that Polaroid might sue for patent infringement, as indeed they did. When the instant camera project was first presented to the board, Bob Hatfield and I asked numerous questions about it. We were repeatedly assured that there would be no finding of patent infringement against Kodak. As it turned out, management was wrong, and Kodak ended up paying a good many millions of dollars to Polaroid when they lost the ensuing suit. In hindsight, the board might have requested outside counsel on the issue; but at the time, that practice was far from typical.

Memorable Management Myopia: The most memorable and frustrating experience I encountered as a Kodak director related to the company's strategy in the face of new competition from overseas. Fuji had entered the U.S. market, selling photographic paper at prices one third less than Kodak's. The company's counter-strategy was to put the Kodak name on the back of the paper and advertise its superior quality.

Having come from a competitive business, I might have accepted that the company could command a three- to five-percent price premium, if they were the very best producer with the highest quality reputation. I didn't see how they could sustain a 50 percent premium. I argued and argued, but Kodak management refused to do anything about their pricing because it would interfere with short-term results.

In 1977, another suit required Kodak to refund money to the photographic developers using its products. The fact that Osco was in the photo development business raised the potential for conflict and hence a question regarding my independence. I wrote the following letter to Kodak's chairman, Walter Fallon:

> It now appears that the Suspension Agreement between Eastman Kodak and Osco Drug, Inc., a subsidiary of Jewel Companies, Inc., in relation to the Berkey litigation may involve a conflict of interest in my status as a director of Eastman Kodak Company.
>
> I have a very strong belief in the importance of completely independent outside directors for all publicly owned companies. Since my independence is now clouded by this potential conflict, I hereby resign from the board of directors of Eastman Kodak Company, effective immediately.

Since I had been a persistent questioner and perhaps even a pest at his meetings, I was surprised when Walter Fallon wrote back to me a few weeks later:

> I guess the old thought—"You aren't really missed until you are gone"—will apply to your departure from the Kodak Board. You certainly were a positive influence in guiding our board toward a fuller appreciation of the role of outside directors.
>
> Don, I appreciate your service on the Kodak board. We are better for it.

• • •

CORNING GLASS

My invitation to join the board of Corning Glass in 1972 is one of many opportunities in my life that I can trace back to education—in this instance, to my tutoring of Amory Houghton while I was a second-year student at the Harvard Business School. I didn't know then that Amo would go on to be the next member of his family to lead Corning, but he did just that.

Amo also kept track of me, and decided in 1972 to invite his former tutor to join his board of directors. As was typical of boards at the time, the outside members of the Corning board constituted a minority, although it was more balanced than many. Adding me to the board resulted in nine of 19 board members being independent, judged by today's standards. Corning was a fascinating and well-managed company; I served on its board for 15 years.

I remember traveling to Corning's ivory-tower research lab on the top of a hill at the time of my first board meeting. There I learned that the company had been working on glass fiber so pure that a light signal could be sent through it several hundred yards, maybe a mile. No one was quite sure at that time what to do with it, but it was clearly a great discovery.

I really liked and respected the people at Corning, especially Amo and then Jamie Houghton, who succeeded him. However, over time, as remaining impurities in the glass fiber were eliminated and the business figured out uses for it related to telecommunications, the market developed to the point where Corning and AT&T were the largest producers of optical fiber, with a combined two-thirds share of the U.S. market.

Since I was by then also serving on the board of AT&T, I became uncomfortable with the growing conflict. The subject of optical fiber was never even discussed at AT&T board meetings because it was minuscule in an immense company, but it was the subject of *every* board meeting at Corning. I decided I had to choose between the two boards, and chose to resign from the Corning board, which I did with regret in 1987.

Memorable Succession Discussion: A couple of years before I left the Corning board, Amo was completing 17 years as Corning's CEO. The entire board admired and liked Amo, but my feeling was that a CEO would have accomplished what it was that he or she could do for a company in a span of 10 or so years. That feeling nagged at me.

For a few years, I had raised questions about management succession and talked about the benefits of change. Eventually,

Amo, in an executive session with Corning's outside directors, announced his plan to step down at the next annual meeting. A few directors tried to argue against it, while others of us were biting our tongues, not wanting to change his decision.

One board member, John Coburn, the Episcopal bishop of Massachusetts, asked a memorable question in response to Amo's announcement. "But Amo," he asked, "if you give up the CEO job, what would you do?" His question epitomized the issue of a director identifying with the needs of an individual CEO, rather than the needs of the company. As much as I admired what Amo's leadership had accomplished for Corning, when his brother Jamie succeeded him, important and necessary changes were made which would not have occurred under Amo's leadership.

• • •

CUMMINS ENGINE

In 1974, J. Irwin Miller, chairman of Cummins Engine and great-nephew of the company's founder, invited me to join the board of the maker of diesel engines and related products and services. Over the years, Irwin became an important role model and mentor for me. The story of our initial meeting also reinforces the role of education and volunteering in many pivotal events in my life.

Memorable Reason for Being Selected for a Board: My retirement dinner at Cummins in 1999 gave me an opportunity to thank Irwin for getting me involved not only in Cummins, but also in AT&T and the Ford Foundation. I told the story of my first meeting with him. In 1973, I had received an invitation to represent Chicago-area Yale alumni at a meeting in Philadelphia with a dozen or so other alumni from around the country; Yale President Kingman Brewster and trustees Irwin Miller, Richardson Dillworth, and Jock Whitney.

The question we had been invited to address was, What can Kingman Brewster do to regain the support of Yale alumni?

In order to prepare for the meeting, I wrote to 30 or so Chicago-area alumni and asked for their input. I was the only one who had taken the time to poll others in preparation for the meeting. One of the criticisms raised by the alumni I heard from related to a situation that had occurred a few years earlier in the midst of a campus protest. President Brewster had sought to quiet the crowd when he agreed with the protesters, saying that he was "skeptical of the ability of black revolutionaries to achieve a fair trial in the United States."

When the press challenged him on that statement, Brewster explained that he was speaking as an individual and not as the president of Yale. Based on the feedback from my survey of Chicago-area alumni, I observed to President Brewster, Irwin, and the other trustees that when the president of Yale speaks, he does so from that office and not as an individual.

I thought my point was a strong one and that I had made it well. In fact, for a long time, I believed that I had persuaded Irwin with my logic. The night of my retirement dinner, though, Irwin told me that he had believed then and still believed that President Brewster had been right in asserting his right to speak as an individual. I learned that I hadn't sold the idea, although I had sold myself. Irwin had been impressed with the work I had done, if not the conclusion I had drawn.

At the time I joined the Cummins board, Henry Schacht was president of the company; he became chairman a few years later. I would have the privilege of working with Henry on other boards, as well, including AT&T (and then Lucent); the Ford Foundation; and the Midwest Regional Committee to select White House Fellows. His story of Cummins's competing for a contract in the Philippines illustrates one of the many reasons I grew to have so much admiration and respect for Henry.

Cummins was very much an international business. The Association of Southeast Asian Nations (ASEAN) had decided that each member country would be designated to build a certain truck part, which would then be assembled in that part of the world. One nation made tires, another chassis, another transmissions, and so forth. The Philippines had responsibility for making engines and held a competition to see which company would be granted the right to build truck engines in that nation. Cummins won the competition.

As I remember Henry's story, just prior to the public announcement of the awarding of the contract rights, the government administrator who had been running the competition escorted Henry to President Marcos's palace. As they walked, he asked Henry, "How has our competition been thus far?" Henry answered that he thought the competition had been run very fairly and that Cummins had bid aggressively. The competition administrator said, "Yes, you did. Now you have won it, and President Marcos will announce that to the press. I just want you to know that from here on, you are on your own."

Henry and the competition administrator went in to join Marcos who proceeded to announce that Cummins had been awarded the contract. As the press conference was ending, Marcos asked Henry to accompany him into the next room. Then Marcos said, "Now I'm sure you're grateful for what we've done…" Henry agreed. Marcos then said, "To show your gratitude, you can do two things. Number one, we need a new passenger jet plane. And number two, your distributor here is incompetent, and I want you to consider appointing 'X' (and he named the firm) as your distributor."

In fact, Cummins and its distributor, who was quite competent, had had a long-term relationship. The distributor Marcos wanted appointed was a relative of his. Henry said, "I can't agree to do either one. It is against the laws of our country to make gifts like an airplane." Marcos asked if he was certain, and Henry said yes. The next day, Marcos announced the change in the award for the rights to build engines to a German company. I can't help speculating that the airplane Marcos used when he fled the country in 1986 could have come from the German company showing "gratitude" for "winning" the contract for the engine business in the Philippines.

Memorable Board Welcome: On our first Cummins board trip to Scotland, we enjoyed an evening at a castle near Edinburgh, not far from the Cummins plant in Schotts. Schotts's bagpipe band, which had recently won a nationwide competition, was playing as we got off the bus at the castle. As the band played, several dozen cattle stopped grazing at the top of a nearby knoll and meandered down to the fence that separated their farm from the castle. When the band finished playing and we were entering the castle, I turned around to see the cows walking back up the knoll to continue their grazing. They had enjoyed the bagpipe concert as much as we had!

Henry Schacht added to my reasons for admiring him when he stepped aside as CEO of Cummins Engine at the age of 60 because he thought the company would be better off if Jim Henderson, his backup and the same age as Henry, had five years to run the company. Jim went on to make great contributions to Cummins, as well as to the boards of Inland Steel, Ryerson Tull, and Nanophase, where he has served with me as a director. And Henry has had no lack of new and interesting challenges post-Cummins.

No executives with whom I have worked have impressed me more than Henry and Jim. Their integrity, their interest in people, and their ability to work with and benefit from their board were unsurpassed. Because I worked with Henry in such a variety of activities, I can say with certainty that we most often thought alike. On one matter we did differ. I felt chairmen should leave their boards when they retired as CEOs, to make it easier for their successors to make changes without seeming to confront their predecessors. Henry disagreed and stayed on the Cummins board when he retired. He later changed his mind.

The quality of the interactions of the Cummins board with Henry and Jim is typified by a situation that Jim described for *Director's Alert* (now *Board Alert*) in 1999, in which he demonstrated the value he placed on board independence and input—mine, in this case:

> "Don is thorough and persistent," [says] Henderson. "If he thinks there's something management isn't paying attention to, he'll bring it up. Again and again, if he has to. He doesn't mind the awkward silences." When Cummins Engine's management was very excited about making a major engine investment, Henderson illustrates, "Don made us think it through. He asked a lot of questions." The company went ahead with the expenditure, but did so from a position of greater understanding.

I served on the Cummins board for 25 years. Some might say that is too long. Obviously, I did not think so. The quality, integrity, and transparency of the Cummins board and its management were qualities that I hold up as models for how boards should operate and how companies should be managed. Much of this level of achieved excellence can be attributed to Irwin Miller. The integrity and management style that Irwin instilled in Cummins made serving on the Cummins board both a pleasure and a confirming experience in developing my understanding of management as it should be practiced.

Irwin helped Cummins in countless ways to become the company it was. After he had stepped down as chairman, but while he was still a director, Cummins was threatened by corporate raiders who had acquired a significant percentage of the company's stock. These raiders typically bought companies, slashed costs, especially in research and development, and then resold the depleted but temporarily more profitable company. Cummins's customers, who counted on the company's research and development efforts—particularly in emissions control and fuel economy—expressed concern about the company's viability if the financial raiders were successful. How could they and Cummins plan years ahead for future engines while Cummins was under the threat of being taken over and having essential elements of the business cut back?

The Miller family responded to the crisis by using their assets to buy out the raiders. As no good deed goes unpunished, the company was sued by a group of shareholders claiming that the Miller family had gotten a sweetheart deal. In reality, they saved the business. The family's investment assured customers that Cummins would continue to meet long-term needs and commitments.

• • •

My involvement on the boards of Inland, Kodak, Corning, and Cummins provided exposure to the ways a variety of other companies were being managed, as well as the relationships between CEOs and their boards—all experiences that could help me at Jewel. Because I wanted to be as up-front with the Jewel board as possible about how I was spending my time, I gave them a yearly activity summary. The summary documented the days I spent away from the business ... how many days I devoted to each of the boards I served on ... and how many days I spent on civic activities, or policy activities such as the Cost of Living Council (with its 20 trips to Washington).

In 1980, as I neared the end of my self-imposed 10-year term as chairman of Jewel, I became increasingly active in external activities, anticipating life after CEO, with the full knowledge and support of the Jewel board. I realized that there was a whole world of corporate board involvement that I could mold into my next career. The management of companies like Cummins and Corning was so superior, and my ability to be of real help and get satisfaction from board service was so promising, that I welcomed the opportunity to explore other board invitations that came my way.

Between 1979 and 1983 when I retired as chairman of the executive committee at Jewel, I accepted invitations to join nine more corporate boards, launching my next career as a "professional director."

CHAPTER 12

A BEHEMOTH BREAKUP
AND A MEGA-MERGER

AT&T 1979-1996
Lucent Technologies........ 1996-2000
Time Warner (Time Inc.) ... 1979-1998

I joined the boards of both AT&T and Time Inc. in 1979. Both were American icons. And while both involved seeing the companies through a fundamental change in their make-up, in one case that meant breaking it up, and in the other case, it meant a merger of already large corporations.

AT&T

The AT&T board is another involvement I can trace back to education or volunteering, in this case to my work for the United Way in Chicago (Chapter 17). In the course of my fundraising activities for the United Way, I met and worked with Charlie Brown while he was president of Illinois Bell (later renamed Ameritech, one of the so-called Baby Bells).

Charlie had also been supportive in Dick Ogilvie's campaign for governor (Chapter 15). When Irv Seaman, a Chicago bank president and volunteer in the Ogilvie campaign, became a member of the Augusta National Golf Club, Irv suggested that we take Dick there for a much-needed vacation after he was elected. We invited Charlie, a dedicated golfer, to complete our foursome at Augusta in February 1969. That golf weekend became an annual ritual spanning 15 years.

In 1979, we decided to celebrate a decade of Augusta golf with a trip to Scotland, along with our wives. Charlie was then COO of AT&T. Just prior to that Scotland trip, AT&T chairman John deButts told Charlie in confidence that he (deButts) was going to retire early and that Charlie was his recommended successor. So Charlie and his wife Annlee came on that Scotland trip with a wonderful secret they weren't able to share with us.

The Browns went to Scotland ahead of the rest of us and, when our group gathered at Gleneagles, Charlie and Annlee told us they'd had delicious salmon the previous night in town. They were enthusiastic about having met the owner. They had learned his name, Younger, from a big sign outside the restaurant. We all went there a few days later and indeed saw a sign out front that said "Younger." It wasn't the owner's name, however, but the equivalent of a sign outside a U.S. tavern saying, "Schlitz."

Augusta and Gleneagles weren't the only places I played golf with Charlie Brown. After the deButts news became public and Charlie was elected chairman, he invited me to play with him at Pine Valley Golf Club in New Jersey. As we played, Charlie invited me to become a director of AT&T. He said, "Don, I want you to come on the AT&T board. You are the first one I am inviting. I want independence and judgment on the board."

A strong independent board was important because Charlie knew that he would be dealing with increasingly intense attacks by Congress, governmental agencies, MCI, and the courts. There were challenges on all fronts, most notably from the Justice Department. It is hard to overstate how much anti-trust litigation AT&T faced at the time.

For the first three quarters of the 20th century, everyone wanted a single phone company with universal service and seamless interconnectivity. A favorite AT&T term for that system was "ubiquity." Eventually, though, the mood to deregulate transformed perceptions; what had been the world's largest company went from being an admirable institution to an unacceptable monopoly. Actions that were acceptable and legal at the time they were taken started to look different later, as anti-trust court decisions changed the precedents.

The first five years I served on the board were tough ones for the company. AT&T had operated since its inception as a regulated monopoly—responsive to regulation, rather than to the marketplace. Much of the time and energy of AT&T people had been spent proving to federal and state regulatory bodies that the company was doing a good job. What had evolved was a different form of enterprise, with a regulated rather than a customer-based culture. AT&T management needed to settle the Justice Department lawsuits and put those problems behind them. I thought AT&T would be a much more interesting place to work once the company realized that its customer was the user of the phone service, as opposed to a government regulator.

In 1983, after four years on the board, I made the motion to proceed with the divestiture of the Baby Bells, an agreement that had been painstakingly negotiated between Howard Trienens (AT&T's general counsel), the Justice Department, and Judge Harold Green. I did not imagine at the time that AT&T could decline over the span of 20 years to become an acquired subsidiary of one of the originally divested Baby Bells—then Southwestern Bell and subsequently known as SBC.

One memorable development in the battle between Congress, the courts, and the Administration to decide the future of AT&T came in the spring of 1982. At that time, Congressman Tim Wirth, chairman of the House

Subcommittee on Telecommunications, Consumer Protection
and Finance, asked for the opportunity to bring several of his
congressional committee members to our May board meeting.
He was trying to pass legislation to break up AT&T. The
congressmen apparently felt that AT&T management was
shielding board members from the wisdom and logic of their
particular legislative proposal. We invited them to meet with
us before the start of our board meeting. Afterwards, we felt
that our congressional visitors left with the knowledge that
individual board members were quite well-versed in the issues,
and preferred a negotiated rather than a legislative settlement
to our dilemma.

I served on the audit committee of the AT&T board
before and during the breakup. One of the questions I asked
during the months before the actual breakup was if AT&T's
remaining assets would have the same value after the divestiture
of the Baby Bells. I knew that GAAP (Generally Accepted
Accounting Principles) rules for utilities were different
from the requirements for other industries. AT&T financial
management's immediate response was that the assets were the
same; so, of course, the value would be the same. The partner
from Coopers & Lybrand, AT&T's auditor, raised an eyebrow,
which I took as encouragement to press further.

Under the accounting rules for regulated utilities, assets
would remain on a company's books as long as there was an
implied promise by regulators that the utility would someday
be compensated for that value. Under normal (non-utility)
GAAP accounting rules, a company would write off whatever
was obsolete. When the Baby Bells were spun off, every part of
AT&T had obsolete assets on its books.

The process that started with an audit committee question
led to a multi-billion-dollar write-off. Had we not taken that
large write-off (which I referred to at the time as "writing off
Central America" due to its size), AT&T would have been in a

lot more trouble a lot earlier in its new divested version. Had we been smarter about identifying assets that were truly obsolete, AT&T would have written off more than it did.

If navigating the legal issues and the breakup was tough, making the transition from regulated monopoly to market competitor was an unprecedented challenge. A *Fortune* magazine article description at the time seems very apt:

> Imagine you're in the class of a business-school professor gone mad. "Ladies and gentlemen," he announces, a wicked gleam in his eyes, "for our next assignment, we're going to take apart what is, measured by assets, the world's largest corporation. Until now, the company has been a monopoly selling telephone service in the U.S. We will divide it into eight huge parts and you,"—he thrusts a finger toward the class—"you will be chief executive of one of these parts. You must convert your company from a full-fledged monopolist to part-monopolist, part-entrepreneur. You must fight off competitors. You must keep the phones ringing and keep almost three million shareholders happy. You will be playing by entirely new rules, but," he smiles slyly—"you won't know what all the rules are."

At the time of the breakup, AT&T was indeed the largest company in the world, with $150 billion in assets and more than one million employees, about one of every 100 employed people in the U.S. The local operating companies would constitute eight of the top nine entries on *Fortune's* list of utilities. Typical of a monopoly, product decisions were made by the company, not demanded by the customer. The culture was based on the leasing of phone equipment and proving to regulators that high quality service resulted.

The divestiture process was completed in 17 months—a time span that may seem an eternity for, say, a 14-year old looking forward to driving—yet the blink of an eye for an institution with the history and size of AT&T.

The breakup of AT&T set off a frantic scramble by AT&T executives who, many for the first time in their lives, had to grapple with strategic planning; devise new ventures; restructure their organizations; control costs; reconstitute their corporate personalities; and even come up with new business names. The chairman of one of the local Bell companies described it this way: "It's like taking apart a 747 in midair and making sure it keeps flying."

In my first year on the AT&T board, I had spent extra time in connection with each of the 11 board meetings visiting with key people to increase my knowledge of the company. One such visit was with Don Prochnow, chairman and CEO of Western Electric, the manufacturing subsidiary of AT&T.

Alongside much more complicated switching systems, Western Electric produced virtually all the telephone instruments used in the United States by monopoly Ma Bell. I asked Prochnow why AT&T was not producing the instruments in the Far East, where I had visited Sony and observed them training dexterous young women to make their low-cost products. Prochnow answered, "We produce everything in the U.S. You must understand how efficient we are!" Less than five years later, after divestiture, the telephone instrument business was losing money and CEO Charlie Brown told the division's management to make money or exit the business. Within a year, there was not a single telephone instrument being produced for AT&T in the U.S., and the business was once again profitable. Don Prochnow was just one of many at AT&T who did not anticipate the meaning of moving from monopoly to competition. AT&T's major manufacturing facility in Oklahoma City was vacant and sold in 2004.

In August 1984, I spoke to a group of managers at an AT&T forum and shared with them my thoughts about managing a competitive business and serving the customer. As I told the group, I had many strong and positive feelings about what was being achieved by the new AT&T. They were more interested in the issues I could see facing them—especially those within their control. I described seven.

Would the world's greatest communications company communicate?

One of the major challenges I saw was whether management (including Bell Labs) would learn quickly enough about the rapidly changing needs of their many and varied customers. I talked about the tremendous cultural shift involved in changing the company's view of who the client was, in reorienting service to customers rather than regulators. I used the Jewel upside-down organization chart to underscore the concept of being customer-driven. To illustrate the point, I described the introduction of low-priced, plain-packaged generic groceries at Jewel during a time of double-digit inflation and growing consumer concerns about grocery prices. Older, more experienced grocers had said it wouldn't work; 40-year-olds designed and implemented it; consumers loved it.

How long would it take to have customers and competitors fully replace regulators as the controllers of AT&T's destiny?

I used the 1983 year-end write-off of AT&T's obsolete assets necessitated by the difference between normal and regulatory GAAP accounting rules to illustrate how dramatically and fundamentally the rules of competition had changed for the company. I contrasted the traditional AT&T assumptions that consumers would continue to pay AT&T to lease phone equipment, creating an annuity, with Jewel's reaction to National Tea's price reductions. In that situation, we triggered our competitive response over a single weekend, knowing that maintaining our market share was more important than maintaining short-term profits (Chapter 6).

How long would it take AT&T to switch from defense to offense?

Before divestiture, one senior AT&T executive asked me to react to studies on long distance call pricing after divestiture. He said his analysts believed that the AT&T name would permit the company to charge a 15 percent higher price than competitors. I described how a two percent difference in grocery prices supported by high-quality operations was accepted by consumers, while a five percent difference was unacceptable. There was every reason to believe that long distance service would become a commodity and that long distance rates would follow a similar pattern. The challenge for AT&T, I said, was to figure out how the company could be the low-cost producer of goods (Western Electric) and services (long distance).

A Cummins Engine example made another point about competition in a world rather than just a U.S. market. Cummins had reduced prices 30 percent to meet Japanese competition on diesel engines and then proceeded to reduce costs to afford the price reduction.

Would the child of a wealthy mother spend money wisely?

I wondered whether the information flows and analytical techniques at Ma Bell were strong enough to support optimal capital allocation decisions. Good investments in a regulated environment were whatever the regulator would permit to be included before the application of a predetermined regulated percent return. There was no promise of a return in a competitive environment.

Time Inc. provided a provocative example. I described how, when I joined the Time board, I asked to see ROI calculations for each of its businesses. Time management had never done the work to figure it out. When they did, the Time magazine business came back with investment numbers in brackets and an asterisk to the following note: "The return on a negative investment is infinite." The magazine business had little capital invested and received subscription revenue in advance—making the net investment negative. That was a prime example of using other people's money.

Could a company successfully sell to its major competitors?
My opinion was suggested by my question. Selling equipment to AT&T's competitors was not sustainable long-term. I described how Jewel's manufacturing had been only for our own use—we had not been able to sell our products to our competition. They did not want to contribute to our retail financial health by buying from our manufacturing arm. The Justice Department's agreement to keep manufacturing within AT&T did not make the strategy the right one in the real world of competition.

Could conservative AT&T be a risk-taker without losing its spirit or its shirt?
I restated the question another way, "Will your pride permit you to cut your losses quickly when you smell a loser?" Time provided another example. Time had successfully launched a number of magazines, including *People* and *Entertainment Weekly*, and the company decided to put out a competitor to *TV Guide*, called *Cable TV Week*. It turned out that *Cable TV Week* couldn't compete with *TV Guide* and failed to match the projections that had been made for it. Time discontinued it after five months.

Would AT&T afford to stay in the forefront of management-labor relations?
I asked the group of managers what could be done to make the goals of hourly workers the same as the goals of management. Cummins and Firestone, like AT&T, were heavily unionized and had traditional benefits packages. Jewel, by contrast, was heavily unionized but had profit sharing (a defined

contribution program) rather than a traditional pension plan. A traditional defined-benefit pension plan and lifelong retiree medical benefits can become major problems when a company shrinks, as my later experience at Lucent would emphasize.

As I continued to serve on the AT&T board following the break-up, one of the issues the board naturally considered was management succession.

Memorable Executive Session: By far the most poignant business meeting I ever participated in, at AT&T or anywhere else, occurred in April 1988. Jim Olsen had succeeded Charlie Brown as Chairman and CEO just two years earlier. In contrast to quiet, cerebral Charlie Brown, Jim Olsen was an outgoing natural leader and salesman. Jim had chaired the March board meeting, flown to Augusta to play golf, thought he had the flu, and returned home to be diagnosed with cancer. Following that diagnosis, he wrote to the board that he would be managing from his home and would be in regular contact with Bob Allen, AT&T's president. The next board meeting was to take place in Denver at the time of the annual meeting, five weeks after the March meeting.

A week before the Denver meeting, I was called to participate in a telephone meeting of the AT&T board's executive committee. Jim opened the meeting with an explanation that he had asked for a session with the executive committee because he didn't think he could handle talking to the whole board. He reassured us that Bob Allen was qualified to run the company and to succeed him.

Jim then spent 15 minutes or more in a monologue reviewing his modest beginnings as the son of a North Dakota barber, dropping out of North Dakota University to work for AT&T. He described emotionally how he had been much more successful than he had any right to expect. He repeated several times, "I am going to lick this!" But he added that it would take time; he hoped that his AT&T medical insurance coverage would continue.

When the conference call ended, I called Raleigh (Bud) Warner, chairman of Mobil Oil and the senior AT&T director, and suggested that we should call a meeting of the board on the evening before the upcoming annual meeting. My concern was to find out what problems Bob Allen was facing and what programs might be delayed with Jim out of action. Jim died that weekend and the newly scheduled board meeting the next Tuesday became instead the one at which we elected Bob Allen AT&T's new CEO.

Ironically, I was reminiscing with Bob Allen in February 2003 about those difficult times. When I referred to the extraordinary and poignant executive committee telephone call, Bob asked me, "What call?" He had not participated in the call, and none of those who had been on the call had ever told him about it.

When Charlie Brown had become CEO of AT&T, the board began having annual strategy sessions, held at The Greenbrier or on Cape Cod, or some similar resort. Bob Allen continued that practice, and I was impressed by one such meeting that Bob approached in a way I consider the ideal example of how a chairman should use a board. He said, "Instead of spending these days reviewing each part of the business, I want to spend the entire time talking about the one issue we're most concerned about. As a management team, we know that we will have to make a decision in the next few months regarding the cellular phone business, but we would like to have your input now as we consider the matter." He stated specifically, "We do not want to make a decision at this meeting, but we would like to tell you what we know and get your input."

Why had AT&T not leveraged its experience in wireless communications before then? The story may be apocryphal, but I was told that a McKinsey consulting study conducted in the 1970s had concluded that mobile telephony would appeal only to a few rich people, not to a mass-market product. When AT&T first divested the Baby Bells, the remaining company decided it needed to be more like IBM. The unfortunate and erroneous thinking was that IBM would be getting into telecommunications and, therefore, that AT&T should be in the computer business. After all, a large telephone switch was a computer.

AT&T spun its wheels trying to get into the computer business (including the unfriendly acquisition of NCR). The company lost money getting into and then trying to get out of computers, when it could have been using its capital to serve the wireless market. In addition to neglecting the retail wireless opportunity, the company had even sold its interests in manufacturing wireless equipment.

It turned out to be very expensive for AT&T to get back into wireless with the purchase of McGaw Cellular. However, when it came time for the board to take action on management's recommendation to proceed with the McGaw purchase several months later, as expensive as the action was, the board's prior discussion at that weekend strategy session make it an easy decision. We had all had ample opportunity to ask questions, to understand management's position, and to have input months before the acquisition vote was taken.

The possibility of spinning off Western Electric, the manufacturing arm of AT&T, was the subject of another weekend board strategy session. I was immediately supportive because of my strong feeling that selling to AT&T competitors was not sustainable. At the same time, the board was also considering the spin-off of NCR, thus admitting the mistake inherent in that unfriendly acquisition.

After a very full discussion of Western Electric without seeking a final resolution, Bob Allen said, "Rich McGinn is qualified and would be the natural choice to lead the new spin-off, but he has had no experience heading a publicly owned company. If any of you have a suggestion for a manufacturing executive who would qualify, let me know." Frank Thomas, president of the Ford Foundation and a fellow director of AT&T, and I both immediately looked at Henry Schacht (who modestly stared at the papers on the table in front of him) and then at each other.

When the meeting ended a few minutes later, I rushed to Bob Allen, beating Frank to his side by a few seconds. I said to Bob, "You have that experienced manufacturing leader right here in this room ... Henry Schacht." Frank Thomas enthusiastically agreed. I don't know whether Bob's response was premeditated or a matter of quick thinking, but he fired back, "I just wanted to test you to see if any of you thought of Henry." The spin-off of Western Electric would later be renamed Lucent, and Henry Schacht would be its first CEO.

These strategy discussions illustrate my definition of a good CEO—someone who can bring questions to the board without having answers. It requires a CEO with self-confidence to work with a board in that way. A person without that kind of self-confidence is inclined to think he or she needs to have answers to everything or be judged badly. The opposite is the case. Show-and-tell sessions make for ineffective board meetings; in-depth strategic discussions make them worthwhile.

Memorable Management Search: When John Walter did not succeed Bob Allen at the helm of AT&T, a subsequent search led to a set of contacts I found most interesting and unusual. The internal candidate was John Zeglis (who later led AT&T Wireless), a person I knew well and had been close to when I was on the AT&T board. The outside candidate was Mike Armstrong, then CEO of Hughes Electronics, and a fellow director of TBG. Heading the search was Tom Neff of Spencer Stuart, a leading executive search firm on whose advisory board I served.

Jane and I had dinner with Ann and Mike Armstrong in Bermuda at the time of a TBG board meeting during the search. Mike was seriously considering the possibility of taking the AT&T job, should it be offered to him, and we discussed the pros and cons. One of my comments to him was that, if he took the job, he should make John Zeglis his partner because John was a strong manager who knew the business. I also counseled John, who was acting CEO during the search; my advice to him was, "Act as if no search is under way; do what your judgment dictates." And I had conversations about each of the two candidates with Tom Neff.

In subsequent days, I had numerous phone calls explaining Mike to John and John to Mike and each to Tom Neff. Others may have known these three, but no one had worked as closely with all three as I had. Mike, of course, became Bob Allen's successor at AT&T.

• • •

LUCENT

Given Lucent's subsequent struggles in the telecommunications market downturn which coincided with the "dotcom bust," it is hard to recapture the feeling of optimism and energy of the early days when Lucent was spun out of AT&T. It was very exciting to watch Henry Schacht, who had retired as CEO of Cummins, take the reins of the new company. The nominating committee of the AT&T board, which I chaired, discussed which of the AT&T directors should become the nucleus of the new Lucent board. Moving to the Lucent board eliminated any budding conflict with Time Warner for me, as it did for Carla Hills (former U.S. Trade Representative): a conflict stemming from the fact that Time Warner was experimenting with telecommunications by competing with AT&T through Time Warner Cable.

Moving over to the Lucent board similarly resolved a conflict for Drew Lewis, chairman and CEO of Union Pacific, between

American Express, where he also served on the board, and the AT&T Universal Card. Of course, Henry Schacht was to be chairman and, since we joked that Henry and Frank Thomas were joined at the hip, having served together on the boards of Alcoa, Cummins and the Ford Foundation, Frank also transferred to the Lucent board, where he served as the lead director.

For one brief moment, Lucent had the largest market capitalization of any public U.S. company. Things went well during the boom time as telecommunications companies popped up and demand soared for the equipment that Lucent supplied. The opportunities seemed endless, as captured in an often-repeated, optimistic one-liner of that period: "Half of the people on earth have never made a telephone call." However, there were some aspects of the business that generated extensive discussion at the board level. Lucent supplied equipment to start-up telecommunications companies on credit, and I remember in-depth questioning of the soundness of those sales.

The rationale at the time was that these telecom companies had franchises purchased in government auctions. Those franchise rights had value and would serve as collateral for equipment loans. Furthermore, the loans the company made to those telecommunications customers were immediately resold to investors, and the early ones were sold with little difficulty and at a small discount. When industry overcapacity ensued, however, the value of the franchises was inadequate to cover what was owed; Lucent's equipment "sales" ended up looking more like "gifts." The board put limits on the amount of customer financing Lucent could have outstanding at any time. Only in hindsight is it clear that the limits we established were too high.

As Henry Schacht and Rich McGinn assembled their management team, the top 13 all came from the ranks of AT&T executives. We were particularly proud that only six of the 13 were white males. Among the women executives were Carly Fiorina, who later became CEO of Hewlett Packard, and Pat Russo, who would become CEO of Lucent after a stint as president of Kodak.

For four years or so, the business grew quickly. In due course, Henry came to the board and told us that he was ready to turn over the CEO's role to Rich, who had been president and COO of the company since the spin-off. Rich's style was always "go-go" and, as CEO, he pushed Lucent to keep up with the fastest growing companies in a very fast-growing market. As long as the market was expanding, it seemed to work.

When the business turned south, however, it was a disaster. Between February 2000 when I retired from the Lucent board and October of that year, the company's stock fell from $50 a share to a few dollars a share. It was stunning how quickly the outlook for the company changed. It was also stunning to watch the value of the Lucent stock I owned plummet.

Lucent went from being a darling of the telecommunications-stock boom market to being on the verge of bankruptcy within a period of months. Thanks to the effective work of Henry Schacht and Pat Russo following the departure of Rich McGinn, many of Lucent's problems were resolved; the company merged with the French equipment maker Alcatel in 2007.

The decline in the size of the company, as well as its revenue and profit potential, highlighted a problem many U.S. companies have been facing. The cost of retiree pensions and medical expenses become overwhelming when a large number of retirees must be supported by a shrinking active workforce.

• • •

TIME WARNER (TIME INC.)

The only Time director I knew before I was invited to join the board was Gaylord Freeman, chairman of the First National

Bank of Chicago. I have always assumed that he supported me as a candidate. A few years earlier, the Time board, like many others of the day, had been composed entirely of insiders. They had added three outside directors as required by the New York Stock Exchange when they went public. My involvement began at a luncheon meeting in 1979 with Andrew Heiskell, the company's chairman. Heiskell and I talked about the things I was concerned about as a corporate director.

By then I was beginning to question the independence of many boards and to see the need for truly independent directors who would challenge management, who would evaluate the CEO, and who held executive sessions without the presence of management. Heiskell, an old-style rather dictatorial chairman, phrased his invitation at the end of our lunch in curmudgeonly fashion. He said, "You know, Don, I don't need you, but I suspect my successors will. I've been encouraged to invite you, and I'm going to invite you, and we'll live with that."

Heiskell retired shortly after I joined the board. He illustrated his leadership style down to his last act as chairman when he insisted that Ralph Davidson become chairman of the board and Dick Munro become president and CEO. In his mind, the strengths of each would complement the other, and the combination would be almost as good in total as he himself had been individually. Other board members, particularly Jim Beré (chairman of Borg Warner) and I, argued strenuously for choosing a single leader, but to no avail. Before voting on Heiskell's proposal, several of us demanded that the board have an executive session of the outside directors with Dick Munro, who would have been our choice as a single leader of Time Inc. Heiskell grudgingly agreed to such a session.

In that private session, Dick admitted that the two-headed leadership structure wasn't the best solution, but told us he didn't think it was productive to disagree with Heiskell's last act as CEO. So the dead hand of the retiring king prevailed.

The notions that patience is a virtue and will be rewarded were reinforced when, just a few years later, Ralph Davidson took early retirement and Dick Munro became chairman, president, and CEO.

Memorable Board Oversight Challenge: The Time board was faced with some unique issues, and one I pressed on in particular was the board's responsibility for editorial integrity. While the company was still Time Inc. under Henry Luce, the magazines operated as independent editorial units under the oversight of an editorial director: first Hedley Donovan, then Henry Grunwald. A company policy required the editorial director to report to the board, but that didn't happen in practice.

The lack of board reporting became a serious issue when Ariel Sharon, then Israel's Minister of Defense, sued *Time* over the magazine's reports regarding his role in Lebanon and the killing of Palestinian refugees during an Israeli raid. When the suit was filed, Henry Grunwald decided to defend the suit. Neither the board nor the business management of Time knew about it. Even Time's general counsel had little knowledge of it.

Time prevailed in the libel suit—but only by the skin of its teeth. At the conclusion of a presentation to the board about the resolution of the suit, Time's chairman—then Ralph Davidson—said, "Well, we got out of that one and can move on to the next item of business." I interrupted, "Before you go on to the next business issue, what did we learn from this experience and what are we doing about it? Who makes the decision to sue versus settle when the next issue comes to light?" This began a months-long discussion about the role of the board in relation to defending editorial positions that would likely become lawsuits. We appointed a board committee that would meet when needed to review matters of editorial integrity. We didn't want to interfere with the editorial process, but we were anxious to protect editorial freedom in a way that also protected the corporation from dumb decisions.

We ended up revising the charter for the editorial director, over Henry Grunwald's initial objection. At one private meeting with Henry, I stumped him with my question: "Why should you be the only one at Time who reports to no one?" Henry agreed to a carefully worded reporting relationship with the board.

As scrupulous as he was about editorial integrity, Henry had to be nudged into retirement when Time management discovered through their Washington bureau that he was being considered by the Nixon administration as ambassador to Austria. Henry thought he could simply recuse himself from coverage of the Nixon administration while he was going through the confirmation process. It was my job, as chair of the editorial board committee to whom he reported, to call him and tell him that the board did not agree with him.

As unhappy as Henry was about the decision, he wrote me a personal letter after his appointment as ambassador, which said in part: "Above all, I want to thank you, and the board as a whole, for your personal support and understanding over these past years. I can think of no group that could have been more scrupulous in its regard for editorial independence and quality. I will miss you and the board."

Memorable Legal Precedent: Strategy Becomes a Defense: Through our annual strategic reviews at Time, it became clear that the company was a predominantly domestic entity competing in what would soon be a world of international media giants. We challenged management about this matter several years running, and they finally recommended the idea of merging with Warner. At that point, 45 percent of Warner's revenues and profits came from international operations, in contrast to 3 to 5 percent of Time's revenues and profits. By then, the Time board included eight outside directors, covering a full spectrum of experience and philosophy related to buying and selling businesses. At one extreme were Mike Dingman (from Wheelabrator-Fry) and Jim Beré, both leaders of companies that had been active in buying and selling businesses. At the other extreme were John Opel, chairman of IBM, and Hank Luce, son of Time's founder, who were more conservative.

That broad spectrum of philosophy and experience turned out to be a real advantage as we were considering the merger. The ultimate agreement amounted essentially to a merger of equals. We had already received the proxy votes to complete the merger at an upcoming special meeting of shareholders. Suddenly and without warning, Paramount threw an offer for Time "over the transom" with a high price. During a very intense 10-day period, the outside directors got together repeatedly without management to figure out what should be done.

In the end, we rejected the Paramount offer and voted to move forward with the Warner merger. The terms for the merger were drastically revised as a consequence of the Paramount offer, and substantial amounts of money were borrowed to complete the transaction. The decisions to reject the Paramount offer and to move forward with the merger were made on the basis of strategic fit, with particular emphasis given to Warner's international business. But because the cash value of the Paramount offer had been so high, the Time board was first pilloried in the business press and then challenged by Paramount in the courts.

The Paramount lawsuit against Time in the Delaware courts became the classic case defining whether boards of directors are within the scope of their rights and responsibilities when they refuse a high bid from a would-be purchaser of the company. Time's board actions were upheld because we had a history of examining strategic opportunities and their impact on the business. Boards, the court said, in essence, were protected if they had a record of coming to decisions and acting for strategic reasons. Every business, the courts concluded, is not for sale, just as every private home is not for sale.

Some years later, I had the opportunity to meet Chancellor Allen of the Delaware Courts at the time of the Time case. I told him that when I read his 77-page opinion, it was as if he had been with us in the boardroom. I told him that he really seemed to understand what we were doing and why. He considered that a very high compliment. "In my role," he said, "I'm never sure whether I'm being realistic and relating to the real world." Not only was Chancellor Allen in touch with the real world, the case itself has had quite an impact on that world. Influenced by that case, boards have had more and more involvement in the strategic directions and decisions of companies.

Time Warner was not finished with acquisitions when the merger with Warner was completed. Some time later, Ted Turner decided that he wanted to preserve the monument he had built at CNN and told Jerry Levin, Time Warner CEO, that he would be amenable to putting the two companies together. He was concerned that, when he died, someone like Rupert Murdoch would grab CNN, and he did not want that to happen. Perhaps a year passed between agreeing to the deal and completing it. Although the price of Time Warner stock dropped during that year, Ted never asked to renegotiate the deal. He was looking for the right place to put CNN, not just the highest price.

Ted did not enjoy being a manager, but he had built a successful business and would have a great deal to say about the Time Warner organization. When Ted attended his first Time Warner board meeting, I wondered how long it would take him to make his first comment, given his reputation for volatility and outspokenness. He kept himself contained for exactly one hour. I was pleasantly surprised at how he handled himself with self-control at board meetings.

I have observed several CEOs who try to hold on to their positions longer than they should and behave imperially if their "right" to their leadership role is questioned. Steve Ross, who became co-CEO of Time Warner following the merger, exemplified this pattern. Steve brought his imperial demeanor as well as his spending habits from Warner to the merged company. While Andrew Heiskell had also been dictatorial, Steve Ross made Heiskell seem almost egalitarian by comparison. We were able to have some oversight influence at the board level, but the only event that really changed Steve's control at Time Warner was his death.

The Time Warner merger was approved in late 1989 and envisioned the retirement of Dick Munro as CEO of Time after a period as Steve's co-CEO at Time Warner. Nick Nicholas was slated to replace Dick as co-CEO. It was not long before Steve's approach and style led to significant concerns and frustrations on the part of board members. His perquisites bothered some of us greatly.

At the same time, Steve refused to address significant corporate governance issues. These included the need for a retirement age for directors, the need to control compensation, the unwieldy size of the board itself, the need for the board to discuss strategy, and the need for communication both at and between board meetings. I chaired the nominating and governance committee of the board, and my contacts with Steve became predictable. Each of my suggestions drew a response along these lines: "Don, you are absolutely right, but not now. There are other things we need to do first." Time Warner had gone deeply in debt to complete the merger; Steve and his advisors were focused on trying to reduce that debt. In essence, Steve had control of the Time Warner board and wanted nothing to change that.

As some board members' frustrations continued to build, Steve was diagnosed with and treated for prostate cancer. The last board meeting he attended was in September 1991. He participated by telephone in the December 1991 meeting, and I saw him at his apartment in February 1992 when he and Jerry Levin engineered the firing of Nick Nicholas. My first inkling that something like that was in the works came in a January 1992 call from Jerry Levin, saying he had decided over Christmas that he could not work for Nick. He added that Steve was siding with him. Nick would have to go.

I was stunned and immediately flew to New York to see if the decision could be changed. As I talked to Steve and Jerry, I realized that it was a fait accompli. Then I was presented with a dilemma. Nick was on a family vacation skiing in Colorado. Steve and Jerry wanted me to call Nick and tell him of their decision. The alternative was for Steve's lawyer, Arthur Liman, to make the call.

Given the limited options, I opted to make the call to Nick. I began the phone conversation with, "Are you sitting down?" Nick couldn't believe that Jerry would do this to him. I had to tell Nick that, in my judgment, Steve and Jerry would easily have the board votes to replace Nick with Jerry, and that retired CEO Dick Munro, who might have stopped the "coup," had sided with Jerry and Steve. That was the last time I saw Steve Ross in person.

On February 21, 1992, I wrote to Steve and Jerry:

On my way home from the board meeting that completed three most difficult days with Time Warner, I wrote down questions for you to consider for the March board meeting...

Nick and Steve seemed mutually supportive in their relationship at the time of Dick Munro's retirement. What happened between then and February 20, 1992?

What brought the strained relationship to a head? Why was the process condensed into a matter of days, giving many directors only one day's advance warning that a problem existed?

What were the differences in corporate strategy between Steve and Nick? Could those differences have been kept from becoming terminal by testing them with the board for their reactions?

What is there about our board/management relationship that could permit a rift to exist for seven months and not be discussed at dinners or meetings? How can we change that?

I did not receive answers to these questions. I had one further communication from Steve in 1992, an unsigned August memo with his name typed in. He was disagreeing with the nominating committee's decision (which had my strong endorsement) to set a retirement age of 70 for directors. When I drafted a response to Steve, I was advised by Jerry Levin and Arthur Liman not to send it. Instead, my frustration with the board that year was communicated in letters and memos to Jerry Levin. Typical of my comments was the following communication I sent on March 16, 1992:

> In the opinion of this director, neither the agenda for board meetings nor the nature of pre-board dinners has provided the needed climate or, importantly, the time for 12 independent directors to fulfill their responsibilities regarding strategy, succession, or executive compensation and evaluation. The size of the board and the presence of 10 inside directors make it difficult to hold board discussions of succession, compensation, or other sensitive personnel issues.

When Jerry was interviewed in 1999 by *Director's Alert* (now *Board Alert*), he described me as one of the directors who always asked the tough questions and "held our feet to the fire in a very constructive way." My needling and Jerry's natural inclination to want Time Warner to be a leader in corporate governance led to a board decision to cut the size of the board to 12 and to retire most of the insiders on the board. An ad hoc committee of two, Dick Munro (of Time) and Hugh Culverhouse (of Warner), were appointed to speak with each director to solicit input about who should leave and who should stay on the board.

The process of downsizing the board was filled with acrimony. Everyone agreed that the board was too large, and everyone was concerned that there was little privacy regarding board matters. *The New York Times* and *The Wall Street Journal* reported on Time Warner board meetings as if they were public events. But the specifics of who would stay and who would go were highly controversial and emotional. Martin Payson was asked to stay as an employee but not as a board member. He resigned instead. Bert Wasserman, CFO, was dropped as a board member although some thought that would be a bad sign to the financial community.

And Bill Vanden Heuvel, a board member, wrote a four-page memorandum with a cover letter to Jerry Levin, asking him to direct the ad hoc committee to cease its efforts. He criticized the decisions regarding some board members. In his view, they should be retained because they were "totally loyal" to Jerry's leadership—as if that was a determining factor in the development of an independent board!

Because the ad hoc committee completed their work by early December, we were prepared to announce the new board composition on Monday, December 14. This announcement might have been made some days earlier, but was delayed to give each departing director a choice of resigning immediately or not being slated for re-election at the next April annual meeting. Steve Ross died that weekend. Not surprisingly, some press coverage accused the Time Warner board of "not waiting until the body got cold" before removing Steve's buddies from the board. In reality, the announcement was just the culmination of an arduous process and was in no way a response to Steve's death.

To say that Steve's death came as a surprise would be an understatement. In a letter dated Friday, December 11, and forwarded by Arthur Liman, Steve's doctor wrote that he had seen Steve on December 7 and: "… I anticipate that Steve should be able to have some discussions with his colleagues about business decisions by mid-January." It seemed obvious at the time that the letter was designed more to slow down the board reorganization than to accurately report on Steve's illness. The changes in the size and membership of the board finally led to meaningful change in Time Warner corporate governance.

One of the most distressing experiences during my years on the Time Warner board culminated in the annual meeting of 1992, which lasted almost five hours. It was the longest annual meeting for any company that I have ever attended. The controversial subject was the recording of "Cop Killer," a song by rap artist Ice-T, which was being distributed by a 50-percent-owned subsidiary of Time Warner. The song was alleged to have influenced a policeman's murder in Texas and, in any case, had despicable and incendiary lyrics. Over several meetings, considerable board time was spent on the subject.

Jerry Levin originally supported freedom of expression. With pressure from the board and innumerable and very vocal outside critics (many of whom were represented at the annual meeting), he later agreed that Time Warner's music management would be expected not to publish such extreme material. The 50-percent ownership in the music subsidiary was sold the following year and has been reported to be highly profitable for the 100-percent owner. As we discussed the issue, the board concluded that the reputation of Time Warner was more important than defending freedom of expression for the Ice-Ts of the world.

Serving on the Time Warner board also provided many wonderful and positive experiences—among them the series of trips called Time Newstours. *Time* magazine created the Newstours as a promotional effort, a way of educating and getting closer to the CEOs of the magazine's major advertisers. It was also true that traveling with a group of CEOs allowed *Time* to get access to world leaders in a way that wasn't normally possible for the magazine's reporters. Once CEOs were committed, board members were invited to go, as well.

Between those Newstours and my numerous Ford Foundation trips, I have managed to meet some extraordinary people and to have some experiences that greatly broadened my view of the world. Some of those memorable experiences are recounted in Chapter 19.

CHAPTER 13

OF BOARDROOMS AND BARONS

LaSalle Partners 1979-present
LaSalle Street Trust
LaSalle Income and Growth
Funds, I, II and III
LaSalle Hotel Properties
Freeport McMoran 1980-1984
G.D. Searle & Co. 1981-1985
TBG
(Thyssen Bournemisza) ... 1981-1993

LaSalle Partners

The third of the three boards I joined in 1979 was the Chicago-based LaSalle Street Trust, a Real Estate Investment Trust (REIT). It started with a visit from Bill Sanders, founder of LaSalle Partners, who was looking for someone with a retail background for the board. Art Wood, chairman of Sears, had turned them down; I was next on Bill's list. That started what is now more than a quarter-century of involvement—20 years between the origination and the closing of the LaSalle Street Trust—plus service on the boards of three successive LaSalle Income and Growth Funds, as well as the board of LaSalle Hotel Properties. I chaired the audit committees at each of the LaSalle boards on which I served.

My LaSalle Partners involvement has given me the opportunity to work closely with Stuart Scott, Bill Sanders's successor at the company, which is now called Jones Lang LaSalle. Stuart is an energetic and creative leader. It is hard to imagine that many of the innovative developments at LaSalle would have come about without him. He managed the merger of LaSalle with Jones Lang Wootton to create Jones Lang LaSalle, a firm with true world-wide reach. I will always admire Stuart for his reactions to questions of who should bear the cost of any issue that was a close call. Invariably, Stuart decided in favor of the investor rather than for his own company.

The LaSalle Street Trust was a REIT with corporate and state pension funds as the major investors. The trust owned buildings such as the Daily News Building in New York, the Field Building in Chicago, and Fox Plaza in Los Angeles. The trust also owned several malls, including one in Kansas City and the Valley View Mall in Dallas. The LaSalle Street Trust has now been liquidated, which in and of itself posed some interesting problems. It had been set up with a prescribed time limit, the end of which came at a low point in real estate values. We did our best to try to persuade the investors to extend the time period, but they didn't agree, and we ended up having to sell the properties in a down market. LaSalle learned from that experience in designing successive trusts.

The three LaSalle Income and Growth Funds have been quite successful, to the delight of their investors, which have included the unlikely combination of the government of Kuwait and General Motors for one fund and Kuwait and Colorado PERA (Public Employees' Retirement Association) for another.

LaSalle Hotel Properties

My board work for LaSalle Hotel Properties (LHO) started with joining the initial board as the company became public in 1998 and then somewhat later helping to make it fully independent of Jones Lang LaSalle. LHO management believed (and it turned out to be the case) that some investors who normally invest in REITs would not invest in the company while it was controlled by Jones Lang LaSalle.

The audit committee, composed of independent trustees and which I chaired, was key to the process of separating the two companies. Hans Weger, the CFO, was careful to check each development with our committee. The board often met in executive session without management participation; the process was an excellent example of avoiding conflicts of interest. LHO made certain that the right questions were being asked and that shareholders' interests were carefully represented.

In the spring of 2004, I was completing my second three-year term as a trustee of LHO. Because I was 77, re-election for another three-year term deserved scrutiny. Stuart Scott, chair of the board's nominating committee, is a long-time friend but a stickler for good corporate governance. Unbeknownst to me, Stuart arranged for a telephone conference call discussion by the board and key management about whether I should be invited to run again. Because of their independent review and decision, it made it much easier for me to agree to continue when the invitation was extended. I saw their prior meeting as an appropriate evaluation of me as a trustee and chair of the audit committee and consistent with good governance.

A similar evaluation procedure in 2007 led to my continuation as an LHO trustee. Both reevaluation experiences reminded me that a set retirement age is a poor substitute for a thorough evaluation of a director or trustee prior to being reslated for election by shareholders—regardless of age.

LHO has been and remains an excellent example of the impact of outstanding management in building a successful enterprise and the contribution that can be made by a strong and involved board. John Bortz, Mike Barnello, and Hans Weger have produced results than compare favorably not only with other hotel REITs but also with other REITs in general. In both 1999 and 2004, LHO's total return put it in first place among all publicly traded U.S. REITs.

• • •

FREEPORT MCMORAN

My experiences at Inland Steel, LaSalle, AT&T, and Cummins, to name a few, had reassured me that there were many CEOs in whose hands my reputation was being well served. I cannot say the same for all my board experiences. Perhaps the clearest example of disappointment was my experience on the board of Freeport McMoran.

Freeport McMoran, among other interests, was the major U.S. producer of sulfur and owned the rights to the largest copper deposit in the world in Irian Jaya, a westerly island in the Indonesian archipelago. In late 1979 Paul Douglas, son of former Senator Paul Douglas of Illinois, who was the CEO of Freeport Sulfur invited me to join their board. Freeport Sulfur would soon merge with McMoran.

George Putnam of Putnam Funds (a family of mutual funds), who was already serving on the Freeport board and who had been a classmate of mine at the Harvard Business School, had recommended me to Paul. I liked Paul immediately and agreed to join the board. Unfortunately, over the next two or three years, Paul, who had been Freeport's leader before the merger, was pushed out by the McMoran contingent. The McMoran contingent supported one of their own, a former Texas football player named Jim Bob Moffett.

Benno Schmidt, Sr., (father of a future president of Yale), who was on the board, originally having been put there to represent prominent Freeport investing families, also backed the McMoran contingent. To my dismay, Jim Bob Moffett won out and Paul was pushed out of the company. Also to my dismay, Benno Schmidt held onto the chairmanship of the board following Paul's departure.

The internal clash between Paul Douglas and Jim Bob Moffett had been a challenge to Benno, who tried initially to keep them apart by dividing the company into two parts, with gas and oil under Jim Bob and the mining business under Paul. Because I identified with Paul and the integrity that he represented, I counseled him frequently and in private as he tried to regain control over the business he had once managed. Had he been the leader, I would have remained a director. The fight was heated; my candidate lost.

Perhaps too late in the leadership battle, I went to Benno privately and said that I thought we needed to have an executive session of the board to talk about succession. His answer: "No, that would be dysfunctional for the company and would upset management."

I challenged him, pointing out that directors should be able to talk about whatever concerned us. Benno still refused to hold an executive session of the board, saying, "If you want to challenge me, we'll bring it up at the board and vote on whether to do it." That made my course clear; if I didn't feel comfortable with management, one of us would have to go. I said, "Thank you very much. I won't run for reelection at the upcoming annual meeting." I let the other directors know my reason for leaving and within six months they were having the kind of meetings we should have been having all along. As I said in a *Chicago Tribune* interview in December 1986, in answer to the question of what to do if a CEO isn't open to advice or help from directors, "The directors who aren't getting what they ask for ought to get the hell out."

Benno, since deceased, continued as chairman for several years. That entitled him to use the corporate jet to travel between his New York home and his Hobe Sound, Florida winter retreat.

• • •

G.D. Searle & Co.

My second invitation to join the board of G. D. Searle & Co. came 15 years after the first. Once again Dan Searle, still a director but no longer an officer of the company, paid me a visit. This time, he was accompanied by Searle Chairman and CEO Don Rumsfeld. I joined the board in 1981.

Don was an outstanding chairman, especially in his use of the board. I admired the way he brought questions to the board in advance of when he needed decisions. The board always participated and was never surprised. Typically he would bring something up for discussion at one meeting, go back and think about it, and then bring it up in an improved version for a vote at a subsequent meeting. The consensus-building Don Rumsfeld I worked with then was very different from press reports of a strong-willed and isolated Secretary of Defense in the George W. Bush administration.

When I joined the board, the Searle family still owned a significant portion of the company's stock. Soon thereafter, they decided, wisely, to diversify their interests. There were two parts of the business. The first was the pharmaceutical business, where making money was always a problem because of the uncertainties of the company's new drug research and development efforts where Searle's small size made it difficult to compete.

The second component was NutraSweet, the division formed to commercialize the sweetener aspartame approved by the FDA in 1981. NutraSweet® was introduced to the market in the form of Equal® tabletop sweetener in 1982 and then in diet soft drinks. The family and the board insisted that the two parts of the business be packaged together in any sale.

Monsanto made an offer for the drug business without the sweetener business, which the board and management fully considered. We decided we did not want to be left with what would then be a one-product company. We turned down the offer, and Rumsfeld went on running both businesses. Later, Monsanto came back and made what we considered to be a fair offer for both parts of the company; we ended up approving that deal.

During the various offers and negotiations for the business, Rumsfeld asked Ed Brennan, then CEO of Sears, and me to serve on a transaction committee of the board, so that he could talk to us frequently without having to convene the whole board. In the last year I was a Searle director, I participated in 40 meetings, counting regular board meetings, regular committee meetings, special meetings of the full board, and telephonic and in-person meetings of the transaction committee.

In addition to his skill in working with his board, Don had the ability to attract good people. One of those was John Robson, president of the company. John did a job that none of us thought could be done. At one meeting, he told the board that he was going to try to get the patent for NutraSweet extended beyond the usual 17-year term. "How could you possibly get that done?" we asked. But John knew how to work Congress, and how to make the case that an extension was warranted because the FDA had taken so long to review and re-review the product prior to its ultimate approval. Robson got the patent extension almost single-handedly.

After the sale of Searle to Monsanto, Rumsfeld explored running for U.S. President. His affinity for the political world extended back to his days as a young member of Congress, where I had originally met him, followed by service in the Office of Wage and Price Controls, as Ambassador to NATO, and as White House Chief of Staff and Secretary of Defense under President Gerald Ford.

Despite hard work, including that of my son-in-law, Joel Getzendanner, who worked for the campaign for a period of time, Don's campaign fizzled in Iowa, and he dropped the idea. Although Don's presidential aspirations may have been dimmed, he has found his way back to Washington, where, in the aftermath of 9/11 and the country's wars in Afghanistan and Iraq, he became a controversial Secretary of Defense. No one who worked with Don at Searle could have predicted that he would become the focal point for blame for the unpopular U.S. involvement in Iraq.

• • •

TBG(Thyssen Bournemisza)

The saga of my service on the TBG board is the tale of an experience so surreal that one would be hard-pressed to accept it as a work of fiction. It started in 1980 when Bob Genillard, a fellow Corning board member, was general manager and CEO of TBG, then called Thyssen Bournemisza. Bob knew I would be changing my role at Jewel, and he invited me to consider the TBG board.

I visited Baron Heinrich Thyssen-Bournemisza in his suite at the Waldorf Astoria in New York to discuss the matter further. I asked him, "What do you want a board for? You own the whole company." He said to me, "I concluded a long time ago that my family and I would be better off if we had a board of independent directors and if we counted the votes." And he did count the votes, too. "What do you want out of it?" I asked him. He replied, "I take a third of the earnings out of the business each year and leave the rest to be reinvested. That is what I would like to keep doing."

TBG was then a conglomerate, with a shipping and barge business, an ocean-going container business, a bus manufacturing company, and an information processing company. There was also an investment arm to provide a return on sizable cash holdings. This was how the corporation had evolved since Baron Thyssen's father had decided to sell out of the family's Thyssen steel inheritance in Germany and to diversify.

The company was often buying and selling other companies. TBG paid taxes on whatever they made in the U.S., but virtually everything they owned overseas was owned through subsidiaries in Bermuda or Curaçao, where there were no taxes. The headquarters of the company was in Monaco, which has no personal income tax. The firm knew how to manage their businesses legally with a minimum of taxes better than any group I have seen.

The membership of the TBG board was itself quite interesting. Freddy Heineken, the brewer, was on it for a time, as were Umberto Agnelli (of the family that controlled Fiat in Italy) and Tony O'Reilly, then CEO of Heinz. The board met four times a year, usually one or two of the meetings taking place in the U.S., others in Holland, and one each year in Monaco. It is hard to get to Monaco from Chicago for a one-day meeting. But I learned that because of the time changes, I could leave Monaco at 2 P.M., get a 4 P.M. flight from Nice to London, catch the Concorde that left at 7 P.M., be at Kennedy Airport in New York at 7 P.M., and catch the last flight of the day on United to Chicago. It was sad to see the Concorde pass into history in 2003.

Perhaps the most important thing the Baron did in the early 1980s was to set up a Continuity Trust in which he placed all of the shares of TBG. Providing for succession and continuity is always important for a family-owned business, but the Baron's assets and family were even more complicated than most. The Baron collected art and wives. His art collection was often described as second in value only to that of the Queen of England. Thanks to a sale of some of the artwork to a public foundation in Spain, many pieces now reside in the Thyssen Bournemisza Museum, which is near the Prado in Madrid.

At the end of his life, the Baron was married to his fifth wife, Tita, a former Miss Spain, former wife of Lex Barker (Tarzan in the movies), and a person I can only describe as a gold-digger extraordinaire. Of the Baron's five wives, I met four. The more I learned about the art and the wives the Baron collected, and the longer I observed his interest in wine, the more I understood his dysfunctional family. The one exception was his oldest son, Heini, who succeeded Bob Genillard as CEO of TBG.

When the Baron established the Continuity Trust, I was impressed, and I congratulated him on solving the problem of how to keep good managers in the business. He had realized that it would be a serious challenge to keep management together with four children and five wives waiting in the wings at his death, eager to claim the Baron's assets for their own. The Continuity Trust was an ingenious mechanism to protect the company from the family.

The Baron's plan included the continuation of the company's supervisory board, on which I served for over a dozen years, and the establishment of independent trustees to represent the beneficiaries. To add a further layer of insulation between the family's trustees and the company's supervisory board, the trust provided for "protectors." The protectors' role—and I can say my role, since I became one of the protectors—involved making sure that trustees were appointed to represent the beneficiaries' interests and that the members of the supervisory board were appointed to represent the company's interests. Protectors approved the appointment of both trustees and directors and provided a buffer between the two sets of interests.

Any prediction of a battle over the Baron's assets was to prove a gross underestimate. Despite the existence of the Continuity Trust, and while the Baron was still alive, the fifth wife, Carmen "Tita" Cervera, who was keeping the Baron isolated from the rest of the world, challenged the trust, saying that he had not been well-advised and that he had been lied to and misled by his son, Heini, when he signed the trust documents. This accusation was bizarre, particularly as the Baron had taken considerable pleasure in Heini's becoming CEO of TBG! Despite the fact that scores of people (including me) were witnesses to the Baron's health and sanity at the time he created the trust, Tita alleged that he had not been competent. Before the whole affair was decided, over $90 million of the family's assets would be squandered on legal fees.

Tita filed suit in Bermuda, a decision that contributed in its own way to the bizarre TBG saga. Bermuda is a small country with few judges. When the first judge to whom the case was assigned was elevated to a higher court, another judge was needed. The replacement judge was hired from Hong Kong. He continued to listen with absurd patience as the plaintiff lawyer prolonged the case for a year.

The plaintiff lawyer's goal was to make it so uncomfortable for the defense that there would be a settlement. But the more that lawyer got into the case, the more he discovered testimony from many credible witnesses who could relate specific discussions with the Baron, including the Baron's statements to the board at the time the trust was signed. I dutifully recorded my testimony regarding the Baron's intentions for the business, his announcements to the board, and the conversation in which I had congratulated him on his solution to management continuity of the business, balanced with the interests of the family.

The trial went on and on until the judge from Hong Kong completed the time period he had agreed to spend in Bermuda. At that point, he declared that he would stay in Bermuda to complete the case if they increased his pay—trying to hold up Bermuda! He left, and the case was assigned to a new judge in England. By that time, Tita apparently realized that reaching a settlement was increasingly urgent as the Baron's health declined and her need for cash increased.

At that point, it should have been an easy matter to bring the suit to its agreed-upon end. However, it still took a long time for the lawyers to get Tita to agree to the documents, during which time she continued to isolate the Baron and refused to let anyone see him. As the story was told to me, it was several months before the family finally assembled at a hotel in Basel, their first gathering in eight years. All that remained was for the Baron to sign the settlement documents. He was upstairs in bed and a notary was present to witness the signing.

In Europe, notaries have different roles than in the U.S. In Swtizerland, the notary was required to attest to the fact that the Baron was mentally fit to sign the settlement. After spending some time with him, the notary came downstairs and said he did not think that the Baron was mentally fit to sign.

Tita realized that having the Baron sign the settlement was the only way she was going to get some of the money she wanted. So she allowed Heini to go upstairs to see his father. This was the first time Heini had seen his father in years. Heini helped the Baron rally to the point that the notary could go back and conclude that he was competent to sign the settlement. At last, the papers were duly signed and notarized.

Eight weeks later, Baron Heinrich Thyssen-Bournemisza died. The Continuity Trust survived Tita's legal attacks and was subsequently distributed to the separate trusts for each of the beneficiaries in 2007. That ended my role as a protector. The tensions among the siblings made the distribution difficult with disagreements over valuations and the rights of existing and unborn children of the four.

At my final TBG meeting in September 2007, I was told of press coverage of the marriage of Tita's son, whom the Baron had adopted at Tita's urging. The Spanish newspapers were reporting that Tita did not plan to attend her son's wedding. She reputedly did not approve of the bride because she was only after her son's money.

• • •

REFLECTIONS

In retrospect, all of my board experiences ... from my first declined invitation to serve on the Searle board to the extraordinary denouement of the AT&T monopoly ... from the exemplary leadership examples of Charlie Brown and Henry Schacht to less admirable CEOs ... from the Irwin family's commitment to the survival and success of Cummins, to the dysfunctional family battles of the Thyssen-Bournemiszas ... have contributed to my evolving views of the relationship between CEOs and their boards, especially the role of independent directors. In a *Harvard Business Review* article published in 1979, "What the CEO and board expect of each other," I concluded that it all comes down to people:

> Much of what we read and say about boards of directors uses abstract terms like responsibilities, liabilities, accountability, legal requirements, disclosure, shareholder representation, and federal chartering. These are ideas superimposed on what are human relationships. I believe that if the attitudes and relationships of a CEO and a director are right, most of what some want better defined and others want better legislated develops in the normal course of events.

What I wrote in 1979 seems equally appropriate today.

CHAPTER 14

A Reputation for Independence

Firestone 1982-1986
Putnam Funds 1982-1999
Aon 1983-2001
Springs Industries 1984-1999
Illinova (Illinois Power) ... 1988-1997

FIRESTONE

John Nevin was CEO of Zenith when I first called on him on behalf of the United Way and later when I invited him to join the Northwestern University board. He was a Harvard Business School graduate, had worked as a controller at Ford and its Philco subsidiary, and was very facile with numbers. We traveled to Poland together on one of the Time Newstours, and I genuinely liked him.

In the 1970s, Firestone experienced a problem with tire quality reminiscent of the company's more recent difficulty with the tires on Ford SUVs. In the earlier case, however, the defects had affected a whole series of tires, and the company had sustained huge losses. After John left Zenith and was brought in to clean up Firestone, he invited me to join the board.

We dealt with a variety of issues as a board during my four years as a director. One was an issue faced by many companies at the time, though it is rarer today. In the early 1980s, many companies were vulnerable to a phenomenon that came to be called *greenmail.* Greenmail referred to a situation in which corporate raiders sought to extract a premium over market price for shares they acquired in a company. Since many companies had a "poison pill" in place—a device that would increase the cost of a hostile takeover—the greenmailers would accumulate the company's stock until their holdings were just under the trigger for the "poison pill." They then sought to have their interests bought out at a greater-than-market price, or to use the leverage of their ownership to co-opt management to favor a greenmail minority takeover.

In their efforts to co-opt management, raiders would frequently approach management with what was really a thinly veiled bribe. "Why don't you go talk to Mr. X at ABC Company," they would say to the CEO of the target company, "and see what happened when we worked with him." Generally, Mr. X had received substantial compensation when the raider purchased ABC Company.

Some corporate executives at the time succumbed to the temptation and paved the way for the corporate raiders to acquire the company, whether or not the acquisition was in the long-term interests of the company's stakeholders or consistent with its strategic direction. John Nevin was approached by greenmailers while I served on the board, but his integrity, ethics, and loyalty to the company caused him to reject such overtures.

Although John frequently asked for help from the board, I discovered that he found it difficult to accept advice from others. As I commuted to Firestone board meetings in Akron, I became increasingly frustrated with him. When the invitation to join the Kmart board came along in 1985, I told John that the Kmart and Firestone boards met on the same days, and that I felt I could contribute more to a retail board than to a tire company board. "Besides," I said, "there's something I want to tell you. You seem to listen, but you don't always hear. You're the most difficult person I have ever tried to help in the business world!"

I expected John to disagree and had my comeback ready for him. But he surprised me and replied, "Yes, you're right. I won't argue with you." I couldn't resist using my rejoinder anyway. "I'm sorry you won't argue with me," I said, "because I had the perfect answer ... Just ask your wife!"

Later, John managed the sale of Firestone to Bridgestone and made a lot of money for Firestone shareholders, but by then I was no longer on the board and had traded trips to Akron for trips to Troy, Michigan, to tackle the issues at Kmart.

Memorable Board Member Misstep: A fellow director of Firestone, who was then chairman and CEO of RJR Nabisco, needed a general counsel. Without telling anyone in advance, he hired away Firestone's general counsel. He did not see it as a big deal and expected to continue on as a Firestone director. The Firestone board's response was succinct: "No way!"

• • •

PUTNAM FUNDS

George Putnam, son of the founder of Putnam Funds, and I had been classmates at the Harvard Business School. Like Amo Houghton at Corning, who graduated in the class behind us, George and I had kept track of each other; and when I was finishing my Jewel career, George invited me to join the board of trustees for what would grow to be more than 100 Putnam funds. During the 17 years I served on the Putnam boards, I learned a great deal about mutual funds and investment company regulations, and I watched Putnam grow from about $6 billion in assets when I became a trustee to over $300 billion when I retired from the board.

While I was still at Jewel, I had declined a number of invitations to join the boards of various banks. The primary reason for turning them down was that I wanted to avoid any pressure on Jewel's financial leadership about where to place Jewel's banking business, thereby avoiding any conflict of interest. It is also true that I didn't think being on a bank board would be all that interesting. It seemed to me that a bank director would never really know the fine points of bank loans, but would still have to approve them. In any case, the fact that I was not on the board of a bank meant that I could join the Putnam board without any conflict with mutual fund regulations.

Being a trustee of a mutual fund is different from being a director of a corporation in a number of ways. For one, mutual fund trustees rehire the management of the funds every year. So each year required the negotiation of management contracts. We would go through a process of rigorously reviewing the management team's performance and analyzing each fund's costs and profits before establishing the contract terms for the following year.

Another difference is that mutual fund trustees fulfill a watchdog role, quasi-regulatory in nature, for which there is no parallel on a corporate board. On two occasions while I was a Putnam trustee, we found that the management of a fund had not adequately done its job. In one case, the fund owned a particular, rather illiquid, security, which management had not re-priced in months.

In another situation, the fund involved had a limit on the percentage of the fund that could be invested in any single security. Somehow, the management of that fund, one of Putnam's smaller ones, lost track of that limitation and invested more than should have been invested in a pig farm. In both cases, we required the management company to make the shareholders of the funds whole. In one instance that entailed a "fine" of $750,000 payable to the fund.

Being part watchdog and part regulator, on top of being trustee and counselor, was a fascinating and unusual experience. While there is no corporate parallel, my Putnam experience has made me wonder whether there might be a need for more of that type of oversight in the corporate world.

Memorable Nominating Committee Lesson: Serving on the Putnam boards gave me an opportunity to address the problem of a weak board member. Traditionally, once elected to a board, directors have expected to stay on the board until retirement, or until the company is sold—really as long as they cared to serve.

One of my fellow Putnam trustees, although a successful businessperson, constantly took board discussions off onto unproductive tangents and was not a major contributor to board deliberations. At a meeting of the nominating committee, we discussed a series of much stronger candidates and debated whether we felt strongly enough to ask the ineffective board member not to stand for reelection.

Mutual fund boards often have their own counsel independent of the management company's. As we debated the issue of whether or not to re-slate that director, our counsel asked us a question that has become my model for evaluating members of any board on which I serve. "How would you feel," he asked, "if there was a major lawsuit against all of you as directors and this person was selected to give the deposition?" I have repeated that question many times in other board situations when someone says, "So-and-so is not very strong, but is it worth the fuss to do anything about it?"

Beginning with that experience at Putman, I have become a strong and often needling proponent of requiring boards to have an evaluation process in place before re-slating directors. I served on the nominating committee of another board during a discussion of re-slating existing directors. We had three outstanding new candidates whom we wanted to add. Two of the company's existing directors were coming up for re-slating. I said, "Does anyone on this committee think that the two we are talking about re-slating are equal to or better than the three on our list?"

We decided not to re-slate the two whose terms were up. One of them understood; the other was angry and challenged us with, "What right do you have to make that decision about me?!?" Making needed changes in the composition of a board is difficult. Once a director is elected, only a vote of the shareholders can remove him or her. That makes it even more important that the nominating committee and the board do a careful job of evaluating directors and not just automatically re-slate them.

When the Putnam trustees decided to support a program to evaluate trustees, Bill Pounds, retired dean of the Sloan School at the Massachusetts Institute of Technology (MIT's business school) and I chaired the subcommittee that developed the evaluation process. We decided to call it an *improvement process* rather than an evaluation program. The first step evolved from board of trustees discussions, during which we identified the attributes that we wanted to see in a Putnam trustee.

Once we had defined the desired attributes, we developed a questionnaire covering the operation of the board and its meetings, the performance of the chairman as a board leader, and the performance of each individual trustee. The key question regarding individual trustees was open-ended: "If I could make a suggestion to 'Trustee by name' to improve his or her contribution to the board activity, it would be
_____."

Management members who sat in on board meetings and therefore had opinions about the board were asked to fill out the questionnaires, as well. (As I recall, management was often more critical of trustees than were the trustees themselves.) The completed questionnaires were sent to the board's outside counsel to be tabulated, and each individual's results were returned to him or her. The chairman and vice-chairman of the board saw all of the results.

Though they were unsigned, individual evaluations could often be recognized for their source. While the evaluations of my performance as a trustee were generally complimentary, one evaluator, who I guessed was Putnam President Larry Lasser "credited" me with often trying to turn a "spark into a fire." That comment came to mind when I learned of Putnam's travails that came to light several years after my retirement from the board. The firm's difficulties illustrate a board truism: If management keeps the board in the dark, there is no way that board members can exercise their fiduciary duties.

Putnam's board of trustees was strong and independent. If what I read in the business press is correct, management did not inform the Putnam board when they discovered fund managers doing short-term trading in their own funds. It was reported that Larry Lasser knew about this and stopped it, but he did not tell the board about this "spark." The fact that the trustees were unaware of the spark allowed it to turn into a fire.

In a letter to me after I retired from the Putnam board, Larry was generous in his comments:

> It seems ironic to me that you as a passionate advocate for corporate governance have been retired by the very governance you advocated. I admire your advocacy, but am disappointed personally and for Putnam we have lost your wisdom, guidance, challenge, and high standards. That they were sometimes communicated in the form of criticism or gentle needling (and sometimes not-so-gentle needling!) never confused that your messages were almost always on target and constructive. If I didn't always show it, I almost always knew it.

The fact that I reached retirement age and left the board seemed more natural to me than ironic. I truly liked Larry

Lasser and was genuinely sorry to hear of his early departure from Putnam.

• • •

AON

When I think of my years on the Aon board (called Combined International at the time I became a director), I think, of course, of Pat Ryan, Aon's CEO, but first I think of Harold Hines. I became fond of saying that Harold and I met in kindergarten—not our own, but as fathers of Bill Hines and Jerry Perkins. I suppose we would have become equally good friends had we met in some other way, but the symbolism of what brought us together was never lost on either of us.

When I first knew Harold, he worked for Marsh & McClennan. When he became president of Marsh & McClennan, he was under pressure to consider moving to New York. I remember more than one conversation with Harold on the subject. In every conversation, we discussed his overriding consideration—what was right for his family. Harold ultimately decided to give up the presidency of Marsh & McClennan rather than move to New York.

Harold would have made a marvelous professor or clergyman. Instead he brought his ability to teach and to care about people to his workplace. Harold never hesitated to express his philosophical outlook. Once, my son-in-law Joel, having transferred from divinity school to business school, was interested in knowing more about business leaders who felt strongly about ethics. In the resulting interview, which was published in the University of Chicago business school newspaper, Harold revealed the depth of his convictions:

> The real essence of being a human being is being able to recognize the difference between what is ethically sound and

ethically unsound. If you can't make that differentiation, then you're not fully conscious, you're not fully human. There are no business decisions without ethical dimensions.... Ethics matter, ethics have economic significance, ethics are the very foundation on which civil society functions effectively.

When Harold decided to stay in Chicago, Pat Ryan hired him at Aon. Unfortunately, Harold died of a sudden heart attack in 1984, at age 60. In the meantime, however, Harold had recommended me for the Aon board. Pat, whom I knew from the Northwestern University board where we served together, was seeking experienced directors for the Aon board and asked John Swearingen, CEO of Standard Oil/Amoco, and me to become directors. Andy McKenna, part owner of the Chicago Bears with Pat Ryan and one of the most active people in Chicago civic matters, also served on the Aon board.

I sent Pat a letter with questions prior to a luncheon meeting to discuss my joining his board. One question was, "Are you expecting one of your sons to be brought into the business to succeed you?" Pat's answer was emphatically, "No." He added that the company had had enough of a problem with nepotism when W. Clement Stone's son was Stone's unsuccessful successor. Pat's merger of his Ryan Insurance into Combined had been particularly attractive to the board of Combined because it had positioned Pat to become CEO.

A few years later, I had a similar conversation with Bill Marriott, CEO of Marriott Corporation, regarding the lodging company founded by his father. One of his directors, Harry Vincent (former senior vice president of Booz Allen Hamilton), arranged for us to meet for lunch to discuss the possibility of my joining the Marriott board. I asked questions such as how long his parents would stay on the board and how long he expected to remain CEO. My questions were too pointed. He called me 10 days later to thank me for coming to lunch and then said, "Don, I'm sure you are a fine director, but we are not ready for you yet."

High on my agenda the entire time I served on the Aon board was the issue of CEO succession.

In 1989, *Directorship*, a monthly publication for corporate directors, asked to interview me. The resulting article, "Talking Succession with Your CEO" (May 1989), summarizes thoughts about dealing with the issue, both personally and as a director, over many years on many boards. When asked whether most corporate leaders have someone waiting in the wings who has been groomed or considered very seriously as a successor, I gave the following response:

> Absolutely. Remember, we're talking about executives who have given a good part of their lives to their business and who usually care very much about it. They care about its future and know too that the final judgment of the quality of their leadership will include the performance of their successor.

The Aon board did not agree that the right person was waiting in the wings to succeed Pat. Four years after I retired from the board, Greg Case, a McKinsey partner, became CEO. Pat remained and has worked with great diligence to bring the 2016 Olympics to Chicago.

Memorable Compensation Committee Lesson: When I became chair of the Aon compensation committee, I encouraged the board to institute a more formal evaluation of the CEO. At the beginning of each year, we would meet with Pat Ryan as the CEO to review both quantitative and qualitative goals. During a subsequent executive session of the independent directors, the CEO's goals were discussed, revised, and finalized.

At the end of the year, the CEO personally assessed his achievements against the goals previously set. Once again, that review was followed by an executive session of the independent directors who completed the evaluation. Then, and only then, was CEO compensation considered. Importantly, the evaluation process was conducted by all of the independent directors on the board, not just the compensation committee. Equally importantly, the final approval of the CEO's compensation came from all the independent directors.

• • •

SPRINGS INDUSTRIES

When I served on the board of Springs, I had a second opportunity to see what an able executive Walter Elisha was. I had been disappointed when Walter left Jewel to run Springs Industries, but a few years later, he invited me to join the Springs board, which I did 1984 until 1999. (I stepped down from the board for some months in 1995, while I was non-executive chairman of Kmart, a major Springs customer, to avoid a conflict of interest).

I admired how Walter modernized, rationalized, and grew Springs over the years I served on the board. His acquisition of competitor Lowenstein Corporation in 1985 was a milestone in his career. It enhanced the Springs product line dramatically by adding the Wamsutta brand and helped make Springs one of the largest U.S. textile firms.

Walter was a capable leader and I enjoyed the opportunity to work with him again, but in 1997 it came time for Walter to retire as CEO, which gave rise to a series of difficult, even painful moments. Like many CEOs, including me, Walter would have liked to remain a board member following his retirement. The board greatly admired and appreciated Walter, but we didn't think it would be a good idea for him to continue as a director. This was not a reflection on Walter's leadership, but a more general realization that it is a mistake for a CEO to stay on his board after he or she has retired.

That was one mistake I made when I left the chairman's job at Jewel. Even though I stuck to my guns and passed along the CEO baton after ten years, I mistakenly stayed on the board for three more years. With the previous CEO on a board, it is harder for a successor to change things. Even if, or especially if, you have an extremely talented and respected retiring CEO, the right thing is for him or her to leave the board upon retirement. I will never forget Walter's last annual meeting and the board meeting that followed it.

Memorable CEO Transition: Walter had announced his plans to retire following the annual meeting in 1997. As he had been doing for 15 years at that point, he finished running the annual meeting; but then, instead of accompanying the rest of the board members to the board room, he just went home. It was terribly hard for me to watch him leave.

The board, minus Walter, went into its regular meeting with his successor, Crandall Bowles. Although the meeting started without any specific agenda, it went on for two hours. I realized that, because Walter was so smart and able, the board and his top management had been less likely to challenge him. They had respected his intellect and reasoning; yet, there were pent-up questions from the directors which would never have come out had Walter been at that board table. For better or worse, the board discussion was different than it would have been in his presence.

Walter was the one who suggested Crandall Close Bowles as his successor. She is the great-great-granddaughter of Colonel Elliott Springs, the company's founder. Crandall had gone to Wellesley and the Columbia University School of Business, and had worked for Morgan Stanley before she joined Springs, starting as a financial analyst.

When Walter told the board that he thought Crandall could be his successor, fellow director Art Schultz (retired chairman of Foote, Cone and Belding) and I said we'd like to talk to her.

"Crandall, you don't need the money," we said. "Why would you want to do this?" Because it is there to be done, was her answer. The message from Art and me was clear: "We want you to know that as long as the two of us are involved, we'll judge you as an executive, not as a controlling shareholder." The family had always tried to have an independent board that made decisions, and Crandall maintained that tradition while also performing as a very capable executive.

Another person I counseled on the subject of CEOs leaving their boards when they retire is Harry Kraemer, former CEO of Baxter International. Shortly after being named CEO, Harry came to a program sponsored by Booz Allen Hamilton for new CEOs. I discussed CEO-board relations with these new leaders. I underscored how difficult it is for a new CEO to make changes with his predecessor(s) sitting at the board table.

As Harry told me the story, not long thereafter, his predecessor, Vern Loucks, asked Harry what his (Vern's) role should be when he retired as chairman. Harry said he wanted to think about it. He went home, discussed it with his wife, and came back the next day with his decision. "Vern, I think you should leave the board." It may not have been the answer he was expecting, but sometime later Vern came back and said, "You know, Harry, I wish I could have done that when I took over as chairman."

In fact, every CEO and every chairman should be thinking at some point about what they want to do with "life after CEO." For too many CEOs, retirement seems to be a synonym for mortality. I have a different view, which I expressed in the 1989 *Directorship* article, where I discussed how I talk to CEOs about stepping down:

> There are various phases of life, and being a CEO is just one phase. Given the fact that people are living longer and that most of us are able to continue to be productive, we ought

to be thinking about what we can do with the next phase of our lives. I strongly believe that there is life after CEO and chairman. The real challenge is to get ready to do things that would be satisfying whether they're in the corporate world or in the not-for-profit world. I begin to talk about "what you do next" instead of implying that when he steps down from the CEO's job it's damn near the end of life. It needn't be that at all.

There is life after CEO ... and the choices for that next phase will be as diverse as the careers that led up to them. It requires the same kind of thought and planning that those CEOs applied to their businesses when they were running them.

• • •

ILLINOVA (ILLINOIS POWER)

Being an outside director with a reputation for independence has provided me with unusual opportunities. In 1987, Wendell Kelly, CEO of Illinois Power, came to call on Frank Considine (former Chairman and CEO of American National Can Company) and me. Certain Illinois Power shareholders had presented a demand for a derivative action suit against the company. This meant that the shareholders were asking the company to sue the management and the board for having acted improperly—in this case, for the decision to build the one nuclear power plant that Illinois Power had constructed.

In order to respond to the request for such a suit, the Illinois Power board was advised by its counsel to appoint a committee of board members who had not been involved in the decisions regarding the building of the plant. The committee would review the actions of the company—both management and board—and be solely responsible for the company's response to the suit. Only one then current director of Illinois Power, who had been on the board for less than a year, could serve on the committee.

Illinois Power needed additional directors to participate on the review committee. The choice of additional directors was extremely sensitive, since the board would be fully delegating to the review committee the decision as to whether the company, on behalf of its shareholders, should sue the board and management of the company. Both Frank and I accepted Chairman Wendell Kelly's invitation to join the board and its special committee.

Learning about nuclear energy was an extraordinary experience. I described it as akin to learning Japanese—it was a fascinating culture with a different language. The review committee spent hundreds of hours on our investigation. We hired legal counsel with experience in derivative action lawsuits but without any previous association with Illinova. We interviewed those in the business who had had anything to do with building the plant as well as people outside the business, including the federal Nuclear Regulatory Commission.

Illinois Power had gotten caught up in the aftermath of the Three Mile Island "meltdown." Following the accident at Three Mile Island, government regulators had halted construction of all nuclear power plants, including the one that Illinois Power was building. When the projects started back up again, the demand for safety redundancy resulted in huge cost increases, far beyond what had originally been projected.

Based on what we heard, we reconstructed the situation and the events leading up to the many decisions to proceed with the plant spread over more than a decade. We concluded that, while building the plant had ultimately turned out to be the wrong decision in its totality and had cost the company far more than planned, the decisions along the way had been prudent based on what the board and management knew at each point in time.

The court dismissed the suit against Illinois Power, and our report became a pattern for what a company needed to do to respond to a derivative action suit.

Not long after that, Cummins Engine received a demand for not one but two derivative action suits. We went against the pattern of getting new outside directors for the special review committee. We did so because of the unusual strength of the Cummins board.

I was asked to chair the review committee because I had been through the Illinova experience. The other members of the committee were Frank Thomas, president of the Ford Foundation; Hannah Gray, president of the University of Chicago; Harold Brown, former Secretary of Defense; and Bill Ruckelshaus, the first head of the Environmental Protection Agency. We felt these five directors, with reputation for integrity and independent thinking, would be able to hold their own in court. We were right. Both suits against Cummins were dismissed based on our committee's findings.

• • •

FURTHER REFLECTIONS

As I think back on the 20 companies on whose boards I served and my years of board service, one observation stands out. I smile to think that my invitation to join boards came, in every case, from the CEO. In those days, there was seldom a nominating committee and, if one existed, it was only advisory to the CEO. Times have changed, and the invitations of today are being extended not by management, but by independent nominating committees. This practice illustrates the shift in power which has taken place ... away from the CEO toward independent directors.

Phyllis and I marvel at our first grandchild, Jeremy Hill, in November 1979.

Bill Beers congratulates me on being named Marketing Man of the Year by the American Marketing Association in 1973, as Larry Fouraker, Dean of the Harvard Business School, looks on.

Governor Dick Ogilvie and Dorothy Ogilvie, and Bill and Fran (Mom) Beers, with Phyllis and me.

In 1978, Irv Seaman, Dick Ogilvie, Charlie Brown, and I pose on the first hole at Augusta National Golf Course, where we were playing golf for the tenth year in a row.

Ann and Arnie Berlin, Jeanne and Jack Cardwell, and Mary and Harold Hines, at the reception following Susan's wedding in 1980.

With Susan, Betsy and Jerry at the party celebrating my retirement from the Jewel board in 1983.

With George Clements, Father Ray Baumhart, and Wes Christopherson at the same Jewel retirement celebration.

With Jerry and Marisa Arango, and Myrna and Wes Christopherson, in 1982.

With Larry Howe, the consummate volunteer.

A reunion of Jewel colleagues in May 1992. From left: Walter Elisha, Howard Wagner, Henry Davis, Larry Howe, Dick Cline … and me.

With Bob Darnall, then chairman of Inland Steel.

I admired the talents and management abilities of three generations of Cummins management—Irwin Miller, Henry Schacht (who would become the first CEO of Lucent Technologies), and Jim Henderson.

With Bob Nakasone, Dick Cline, and Joe Jannotta, in Santa Barbara.

This picture with Harold Washington appeared in the Chicago Tribune *in 1984, as I delivered the results of the Civic Committee study of jobs in metropolitan Chicago.*

With Nicki Mash, the first recipient of the scholarship I endowed at Northwestern University.

Above: With Dolores Cross, then president of Chicago State University.

Right: With John McCarter, president of the Field Museum of Natural History, a role I encouraged him to take on during a mentoring session.

Jane's children, Elizabeth and Frank Phillips, together with Betsy, Jerry, and Susan, join Jane and me on our wedding day, 1985.

With my siblings, enjoying middle age.

Jane and I enjoy Norway and each other on a 1986 trip.

At the Provence home of Jacques and Jacqueline Dopchie in June 2001.

On a Time Newstour in 1985. I was and am a news junkie.

Shaking hands with Fidel Castro on the 1985 Time Newstour. Reg Brack, then president of Time Warner magazines, is in the background.

Meeting Ferdinand Marcos on the 1985 Time Newstour.

With Frank Thomas, President of the Ford Foundation.

Ford Foundation board members and staff pose with the Imam of Xian outside his mosque on our 1989 Ford Foundation trip.

General Obasanjo, president of Nigeria and fellow Ford Foundation board member, and I switch hats in China's Forbidden City

The cartoon that appeared in Crain's Detroit Business *in January 1995, following the announcement that I would be non-executive chairman of Kmart. (Reproduced with permission.)*

One of our very memorable family trips—the Perkinses on safari in Kenya in 1996.

CHAPTER 15

THE BEST SALE I NEVER MADE

T he Perkins family moved into our newly finished house on Drury Lane in Northfield, Illinois, in the early spring of 1958, just weeks before Susan was born. The other houses in the neighborhood were much like ours—mostly ranch homes—and most of the families had young children. The first weekend after we moved in, I looked over at our next-door neighbor's yard and saw a short, overweight man pushing a lawnmower—an old rotary mower—around his small yard. I went over to say hello and met my neighbor, Dick Ogilvie. Dick invited me in for a beer and we got to know each other. Part of getting acquainted included the discovery that we had both graduated from Yale. Were Dick still alive, he would tell you we drank martinis rather than beer, but neither of us had the money for hard liquor at that point in our lives, so I know I am right—it was a beer. It was the most costly beer I ever drank.

Dick was a junior lawyer in a Chicago law firm back then and was active in Young Republicans. He and his wife Dorothy had a daughter a couple of years younger than Betsy. Frequently, Dick and Dorothy and Phyllis and I would get together to play bridge. In the summer, while the children were young, we would put them to bed, leave the windows open so we could hear them if there was a problem, and sit down to play at one of our homes.

One night, as we played, Dick announced that he had made a major decision—he was going to run for sheriff of Cook County. I was not very encouraging. "That doesn't make any sense to me," I told him. "You're short, you're fat, you're ugly, and you're a lousy speaker. And you're honest! How are you ever going to succeed in Chicago politics?" He said he would like to see how far he could go. The only one of those attributes that would ever change was that, with practice, he became a better speaker.

As long as Dick was determined to pursue political office, however, I was going to do what I could to help him. I had never raised money for a politician, but I started raising money for Dick Ogilvie.

Dick already had a strong reputation in law enforcement when he entered the sheriff's race, thanks to his prosecution of organized crime. The case that brought him the most publicity was his prosecution and conviction of Chicago mob boss Sam Giancana. While Giancana's conviction was later overturned, the case put Dick in the media spotlight and helped solidify the public perception of him as a standard-bearer for law and order.

Sometimes we would joke that his anti-crime image might attract attention from someone other than the media. When Giancana's conviction came in, I teased Dick that I was going to put a sign in front of his house with an arrow pointing to it that said, "Dick Ogilvie lives here." That way, a mafia thug wouldn't accidentally put a bomb at our house instead.

Phyllis and I were in Virginia the night of the sheriff's election in 1962, and I was frustrated when I couldn't get any news about the results. Finally, I decided just to call the campaign office and ask about the outcome. The person who picked up the phone answered, "Sheriff Ogilvie's Office." That was how we learned he had won. Dick served as sheriff of Cook County for four years, and then ran for and was elected president of the

Cook County Board. Both of these offices were traditionally held by Democrats; Dick was a Republican.

In 1968, when he had been county board president for two years, Dick decided to cut his term short to run for governor of Illinois, and he asked me to be his finance chairman. I had just become an officer of Jewel; I was young and certainly inexperienced in politics. But I believed in Dick Ogilvie and was committed to helping him succeed as a candidate. I spent most weekends that year working on the campaign, raising money and advising Dick. We raised about $2.5 million for that first campaign and more than $3 million during his second campaign for governor.

In February 1969, on the heels of the 1968 election that made Dick governor, he and I, hosted by Irv Seaman and accompanied by Charlie Brown, made the first of our trips to play golf at Augusta National Golf Club in Georgia. Dick had not taken any time off for a year and a half, and I had never been to Augusta, so we were excited at the prospect. The four of us went to Augusta to play golf that February and proceeded to repeat the outing every year for 15 consecutive years. We were there in sleet, snow, nice weather ... whatever it happened to be.

The first year we went to Augusta, Irv went around the dining room at dinner to introduce Dick as the new governor of Illinois. One of the members there that night was Billy Joe Patton, an outstanding amateur golfer. Unfortunately, Billy Joe had had a little too much to drink that night. When Irv introduced Dick to him, he said, "Illinois! Is that where Lincoln came from?" Dick confirmed that Abraham Lincoln had come from Illinois. Billy Joe swept his arm around the Augusta dining room, encompassing both its Southern elegance and the beautiful course beyond the windows in his gesture and said, "Son of a bitch! If it weren't for him, we'd all be living like this!"

Dick had been advised to take a security person with him to Augusta. The security guard, who happened to be a single-digit

handicap golfer, walked around with us as we played. It was
driving him nuts walking around watching instead of playing,
but he was still very happy to be seeing Augusta. Dick was not
a good golfer, but loved to play, and the security man was all
involved in Dick's game. "Good shot, sir," he'd say, when Dick
hit the ball well. On one hole, Dick had a particularly good
drive and the security guard congratulated him, saying, "You
really got your ass into that one ... um ... sir!"

It is amazing that we could get four busy people together
every year for 15 years, but we would start picking the date
for the following year when we completed each year's play.
By the time we had gone to Augusta for 10 years running, we
started feeling guilty that we had never included our wives in
our trips. So I suggested we go to Scotland with our spouses
to mark a decade of outings. I had been to Scotland with the
Cummins board because they had a plant in Shotts, not far
from Edinburgh and close to Gleneagles and St. Andrews. And
I had played St. Andrews with the Cummins people, who were
very gracious. They had told me that if I ever came back to play
golf, they would help arrange it.

So, we planned a Scotland trip for the four couples. June
Seaman was the best of the women golfers, Phyllis was all
right, Dorothy Ogilvie was a mediocre golfer, and I don't think
Annlee Brown had ever played more than nine holes at one
time in her life. But she played 18 holes almost every day we
were there. We had a wonderful time.

My support for Dick as governor extended beyond golf
vacations. One of the things he asked me to do shortly after
being elected was to help him find out what was going on in
states he thought were well run, so he could adapt those lessons
to Illinois. The best run states in the country, in Dick's opinion,
were Ohio, where Jim Rhodes was governor, and California,
under Ronald Reagan. He asked me if I would take a crew to
one or the other to see what we could learn that would help us

in Illinois. I had a conflict with the scheduled California trip, but took a group of observers to Ohio to meet with Governor Rhodes.

Over cocktails out in the garden of the executive mansion in Columbus, I asked Rhodes how he had succeeded in becoming governor. "Oh," Rhodes said, "it's pretty simple. I just talk about one thing." "What's that?" I asked. "Oh, I just talk about jobs," he said. "I go out to College Corners, Ohio, and I say, 'If you want to keep your children here in College Corners, elect me, because I'm going to provide jobs in your community and in the state. Then your children won't have to go off somewhere else to get a job.'"

When it came time for Dick to run for a second term, one issue outweighed all others in importance. During his first term, I telephoned Dick to discuss a family trip we were planning. "This is a big day in my career," he told me. "I am signing a bill today which will probably make me a one-term governor."

Dick signed the legislation that established the first income tax in Illinois. He understood the political repercussions, but he knew it was absolutely necessary for the state's well-being. "It's a necessary evil and will be greatly appreciated by my successors," Dick said. "It will make the job doable for future governors."

In retrospect, Dick's first race for governor had been relatively easy. His opponent, Sam Shapiro, was a nice guy from Kankakee who had been lieutenant governor under the previous governor, Otto Kerner. Shapiro had become governor when Kerner traded the governor's mansion for a jail cell when he was convicted of bribery, mail fraud, and other federal crimes. Shapiro's campaign slogan was "Love the Gov." Ogilvie's record of being a crusader for honesty in government played particularly well during that first election.

But in 1972, the competition was different. Dan Walker, the Democrat candidate, literally walked the state from south to north in jeans and a red bandanna, portraying himself as the populist champion and contrasting his approach with the "Ogilvie income tax" which, as necessary as it was, was decidedly unpopular. After the campaign was over, however, I observed that, having raised over $5 million for Dick during his two gubernatorial campaigns, I never had to apologize for anything he did. Many still consider him the best governor Illinois has ever had.

Phyllis and I and the Perkins children spent Dick's reelection night in 1972 at the Bismarck Hotel in downtown Chicago with Dorothy and Dick and their daughter Liz awaiting the outcome. The race was extremely close. When we finally went to bed in the early hours of the morning, we still did not know whether Dick could somehow squeak through. It did not look good, and the loss was confirmed the next morning.

Dick asked me to come to his press conference with him. I will never forget the tears in the eyes of some of the veteran reporters at that press conference. They knew what talent Illinois was losing in Springfield. And while the loss saddened me, I had prepared for the possibility in advance.

Following the press conference, I said to Dick, "I have discussed with the Jewel board the possibility that you might lose, and I have been authorized by them to invite you to become a director of Jewel."

So on this "morning after," a low point in his life, Dick was offered his first post-gubernatorial involvement. Dick went on to join the law firm of Isham, Lincoln and Beale, and to be the court-appointed trustee of the bankrupt Rock Island Railroad, before he died just 16 years later of a heart attack at far too young an age.

Dick's successor as governor, Dan Walker, also turned out to be a one-term governor. He had no income tax to blame—only poor management and, as it later turned out, a less-than-honest approach to his personal investments. It is striking that the elected Illinois governors immediately preceding and following Dick Ogilvie both spent time in prison.

Dick's departure from public office did not exempt me from some additional service in the governmental arena. Eight years later, Jim Thompson asked me to take on another role, one that would become a fortuitous failure—the one I call the best sale I never made. In 1984, the State of Illinois learned that the U.S. Department of Energy planned to fund the construction of an SSC (a Super-conducting Super Collider), a device to accelerate, measure, and characterize the smallest atomic particles. The competition was primarily between two states, Illinois and Texas. My role was to create and chair a coalition of business, labor, scientific, academic, political, and community leaders to convince the Department of Energy to site the SSC in Illinois.

It made basic good sense to establish the project in Illinois at the site of Fermilab in Batavia. The obvious rational decision, as far as I was concerned, was to use the infrastructure at Fermilab rather than spend money to reproduce the same facilities starting from scratch in a green-field site in Texas or anywhere else. Fermilab, a pioneer in high-energy particle physics, was then headed by Dr. Leon Lederman, a Nobel Prize-winning physicist and discoverer of the Quark, a subatomic particle.

We built a compelling case for siting the SSC at Fermilab, but when all was said and done, the chairs of the congressional committees were both from Texas—and Texas won the contract. Despite the disappointment, it soon became clear that the project was "the best sale I never made." It was best not just because the Department of Energy cut the funding the following year and the project was discontinued. It was best because we had established a viable, multi-constituent coalition which could work to promote the science and technology interests and capabilities of Illinois.

Walter Massey, then vice president of research at the University of Chicago, wrote an op-ed piece in the *Chicago*

Tribune asserting that this was the most effective coalition he had seen, and challenging the state to use such an organization in an ongoing public-private effort. Governor Thompson subsequently institutionalized the effort and we called it the Illinois Coalition.

At the time, Illinois was last on the list of states in the percentage of federal taxes returned and spent in the state. That became a strong argument for using the Illinois Coalition to begin to correct the imbalance. As a coalition of leaders in business, labor, academia, politics, and technology, we would work together to win projects from Washington. The underlying public-private principle of the Illinois Coalition was to get half of the money for the effort from the state government and raise the other half privately.

As we got the Illinois Coalition off the ground, Governor Thompson had the idea of asking the legislature for money to support awards to emerging high-tech companies in Illinois. The first year we had $20 million to award. The money dried up within a couple of years as the state ran into financial trouble, but that initial state funding helped put the Illinois Coalition on the map. The Coalition continues to be the center of knowledge about high-tech activities in the state.

I never ran for public office and never held a full-time political appointment. The closest I came was when I received an invitation at the start of the second Nixon administration to go to Washington "to discuss one of the domestic cabinet jobs with the President." Had I gone to such a meeting and been invited to join the president's cabinet, it would have been very difficult to say no. At that stage, I was fully occupied at Jewel, where I had been president for only two years; and I did not feel that going to Washington would be right for our family. I was also disenchanted with Nixon.

My decision to turn down that invitation was helped by the fact that Phyllis, even more disenchanted with the Nixon administration and even more realistic than I was about what it would mean if I accepted a job in Washington, said to me, "You wouldn't seriously consider going to work for *those people*, would you?"

CHAPTER 16

REMEMBERING "NUM NUM"

N um Num" is the name Phyllis was called by her
grandchildren—the syllables uttered by her first
grandson, Jeremy. The name stuck. Before she was a mother
or grandmother, though, Phyllis was a leader. Soon after we
moved to the Chicago area, Phyllis joined the Junior League of
Evanston and would later serve as its president. Over time, she
would chair the Woman's Board of Evanston Hospital, serve as
president of the board of trustees of The North Shore Country
Day School (the only woman ever to have served in that role),
serve on the YWCA board, and accept an appointment by
Governor Thompson to serve on the Illinois Health Finance
Authority. In the days when women—especially the wives of
corporate CEOs—did not seek paid employment, Phyllis was the
model of the volunteer leader.

Although I did not write poems for each of Phyl's birthdays
the way I had for the children's, decade birthdays were signaled
with expressions of love and pride, dressed up in the usual
meter, as I did on her 50th birthday. That poem was written in
February 1979 and started off recognizing the most important
part of her life—her children:

Although Evanston Hospital kept Phyllis busy,
And the Y and North Shore make her schedule seem dizzy,

Not a thing in this world brings a light to her eyes
Like her children ... for luckily each is a prize.
For their first, with great calm, two young marrieds were
    waitin',
At Wright-Patterson Air Force Base very near Dayton,
Betsy's birth an occasion for newly born cheer,
With cool Don driving Phyl in their car's second gear.
It was on to Chicago ... the weather there's cruel,
Though at least there was warmth in the smiles throughout
    Jewel.
That's when Phyllis told Don that he shouldn't be nervous,
On a cold winter night when she came up with Jervis.
The apartment was full, but Phyllis was not.
A house would be needed with one more "begot."
It was Northfield where Susan was tucked into bed,
And the family lived happily over its head.

When I thought of all the work I saw her do for her volunteer organizations, I often visualized her standing in the kitchen where she had a desk and two phones, which she would often use simultaneously. This was in the days before conference calls and multi-line phones; the following description is literally accurate ...

Phyllis's work as a leader has tested her powers;
Telephoning alone consumed thousands of hours.
As she'd rise in a hierarchy thanks to her peers,
She required two phones ... one for each of her ears.

The poem also captured a routine in our relationship, one patterned after George Burns and Gracie Allen, whose radio program always concluded with George saying, "Say goodnight, Gracie." I was always an early riser and eager to get to bed at an early hour, as well. Phyllis, on the other hand, was a night owl.

She's a leader, a scholar, a bridge buff, and nurse,
But she's married to "Sleepy," for better or worse.
And when Sleepy Don's drowsy, then ev'ryone knows,
"Say goodnight, Phyllis" means that his eyes will soon close.

I had always assumed that Phyllis would be my companion through life, but that assumption and my image of retirement with her were challenged suddenly in March 1982. The month started with what had become a tradition in those years, as we rented a house in Ponte Vedra, Florida, and prepared for visits from our children and grandchildren.

Unlike previous years, we didn't play golf because Phyllis was suffering from what she said was bursitis in her shoulder. She had been complaining of pain in her shoulder for a few months and had even given me a hard time for travelling after Christmas when she had needed to do snow-shoveling, which aggravated the pain.

As the family began arriving, I flew to New York for a Ford Foundation board meeting. On my way back, I called in from Atlanta as I was changing planes. Susan answered the phone and told me that Phyllis had collapsed and hit her head. At the time, Phyllis was still unconscious, and the paramedics had arrived and were preparing to take her to the hospital. No one could even guess as to what had happened.

Phyllis was in a coma for several days. The head injury complicated the discovery of what was wrong, but it was not the root of the problem. Phyllis had lung cancer. The pain that she had been suffering was *not* bursitis, as she had assumed and assured everyone; it was the tumor pressing against her lung.

An operation took a lot out of Phyllis, as we expected, and the news was not all we had hoped for. Bill Fry, the surgeon, told us he taken out all he could, but he had not been able to remove the entire tumor. On her trips back to the hospital for her radiation therapy, though, there was one highlight: Phyllis was able to visit Betsy and newborn Zachary in the maternity ward.

It was strange to observe that, although she had smoked profusely all of her adult life, she never smoked after she came out of the coma. On several occasions when I visited her in the hospital, she would declare, "Someone's smoking on this floor. Go tell them to stop." Not only had she herself stopped, she was acutely annoyed by anyone else smoking. I would go up and down the hall, but was never able to find anyone smoking. I would go back to her room and say, "I don't smell anything anymore, do you?" Phyllis never accepted the obvious: that smoking had caused her lung cancer.

As if the family needed just one more trial in 1982, Grandpère (Jerry Babb) died that July. He had had a difficult last few years with diabetes and the resultant loss of a leg. This would mean that Grandmère (Ruth Babb) would lose her husband and her only child within six months. She would continue to live in her Sheridan Road apartment for eight more years, becoming increasingly reclusive. I would visit her there most Saturdays to keep her books and do some occasional shopping.

As Ruth became increasingly frail, I asked my secretary to call her each weekday morning; I covered the weekends. One Monday morning there was no answer. Fortunately I was not traveling that day, so I drove from the Loop and found her on the floor with a broken hip. She estimated that she had been there for over 30 hours. Paramedics transported her to Evanston Hospital. From there she moved to the Presbyterian Home, where she would spend the final months of her life.

Despite the limitations of Phyllis's physical condition during the year of her illness, we took two exhausting trips after her operation. One was to a Ford Foundation meeting in South Africa, with stops in Kenya and in Zimbabwe to see Victoria Falls. I suggested canceling the trip, but Phyl insisted she wanted to do it. "I'll do one thing a day," was her approach. We pushed her around in wheelchairs and she would participate in either lunch or dinner each day. One day in Kenya, she even went out in a Land Rover for a few hours to see some of the wildlife.

The second trip was to Scotland, where we had planned to go with three other couples on a golf outing. Again I said, "This doesn't make any sense," and offered to cancel the trip. Again she said, "I can't play golf, but I can do one thing a day." To my amazement, she made the trip and, as she had planned, did one thing a day.

We also bought a condominium at Lost Tree Village in North Palm Beach, Florida, that November. Phyllis made a trip with me in December to make some decorating decisions, but she would never spend a night in it.

We were back in Chicago in time for Christmas. She was under orders from her doctor, Frank Guthrie, to come into the hospital right after the holiday. I remember her sitting in her chair in the den and saying, "I really hate to go in because I know I will never come out."

She was in the hospital the third week of January and had had a blood transfusion the previous Friday that really picked her up. I spent Monday and Tuesday with her, as I had almost every day she was in the hospital during the previous year.

Because she seemed stable, I flew to New York Tuesday night for my third-Wednesday-of-the-month AT&T board meeting. About 10 A.M. that morning, a message was brought into the board meeting: "Come back to Chicago fast." I made it from the AT&T offices to Evanston Hospital in four hours by way of commercial aviation. When I walked into her hospital room that afternoon, she was surrounded by medical attendants. She looked at me, and the last word she spoke was, "Smile."

Phyllis died on January 19, 1983, a Wednesday. We held a memorial service the next Monday at the Alice Millar chapel at Northwestern University. I asked Wes Christopherson, my close partner at Jewel, and Julie King, one of Phyllis's lifelong friends, to deliver the eulogies. I couldn't do it myself. I have seen other people speak at their spouses' funerals, but it was more than I could manage.

Still, I tried to figure out how I could have some input. I woke up at 4 A.M. on the Friday after she died with a clear idea of how I would capture my thoughts and feelings—I would write a letter to her grandchildren. Jeremy was three years old, and Zach was just six months old. Of course, they wouldn't understand the message then, but I felt it would be important to them later to know about their grandmother, so I wrote a letter to be delivered in 1995, when Jeremy would be 16 and Zach 13. I asked Wes if he would include the letter in whatever he said. This was my way of making a statement at the memorial service without having to stand up and try to control my tear ducts, which have never been known for their discipline.

When 1995 arrived and we read the letter, the audience would include all of Phyllis's grandchildren, including the four she never knew: Andrew (11), Shelley (10), Christine (8), and Jessa (7).

January 24, 1983
For delivery in 1995

Dear Jeremy and Zachary:

Now that you are both teenagers, I thought that you might enjoy knowing about someone who loved you greatly. Jeremy, you gave her the affectionate name by which the family refers to her. Listening to your early mumblings as she hugged you, she thought that you said, "Num Num," and it stuck. It sounded like a character from Gilbert and Sullivan, and it must have amused and confused motorists who saw NUM NUM on her car's license plates. Zachary, the reverse was true for you as Num Num suggested your name when your mother and father were looking for a distinctive first name to go with Hill.

The environment of family love in which you have been raised reflects Num Num's influence on all of us. She was always thinking about what she might do for others. She would start each year with scores of birthday cards, already arranged in order of dates so that she would never forget the birthday of a close friend or family member. Most of all, Num Num loved Christmas! She shopped for Christmas the year round and had a closet shelf designated for each of us. It would be a fair guess that she received and looked at a thousand mail order catalogs a year, so we called her the "world's greatest shopper." Whether it was stocking presents tied in tandem and stretched from the mantle across the room or a "big present," she would find just the right idea that recognized a strength or kidded a weakness in each of us. Num Num shopped so far ahead that in the year of her illness, she simply went to her inventory for Christmas. Even at that, the designated shelves were not bare.

Most of our friends think of Num Num at Christmas time in terms of children's pictures appearing on the Perkins Christmas cards. Beginning with a picture of your mother at the age of nine months and continuing for thirty years [Note: the annual Christmas card with family picture still continues], the Christmas card pictures were a chronicle of her children and eventually her grandchildren whom she loved so dearly and in whom she took such pride. If you'll look through the book of cards that we kept, they are certain to make you smile. You'll see that your mother once wore glasses, your Uncle Jerry once had shoulder-length hair, and Aunt Sue spent much of her childhood in pigtails. By the way, when you look at the pictures of Aunt Sue, you'll see a remarkable resemblance to your Num Num during her early years.

For Num Num our home had a special purpose, first to bring up and then to bring together our family. Nothing pleased her more than to have a family event to celebrate and to toast at the dinner table. There had to be a bed for every family member long after your mother and uncle and aunt had left our nest. In fact, Jeremy, five months before you were born, Num Num gave me as a Father's Day present the crib you slept in whenever we were lucky enough to have you visit. Num Num loved to play family games and would even put up with the inferior bridge-playing ability of the rest of us.

As much as home and family were the focal point of Num Num's life, she was the consummate volunteer leader. That reminds me of two signs she kept in the kitchen. One said, "Kiss the Cook." The other said, "Be the job great or small, if I do it too well, I'll get stuck with it all."

I hope by the time you read this it sounds peculiar in your era, but in the 50s and 60s "leadership" was not a word that was readily connected with women. Whether it was the Junior League or The North Shore Country Day School or the Evanston Hospital, Num Num was the leader. She took particular pride in being the first woman to chair The North Shore Country Day School Board of Trustees. She reflected the good fortune of her life by giving of herself and her time. Num Num personified what theologians and philosophers have said for centuries: the more you give of yourself, the more you will receive. That is why she received so much in the way of friendship from so many.

Take a look at one of those old pictures of Num Num holding you when you were very young. It will tell you something about your heritage. You were being held by an able, giving, and loving person. I would wish for you, even in your challenging teen years, that you take pleasure in being like Num Num ... able, giving, and loving.

With all my love,

Pop Pop

CHAPTER 17

MAKE NO LITTLE PLANS

M y involvement in Chicago civic activities grew not only from a desire to do something worthwhile, but also from a long-held conviction that Jewel could not be healthy if the communities we served were not healthy. I started with volunteer fundraising for the United Way in 1962. My involvement in that organization would last another 25 years, including several years chairing the board of the Crusade of Mercy, the overarching organization that comprised the fundraising efforts of the United Way of Chicago, the suburban United Way, and the local chapter of the American Red Cross. In 1979, I agreed to chair the annual United Way campaign. We established a goal of raising $58 million, a goal I knew was a stretch but one that would satisfy many urgent needs in the city and surrounding areas. That year, I made 80 one-on-one face-to-face calls on corporate leaders in Chicago. Of course, I was still chairman and CEO of Jewel with plenty of work demands there, so I would have the Jewel driver take me to my appointments. I'd take work that I could do in the back of the car—and there was a lot I could do, even in the days before cell phones—while we drove between meetings. I would get out, make my pitch, get back in the car, and go back to work on the way to the next meeting. That year set a new standard for personal involvement by a campaign chairman!

The pitch itself was also new. In previous years, we had been asking corporate executives and senior managers for one day's pay—one out of 200 days of work a year, or half a percent. As I approached CEOs in 1979, I said to them, "If *you* give one percent this year, you could certainly ask the rest of your management to follow suit next year." It was those "one-percenters" that got us to our 1979 goal.

That United Way campaign gave me a great deal of satisfaction, something that didn't always carry over to chairing the Crusade of Mercy, where I was frustrated in my efforts to change the way the funds were allocated. There was a disconnect between the philosophy for allocating the funds and the actual practice of giving them out. The Crusade of Mercy *philosophy* was to evaluate the needs of the communities and the recipient organizations each year and to give the money raised where the need was the greatest. The *practice* was that each entity felt entitled to a greater level of funding year after year. The lion's share of the funds was raised through payroll deduction from companies, independent of any arbitrary city/suburban split.

But sometimes it was difficult to get the agencies to focus on where the most acute need existed—often in the city—rather than on historical levels of funding. The suburb-city conflict was not one that I had any success in solving; it took about 20 years before it was resolved eventually through the work of the Civic Committee of the Commercial Club.

When we broke the pattern of giving a fixed percent of the funds we raised to the Red Cross, they had their national leaders come to see me, but I stuck to my guns. Despite that battle, though, I do associate the Red Cross with one of my best golf games ever.

I had been downtown negotiating with the Red Cross one morning and raced to the Shoreacres Club in Lake Bluff for a 1 P.M. shotgun start. I grabbed a sandwich off the buffet and ran to the tenth tee to join the last foursome to tee off in the annual

Commercial Club golf outing. They had been kind enough to wait for me. I parred the tenth hole and the eleventh, birdied the twelfth, and eagled the thirteenth. I was three under par after four holes! Somehow, despite having no time to warm up and trying to finish my sandwich between shots, it was my day to play well, although I didn't sustain the pace of those first four holes. I won the event that year with an 81.

Working in the United Way effort for all those years and then leading the United Way campaign in 1979 were important in at least a couple of ways. First, my involvement enabled me to get to know the business leadership in the city and to establish my credibility. Second, I became aware of many of the problems in the area. The experience helped prepare me for my major contribution to Chicago—or more properly, as I always insist, to metropolitan Chicago—through the Commercial Club of Chicago and the founding of the Civic Committee.

The Commercial Club was composed of more than 300 leaders of the major institutions in the Chicago area. I was invited to become a member in 1967, when I was president of Jewel. Founded in 1877, the Commercial Club had played a significant role in Chicago early in its existence. One of its early contributions was to buy a ten-barrel Gatling gun for the First Regiment "to aid in defending the city." The club in its early days had also been instrumental in educational projects, the Drainage Canal, and "the prosecution and punishment of certain county and municipal officials."

The Commercial Club was best known for its critical contribution to the city just after the turn of the century when the Chicago Plan, now generally known as the Burnham Plan, presented a vision for Chicago's beautification. The plan, adopted in 1914, dealt with saving the lakefront, establishing parks and forest preserves, and improving streets and buildings. Burnham urged,

Make no little plans. They have no magic to stir men's blood, and probably themselves will not be realized. Make big plans; aim high in hope and work, remembering that a noble, logical diagram once recorded will never die, but long after we are gone will be a living thing, asserting itself with ever-growing insistency. Remember that our sons and grandsons are going to do things that would stagger us. Let your watchword be order and your beacon beauty.

At the time I became president of the Commercial Club in 1981, it was a luncheon and dinner club—a good way to get to know people, but nothing more. It had done nothing of note in the almost 75 years since its support of the Burnham Plan. Jim Beré (CEO of Borg Warner), my successor as president of the Commercial Club, and I started referring to the Club as Rip Van Winkle, asleep since Burnham's day. The club had as members all the business and other establishment leaders of the metropolitan area—and all that strength and talent went unfocused. We were a long way from fulfilling the stirring words with which Daniel Burnham had inspired the city in the development of its physical renewal.

Jim Beré and I wanted to change that. In 1982 Jim appointed a Civic Committee with me as chair.

The committee's first effort was to draft a carefully worded letter to Illinois Governor Jim Thompson and Chicago Mayor Jane Byrne. We described the talent in the Commercial Club and emphasized that we did not want to embarrass anyone or to get any credit or publicity for our help. Rather, we wanted to work behind the scenes on whatever problem they might identify where either thought we could be helpful. The letter led to meetings where each of them smiled and shook our hands and told us how much they welcomed our help. We never heard another word from either of them about our offer.

It was obvious that we were not going to get a Civic Committee off the ground if we waited to get our assignment from the governor or the mayor or by approaching it in such an open-ended fashion. Instead, Clayton Kirkpatrick, editor-in-chief of the Tribune Company, suggested, "You know ... we really ought to find out what the problems are ourselves and then decide how we can be helpful. Sitting around waiting won't do any good."

We started a major research effort, influenced by my 1968 experience helping Dick Ogilvie, then the newly elected Governor of Illinois. I recalled my visit with Ohio Governor Jim Rhodes and his advice that elections are all about jobs (Chapter 15). So we determined that the Civic Committee research effort would focus on jobs. We could have looked at an economic measure, but, influenced by my previous experience in Ohio, we settled on jobs as the focal point for our study.

Jobs were a logical place for us to concentrate as a group of business leaders—one where our experience was relevant and where we might be able to have an impact. We decided to look at what had happened to jobs over a 30-year period—choosing that length of time so that the study started after the war years and before the first Mayor Daley came to power.

The next thing we needed was help gathering data, performing the analysis, and preparing the report. I called on McKinsey, Booz Allen Hamilton, and Arthur Andersen, each of which was Chicago-based or a major player in Chicago, and asked for their help. Each of the three organizations provided extraordinary help and contributed incredibly talented people to work on the study.

We also got help from another source. Si Keehn, president of the Federal Reserve Bank in Chicago, offered to support the effort. He told me that they had access to a lot of information. "We're in an unusual position," he said. "We're a private organization, but we have access to public data. Maybe we could be of help."

We accepted, saving ourselves the hundreds of thousands of dollars that it would have cost to collect the data independently, even if we had been able to get data in the quality and depth that the Federal Reserve Bank was able to provide.

The resulting study, entitled "Jobs for Metropolitan Chicago," was completed and ready to present to the full membership of the Commercial Club in June 1984. The results would surprise many. The first Mayor Daley had coined a catch phrase dubbing Chicago "The City That Works," an intentional double entendre. What we found was that at least one of those meanings—the one associated with jobs—didn't stand up to scrutiny.

The 30 years of data revealed two striking patterns. First, in each and every one of those 30 years, Chicago had lost share of the national job market. Second, Illinois was 50th out of 50 states in the amount of federal tax dollars returned to the state compared to what we contributed—an annual net outflow of tax dollars. We were genuinely surprised by what we learned, but it was clear that we had uncovered two very logical reasons to spur on the Commercial Club membership.

The first item of business was to form a fully functioning Civic Committee, which required the support of the Commercial Club's leadership. I approached the two successors to Jim Beré and me—Si Cathcart (CEO of Illinois Tool Works and a director of Jewel) and Karl Bays (CEO of American Hospital Supply and also a Jewel director). I compiled a list of 34 people I thought would constitute a committee with the necessary talent and ability to get things done. Si and Karl told me, "OK. If you can get those people involved, we will agree to support a Civic Committee of the Commercial Club."

I talked to all 34 of the people on my list; 33 said yes. The 34th told me that he was leaving his wife and moving to Arizona.

The Civic Committee was formally established in 1983, the same year Phyllis died, and I poured myself into it. When I wasn't traveling to or attending a meeting of one of the corporate boards I served on, I was working on the Civic Committee. As I told the *Chicago Tribune* in an interview about the work of the Civic Committee in 1986 when they asked about my retirement from Jewel, "I retired from a single title, but I did not retire from trying to get things done."

One of the considerations in forming the Civic Committee was what the composition of the committee should be. Should the committee be composed of business and other major institutional leaders, or should it be more open and democratic, with representatives of other constituencies? I went to New York to talk with David Rockefeller about what he had initiated and called the New York Partnership. I also went to Cleveland to meet with the leaders of Cleveland Tomorrow.

The two initiatives had taken opposite approaches. The New York organization was composed of a broad range of constituencies, while Cleveland Tomorrow was made up of 30 corporate leaders. I learned that the New York Partnership, with every borough and every constituency involved, resembled a local version of the United Nations and was unable to get anything done. Dick Shinn (CEO of Metropolitan Life), John Whitehead (co-CEO of Goldman Sachs), Jim Robinson (CEO of American Express), and others I talked to told me that the business leaders had learned they needed to meet privately to get anything accomplished. The larger meetings were taken over by agendas unrelated to the city—in particular, by people who were there only to gain access to the business leaders for their own purposes.

I recognized the dilemma from my personal observations in the 1970s of an organization called Chicago United. Chicago United had been founded by Tom Ayers, CEO of Commonwealth Edison, after Martin Luther King's march in Marquette Park. The intent was for corporate and black leaders to work together. It was a grand gesture of goodwill but generally ineffective because it was too often used to further individual agendas and as a vehicle for personal contacts and personal gain.

Cleveland Tomorrow used a different model. Del DeWindt (CEO of Eaton Corporation) and Morton Mandel (CEO and owner of Parkwood Corporation), with whom I visited, described how their homogeneous group of businesspeople were able to work together without any agenda other than what they were trying to do for their city. The 30 corporate leaders who made up Cleveland Tomorrow came to the meetings— substitutes were not permitted—and they got things done. So, while some in Chicago were later critical of our approach as being elitist, I felt that a model more like Cleveland Tomorrow offered the best shot at getting things done to benefit our metropolitan area.

I also knew that the Civic Committee needed staff and the leadership of a strong executive director. Serendipity stepped in and provided the ideal answer—Larry Howe. Larry was available because of the acquisition of Jewel by American Stores.

Larry had replaced Grant Gentry, Jewel's general counsel, when the latter left to become president of A&P, taking 20 Jewel people with him and cleaning out the legal department. Larry had been at Bell & Howell and then returned to the law firm for which he had worked prior to his time at Bell & Howell. When I asked Larry back then why he would leave the law firm to come to Jewel, he told me he enjoyed people more than cold legal problems. Following the American Stores acquisition, Larry and I had lunch as he was considering his next steps. "I've been very fortunate," he told me, "and I would like to spend the next several years giving back instead of taking from."

Making the connection between the Civic Committee's need and Larry's interests and capabilities was obvious. It also set a powerful precedent for the stature and abilities of the executive director of the Civic Committee, as Larry was a member of the

Commercial Club in his own right. His successors in the role—Arnie Weber, former president of Northwestern University, and Eden Martin, who had been the managing partner of prominent law firm Sidley and Austin—have maintained the very high standard established initially by Larry Howe.

We wanted to try again to get local political leaders connected with our efforts. The first step was to present the results of the "Jobs for Metropolitan Chicago" study to them. I approached George Dunne, long-time president of the Cook County Board about the study, and he was fascinated. I told him I would like to talk to the presidents of the Chicago-area county boards. Dunne's reaction surprised me: "Well, that would be interesting," he said. "To my knowledge, we have never met as a group." Dunne was a Democrat and all the other county board presidents were Republicans. He brought them all together to hear about the study. They were intrigued, but coming to the meeting was the extent of their activity; none of the county board presidents asked the Civic Committee for follow-up help.

We also briefed Harold Washington, Chicago's first African-American mayor. Not long afterwards, Mayor Washington came to the Civic Committee with concerns about the financial stability of the city. Some months earlier, New York had literally run out of money and had been unable to cash payroll checks. "I worry," said Washington, "that the same thing will happen in Chicago, and I can't get anyone to tell me how long it might be before it happens here. Would you help me answer that question?" This was exactly the kind of project that made sense for the Civic Committee, and we took it on.

The study concluded that the mayor's worries were well founded. We projected that it would only be a few years until the City of Chicago would be bankrupt, or close to it. That was the genesis of FRAC, the Financial Resources Advisory Committee, as a subsidiary of the Civic Committee (later renamed the Civic Consulting Alliance [CCA]). FRAC's analysis found ways for

Chicago to increase revenues and to reduce expenses, through outsourcing and other business initiatives. The current mayor, Rich Daley, continues to rely on CCA for advice and support, and similar work has been undertaken for Cook County and the Chicago Board of Education. Credit and publicity continue to be avoided; the satisfaction is in the work and the health of the community.

The Civic Committee has since expanded its work into an effort entitled Metropolis 2020, a dynamic assembly of volunteer leaders working on long-run solutions to problems in land use, transportation, early childhood education, and affordable housing.

One of the issues the Civic Committee avoided at first was education, despite the business community's serious discouragement at the sad state of the Chicago public school system. Education, as an issue, was just too fraught with politics and special interests.

A few years later, however, the landscape began to shift. By 1986, the Chicago public school system was running out of money for the umpteenth time. The legislature was increasingly frustrated, and that frustration had developed into real anger downstate. The Civic Committee represented the business community in the debate, and an angry and motivated legislature passed the school reform bill of 1986. The legislation established local school councils with the ability to hire their own principals and gave principals more authority to choose their teachers.

And most importantly, a Republican-dominated General Assembly in Springfield, in a fit of spite, transferred responsibility for Chicago's schools to the mayor of Chicago. Accomplished for the wrong reasons, the move has enabled Mayor Daley to bring in strong superintendents and appoint strong members to the Board of Education who could make significant changes.

In a 1987 op-ed piece in the *Chicago Tribune*, as the school reorganization was getting underway, I described the problem as clearly and as forcefully as I could. I compared the Chicago public school system to the Soviet economy, labeling them equally ineffective:

> The Chicago public school system will not work until the two groups who most often rationalize that their activities benefit schoolchildren agree to or are forced to change their defense of the status quo. Until the status quo logjam of the administration of the Board of Education and the leadership of the unions is broken, nothing will change. We will continue to be embarrassed by the lack of results in what is now a minority school system. It is an incredible irony that the knee-jerk resistance to change on the part of the school administrators and union leaders, so many of whom are minorities, perpetuates racial inequality and produces results that serve the purposes of the most ardent racists in our society. When will concerned citizens—all of us, black, white and brown—be angry enough to dynamite the logjam?

Initially, the Civic Committee found a way to contribute to Chicago educational reform through an organization called LQE—Leadership for Quality Education. The formation of LQE, like FRAC and other initiatives, illustrates how the Civic Committee, when the need arises, expands beyond its homogeneous composition of business and major institutional leaders. Whenever the scope of an issue demands, the Civic Committee can form a subsidiary or an associated organization with expanded membership without diluting the focus and productive homogeneity of the Civic Committee itself.

LQE has given me an opportunity to work with John Ayers, son of Tom Ayers. John ran LQE for 15 years, to create charter schools and to help the Board of Education in Chicago.

John came to me some years ago worried about his own education; he had only completed a year of college. I remembered that the University of Chicago and Northwestern would both admit experienced, bright people without college degrees into their MBA programs—and we had encouraged a number of high school graduates at Jewel to pursue MBAs. I supported John's application to Northwestern, and he justified my belief in him by finishing first in his class.

The evolution and accomplishments of the Civic Committee over its first two decades could fill the pages of an entire book. In a short time, a group of business people, whose efforts were fragmented and whose power was therefore dissipated, became cohesive and aligned around a clear set of priorities they themselves set. The Civic Committee became a leading business institution in Chicago.

This is not to say that the Civic Committee has been able to address all of the issues and ills of a huge metropolis, but it has made its mark. I put it this way in remarks given in 1991, seven years after the "Make No Little Plans" report was completed:

> In describing the issues that will be facing our region in the coming years, I do not mean to suggest that the problems are wholly impersonal, fiscal, and governmental. You only have to go one half-mile south or west of where we meet today to know that Chicago is haunted by great areas of unemployment and poverty, racial isolation, inadequate housing and health care, gang and drug epidemics, family disintegration, and all of the other symptoms of modern urban distress. And the daunting problem of how to get more investment into those neighborhoods will not go away.
>
> The Civic Committee obviously does not have answers to these dilemmas; but we are sure that solutions will be much easier to find if the local economy can provide more good jobs for those who do not have them. Which is why we will continue to focus on economic development in one form or another.

At the same time that I was leading the creation of the Civic Committee, I received a call from Bruce Newman, executive director of the Chicago Community Trust. We had lunch. I started by telling Bruce, "I will have lunch with you, but I want to tell you up front ... I am so busy that there is nothing you could ask me to do that I would say yes to."

Bruce talked about his idea—giving young people who had had initial success in business or not-for-profit endeavors the ability to spend a couple of days a month in a program he planned to call Leadership Chicago. The participants in the program would find out what the challenges were in Chicago, meet with leaders, and work on projects. In effect, he wanted to create a local, part-time White House Fellows program. As Bruce had hoped, and despite my earlier assertion that I would turn him down, I said yes.

My first tasks were to help craft the program and to raise the initial funds to support it. The program was designed with two important elements based on my experiences. First, we added a word to the title of the program to make it Leadership Greater Chicago, consistent with my United Way and Civic Committee perspective that it was the metropolitan area that mattered. Second, I felt that it should take no more than eight to ten years for the program's graduates to begin to lead Leadership Greater Chicago and for the program to be sustained by them. In later years, I frequently ran into graduates of the program and current leaders of Leadership Greater Chicago who were participants in the program's early years.

Occasionally over the years, I have been asked by researchers studying the city of Chicago what I consider to be the number-one problem in the metropolitan area. My answer has been and today my answer continues to be ... race relations. The racial segregation of Chicago allows us to live our lives isolated by race, ethnicity, and class. I had encountered the issue in the 1960s when Jewel was challenged by Jesse Jackson and worked with him on the covenant we signed with what was then Operation Breadbasket (Chapter 9). It surfaced again dramatically in the issues of the Chicago public school systems in the 1980s.

The extent of that separation came home to me again in the 1990s when my wife Jane introduced me to Dolores Cross, then president of Chicago State University. Despite the fact that Chicago State was and is the number one university-level educator of minority students in Illinois, it had not been on my radar screen. I have had many occasions over the years to thank Jane for changing what was on my radar screen, and I credit her for the time I have spent in trying to be of help at Chicago State.

When I met with Dolores, she was eager to get my help and support for the university. I told her I would do anything except raise money, as I was already deeply involved in fundraising at Northwestern. As we talked about the challenges facing Chicago State's students when they graduated and were ready to move into the worlds of graduate school and business, I was vividly reminded of my own experiences. The idea we came up with is called the Friends of Chicago State University, a mentoring program intended to bridge the gap between the business establishment, symbolized by the Loop, and the best scholars at Chicago State on the south side. The Friends program was designed to create valuable links between white and minority business leaders and minority students, many of whom are the first in their families to attain a college education.

The program has produced acquaintances and dialog that simply would not have come about in any other way. One young African-American scholar returned from a meeting with his mentor, Art Kelly, a prominent venture capitalist in the city, and commented "that was the first meaningful conversation I have ever had with a white man."

While the CSU mentoring program has evolved, one outcome was that my daughter Betsy Hill, who was an early supporter of the program, joined and then became chair of the university's board of trustees.

CHAPTER 18

THE THOUGHT OF A TRYST

After Phyllis died in January 1983, I immersed myself in work for several months. The Civic Committee of the Commercial Club was the focus of my attention in my attempt to lose myself in work during that time. Later that year I came out of my shell.

Dating in my late fifties bore distinct differences from my recollections of dating in my teens and twenties. Where once I was concerned that the parents might answer the phone, I now worried that the kids would answer the phone! It was also exhausting to give up the early bedtimes I had gotten used to over the years.

One Saturday morning, I got a call from a friend, Georgine Campion, who suggested that I call Jane Phillips. I hung up from the call with Georgine and called Jane. We made a date to have dinner.

The name Jane Phillips was new to me, but Jane had heard about me several months earlier. The previous fall, I had gone to New York for board meetings and had taken Charlie Shaw up on his offer to use his apartment there. Charlie had built the Museum Towers using air rights over the Museum of Modern Art.

He had apparently made the same offer to another person, and when I walked in, I saw an attractive woman who introduced herself as Karen Lawrence. Karen was about to leave, but we overlapped long enough to have a beer together. I stopped "interviewing" her when I learned she was married and had three sons, but she apparently didn't stop interviewing me.

When she returned from her trip, she told Jane, who was her close friend, that she had found the perfect person for her. Jane said, "But he's in New York!" "No," said Karen, "he lives a mile away. And," she added, "you won't even have to change your monogram!" When they inquired of Charlie, he told them I was seeing someone else, but Jane told friends, including Georgine, that she would like to meet me if I was ever available.

Jane's and my first date included dinner at Les Nomades and walking around Michigan Avenue, getting to know each other. One of the things we talked about was limericks. We had managed to squeeze our date in before Jane left to take her mother to Florida to show her Epcot while she was still physically able to enjoy it. Jane sent me the following limerick as she was leaving:

> There once was a girl from Wilmette,
> Who hated blind dating and yet,
>   When matchmaker Campion
>   Came up with a champion,
> 'Twas a date that was hard to forget.

I was impressed!

I knew Jane would be gone for 10 days or so. In her mail when she returned was a limerick I wrote in response:

> I confess that the thought of a tryst
> Is exciting and hard to resist,
>   With a girl of ability,
>   Who displays the facility
> To perform as a limericist.

We each confessed that we had to look up the word "tryst" to make sure it meant what we thought it meant!

Most of the women I dated as a widower had been recently divorced. Jane had been divorced for 13 years from an alcoholic husband, had raised two children and sent them off to college, and had established her independence. I soon realized what an outstanding person she was.

As Jane and I started to get more serious about each other, I told her that she would have to meet Fran Beers, my close friend whom I called "Mom" (wife of Bill Beers, chairman of Kraft). I wondered how Fran would react to Jane since she had been critical of my previous dates. Jane said, "That's fine. She'll know me from Holy Comforter Church." But when I called Fran to set a date to get together for cocktails and dinner, she gave no indication that she recognized the name Jane Phillips.

The night of our date, we walked up to the door of the Beers's apartment and rang the bell. Fran opened the door, took one look at Jane, turned to me, and said, "This one's right!" She may not have reacted to the name on the phone, but she knew Jane as soon as she opened the door and saw her.

Everyone realized how serious we were when I brought Jane to my son Jerry's wedding in June that year. The day after the wedding, after we finished bidding goodbye to all of our out-of-town friends and relatives, I proposed. "I want you to know," answered Jane, "that I don't need you. I love you and I want you, but I don't need you." We often laugh about whether the "I don't need you" emphasized the word "need" or the word "you." The date we set for our wedding in September interfered with only one board meeting—I had to tell the chairman of Inland Steel that I would miss that board meeting for an unusual reason—I would be on my honeymoon!

We decided to limit the wedding ceremony to family and to have a party to celebrate later with a larger group of friends.

The invitations we sent out were for a party to celebrate the one-week anniversary of our wedding. At our small family wedding, I claimed a distinction. Although it was "just family," the participants included Ruth Babb (Phyllis's mother), Jane's mother, and Alice Phillips, Jane's mother-in-law from her first marriage. It is not every groom who has three mothers-in-law at his wedding!

Because I was 58 (the age of Jane's father when he died) and Jane 49 when we married, we laughed about her marrying a much older man. I promised her at least 25 years and am trying diligently to fulfill that promise.

Jane and I discussed where we would live when we were married. I offered her three options—the home at 969 Hill Road in Winnetka, which she could redecorate; her home on Ridge Road in Wilmette, which we could enlarge; or selling both and buying a new home. Jane knew what answer I hoped for, and we have had a wonderful life at "969." What she has accomplished in decorating the house, designing and building an extraordinary kitchen, and planning and overseeing an English garden has made our home beautiful, comfortable, and just right for us.

Whenever we are home and the weather permits, dinner is eaten on the porch looking out at the garden and is invariably accompanied by the declaration, "Aren't we lucky!" Of course, I have been able to tease her about the ongoing process of decorating, as in the poem I wrote for her 50th birthday:

> Just by chance Jane's new house is exactly her age.
> Her new primary color is mushroom, not beige.
> As refurbishing lengthens, I know what's in store.
> By the time we are through, we'll start over once more.

When Jane and I married, she was working at Long Grove Confectionery, based in Buffalo Grove, Illinois. She brought class and good taste to every facet of the company she touched—designing packaging, products, and advertising. When first divorced, Jane had had a small freelance "art agency" in the basement of her home; being home-based was convenient when her children were young. Later, when she went to work full-time for Long Grove Confectionery, she moved to a different basement—that of the Long Grove store in Plaza Del Lago in Wilmette and then to the company's corporate headquarters.

In 1992, seven years after we were married, Jane decided it was time to retire. At "969," she has her drawing board in her second-floor sitting room with north light and a view of the garden, although she uses it infrequently these days. She would tell you that her life is too busy now to sit and paint—besides, she says, "I used to paint all the time because it was how I made my living. It took the fun out of it."

Despite working for the first years we were married, Jane never passed up a chance to travel if she was invited. Trips with the Ford Foundation, the Morgan Bank International Council, and Cummins Engine were highlights. The Cummins trips were particularly memorable to Jane because they occurred over the Fourth of July—her birthday. I have often said that I particularly like her birthday because I never needed to give a party for her … the whole country did.

On one trip, we joined in the dedication of a new Cummins joint-venture facility in Jamshedpur, India, where a wonderful fireworks display was a feature of the evening dinner at the plant. And I know Jane will never forget another trip during which we visited Cummins facilities in the UK and France. She was able to say about that travel-filled July Fourth that she had had breakfast in London, lunch in Quimper (in Brittany, France), and dinner in Paris.

Jane had never played golf in her life when we were married. She took her first golf lesson at Lost Tree Village on our honeymoon—and now has joined me in being a golf nut.

Jane and I have played golf in some unusual places, including memorable outings in Russia, Turkey, and Bangladesh. We played a nine-hole Russian course in the early 1990s when we were touring with Marilou (Ogilvy Public Relations) and Henry von Ferstel. Had we wanted to play the other nine holes of golf in Russia at that time, we would have had to drive 35 miles.

The Turkish course was the best of the three; the most distinctive thing about it was the old Roman aqueduct that crossed it. At times, we walked under it to go from a green to the next tee. It was beautiful.

The most memorable aspect of the course in Bangladesh (and there was only one golf course in the country) was that it was on the property of the president's house. Jane and I were in Bangladesh for a Ford Foundation meeting. The local Ford Foundation representative liked to play golf and knew that I did, too. So, we finished up early one day and went out to play the course.

On every water hole, there were small boys, seven or eight years old with red T-shirts. If you hit a ball in the water, they dove in and retrieved it. They would be given a chit worth a few cents, so they hoped you would hit into the water. We never lost a ball on that course!

In addition to those three somewhat unusual places to play golf, we have played probably 20 courses in France, as well as courses in Scotland, Ireland, England, Canada, Mexico, Italy, Switzerland, Austria, Belgium, Luxembourg, Spain, and Portugal. One of the courses—in Austria—seemed to be particularly hilly. On the ninth hole, there was a sign with instructions on how to get off the ski lift. The first nine holes played up the hill and the remainder down the hill of what was a ski run in the winter! It was a lot easier coming down!

Jane greeted the travel opportunities enthusiastically, and has also brought her organizational and people skills to other business activities. She has, for example, accompanied me to conferences held by Booz Allen Hamilton for new CEOs. While I discussed the challenges of board relations with the new CEOs, Jane counseled the spouses (usually wives) on their roles.

She and I independently emphasized how much a spouse could learn at company events from conversations that occurred naturally and easily. I have often observed that both Phyllis and Jane were outstanding judges of people. Whether they offered praise or raised questions about the people they met, I learned to listen.

When Jane decided to stop working, she was ready to take up a new set of interesting and fun activities. She takes great pride in serving as a trustee of the Shedd Aquarium, as well as the women's boards of Ravinia Festival, Northwestern University (where she served as women's board president), and the Associates of the Art Institute. She has also enjoyed her garden club, where she keeps winning blue ribbons.

Another of Jane's claims to fame is her cooking. Our kitchen is designed with space for the family to join her as she completes preparations for a family dinner. Typical of family appreciation of her culinary skills is Jerry Perkins's answer to the annual question, "Where would you like to go for your birthday celebration?" Jerry's unfailing response is "To my favorite restaurant—Jane's dining room."

While "969" continues to be home in Winnetka, we have traded an ocean view for more space and privacy, selling the Florida condominium I bought when Phyllis was ill in 1982 and moving in early 2002 to a house in the same Lost Tree Village complex. Not only can we no longer hear our neighbors' toilets when they flush, we each have our own offices, a pool where I swim daily when I'm there, and two guest rooms for family and friends when they visit. Having redecorated our Winnetka home, Jane has gotten new satisfaction displaying her artistic and landscaping skills as she redoes our Florida home. As it is in everything she does, her guiding principle is understated elegance and her color, mushroom.

Melding two families is sometimes difficult, as modern American society has given us much occasion to observe. In this respect, we have been very fortunate.

My first impression of Jane's son Frank was of his exceptional verbal prowess. I observed to him that his persuasive skills were so outstanding that he could sell any thing or any idea. My fatherly advice was perhaps less profound than that of Polonius, but I recommended that he always be sure that he believed in what he was selling. Frank was at Duke University when Jane and I met. From there, he spent two years in New York at LaSalle Partners prior to business school, which included a year each at Harvard and Kellogg.

Kellogg MBA in hand, Frank joined Aon where his career has been extraordinary. At the age of 35, he was president of an Aon subsidiary, AIS, responsible for 700 people in 20 offices throughout California writing automobile insurance. He later added responsibility for all of the personal lines insurance business to his role there.

When Frank married Mary Martens, an accomplished journalist and writer, the rehearsal dinner, celebrated at the Shedd Aquarium, included this poetic commentary:

> From our view at the Shedd, this auspicious event
> Just prepares for tomorrow's momentous moment,
> And though Frank and his Mary are très impromptu,
> Both will follow tradition by saying, "I do."

Frank and Mary are less impromptu these days, as the joys and demands of parenthood require. We welcomed Hal (Halvorson Bennett Phillips) to the family in 2002. Hal shows every sign of sharing his parents' aptitude with words and a vocabulary that early on included a clear "Pop Pop," the name I am called by all of my grandchildren.

Elizabeth (aka Sissy to those who have known her from childhood) was a student at Boston University when Jane and I were married.

One of the highlights (at least it was a highlight for me) of the Northwestern Masters degree she earned following BU was a short film she produced based on Marlene Dietrich's rendition of the song "See What the Boys in the Back Room Will Have." She chose to cast her new niece and nephews—Jeremy, Zach, Andrew, and Shelley, the latter as a four-year-old Marlene of the 1920s—mouthing the words to Dietrich's recorded voice. They were all delighted to "pretend" for their talented director.

Following a series of roles at CNN in Atlanta and then at various public relations firms, she became an independent producer of corporate events—and devoted mother to Bennett (Bennett Phillips-Sorich).

When Elizabeth announced that she planned to marry George Sorich, a talented architect, in September 2002, I was honored and proud that she asked me if I would walk her down the aisle. I realized that I had been her father for over half of her life at that point, an admiring fan, and, I think, a good shoulder to cry on occasionally. At Elizabeth and George's rehearsal dinner, I reflected on a time long before I came into her life…

Just three days before Christmas, the whole Phillips clan
Was astir with a birth which completed their plan.
Their Elizabeth joined brother Frank in society,
Thus providing the maximum gender variety.

Both Frank and Elizabeth and their families spent several years living and working in southern California. To our great pleasure as grandparents, both Hal and Bennett and their parents now live within five minutes of us in Winnetka and

Kenilworth, respectively. Jane's favorite description of our grandchildren in 2006 was, "While Don's grandchildren are all in college or graduate school, mine are in nursery school."

Despite the gap in our ages, our children and grandchildren have gotten to know and enjoy each other. A primary vehicle for that has been a series of family trips. Together, Perkins and Phillips clans have played golf in Scotland, gone whitewater rafting in the Canadian Rockies, marveled at elephants and giraffes in Kenya, sailed the Greek Islands, combined the excitement of Paris with a relaxing barge trip in Burgundy, and explored Montreal and the surrounding countryside.

What the itineraries of those trips cannot capture are the countless games of "Spades" and "Oh, Phooey!", the creative version of "Who Wants to be a (French) Millionaire?", the collaboration on a song capturing the trip's memories with which our children and grandchildren have thanked Jane and me on the last night of each trip (always kept strictly secret until the last moment), and the time taken out of very busy lives just to be spent together.

Being fortunate twice in my life is more good fortune than comes to many. Thank you, Phyllis. Thank you, Jane.

CHAPTER 19

UNFORGETTABLE PEOPLE
AROUND THE WORLD

W hen I was growing up, the *Reader's Digest* was the only
magazine that came into our home, and I read it cover
to cover. One feature, "My Most Unforgettable Person," always
caught my interest. Between 1979 and 1990, thanks to Time,
Inc. (later Time Warner) and the Ford Foundation, I visited 13
less-developed countries and met many unforgettable people.
Some of these people were powerful and famous. Others lacked
both power and fame, but their strength distinguished them and
made them memorable to me. They populate the descriptive
reports I wrote for friends and family following each trip.

The Ford Foundation had offices around the world, and
the Foundation leadership regularly encouraged trustees to
make trips to see the Foundation's programs in action. About
every other year, a specific trip was organized for the trustees,
including visits to Africa, South America, and Asia.

The Time Newstours, created as a promotion to the leaders
of the magazine's major advertisers, involved *Time* reporters
and also included board members. One principle of those trips
was that we were all going as reporters. The professional staff at
Time, some U.S.-based, others in the country we visited, would
provide us with background to prepare us for what we would be

seeing. And because the visits were based on the notion that we were reporters, there was ample opportunity to ask questions.

A third opportunity for international travel also contributed to my perspectives on what was going on in the world—the Morgan Bank International Council. John Meyer, Morgan Bank's CEO in the 1970s, knew me from the Kodak board where we served together. He was a crusty man who always wore the same old suits dotted with the ash and burn marks from the pipes he smoked continually—a distinguished banker who dressed more like an impoverished philosophy professor.

I don't know all of the thought process behind his invitation to me to join the Council, but I have always imagined him sitting down with his colleagues, thinking that the other members of the Council were getting on in years and deciding they needed some young blood. I envision John piping up, "I know a young one." The Morgan Bank International Council met every nine months, alternately in the U.S. and overseas.

During the 21 years I was a member of the council, I visited Austria, Belgium, Italy, Hong Kong, Japan, Brazil, Australia, Canada, and Germany. It was an incredible program and gave me great insight into issues—especially economic and financial issues—around the world.

Here, then, are my "Most Unforgettable People," presented in three groups: the Powerful and Famous; The Influential; and The Not Famous, Not Powerful, But Strong. These are excerpts from reports I wrote to family and friends following the trips.

The Powerful and Famous

CHINA—1985 AND 1987

Deng Xiaoping—Time Newstour, 1985

Deng, 81 and the chairman of the Communist Party, was short (less than five feet tall), a chain-smoker and spittoon user, humble and relaxed, with a sense of humor and a nice chuckle. His short stature and personal humility seemed to make him no less effective a leader, however.

During our 70-minute visit and interview, Deng's leadership skills became obvious, but no one would have picked him out of a crowd as the man to succeed Mao Tse Tung. Though none of us truly understands how Chinese leaders are selected, if the Party was looking for the exact opposite of egomaniac Mao, they seemed to have found it in Deng Xiaoping.

In discussing the changes China enjoyed under his leadership, it was striking to hear him say of the Chinese people, "You should give them the power to make money." When we asked about the balance between the socialist system and a market economy, he explained, "What we do in the reforms in the countryside is emancipate the productive forces and bring into play the enthusiasm of the peasants. That's why we put an end to communes and have introduced the responsibility system in production." Four years later, when I returned to China with the Ford Foundation, I would have an opportunity to see a Family Responsibility Farm in action (described later in the chapter).

In another departure from more traditional Communist approaches, Deng recognized that, "Some Chinese people will become prosperous first and others later." While the socialist rhetoric still accompanied economic reforms, the blended approach could be summarized in Deng's statement, "We are adopting the useful methods of capitalism to help us speed up the development of our socialist system."

Premier Li Peng—Ford Foundation, 1987

Our meeting with 61-year-old Premier Li Peng took place six weeks before the drama of Tiananmen Square. While we couldn't anticipate that crisis in the wings, it was fascinating to look back at our visit when we later heard the news of the student protest and the government's reaction.

Before our arrival, we knew that Li Peng was a Russian-trained technocrat who had risen in the Communist Party as a specialist in the power industry. His father had been killed fighting with the Communists against the Nationalists when Li was three. Zhou Enlai, who became Premier under Mao Tse Tung, had taken an interest in Li Peng from the time he was 11, helping him with this education and serving as a mentor in later years. We were told that Li Peng was usually described as stern and dedicated.

We found Li Peng to be pleasant and relaxed, smiling at times, and surprisingly candid. The cordial nature of the dialogue was such that I could ask, "If you'll forgive a typical American question, does your plan for the Communist Party and for China include democratic elections and increased opportunities for more of your people to pick their government representatives?"

Li Peng responded, "You asked an American question; I'll give you a Chinese answer." He went on to suggest that the illiteracy rate and size of the population dictated against popular elections. He also pointed out emphatically that more candidates stand for election to the Peoples Congress than there are seats, so there is some choice. There was some truth to his answer, but it was at least as true that any turnover of those in power was less likely under China's one-party system.

We were startled by how aware Li Peng was of what was going on outside China. At one point, he said, "You in America are lucky to have a tradition that results in an impasse such as the

Eastern Airlines strike. We do not have that discipline and would probably have given in to the workers at the local enterprise level." There were two startling aspects of his comment.

First, we were amazed that he even knew of the strike, which was then only three days old. And second, we were struck by how different his remark was from the usual Communist Party line about the strike showing that the U.S. is anti-worker. Instead he described the management-labor problem in China as both sides "stand on the same line," in effect conspiring against the state to divide up income through bonuses unrelated to profit or merit. And then they would come to the state for additional capital when it was needed.

We were impressed to find a Communist leader, raised in the central planning tradition, wishing for a healthy tension between workers and management, a means of decentralizing dispute resolution, and a way to encourage enterprises to reinvest on their own, rather than coming to the state treasury.

CUBA—1985

Fidel Castro—Time Newstour, 1985

In Castro, we encountered a leader still committed to traditional communist ideals and seemingly equally as committed to wearing us out with talk. The six-foot-three-inch, 69-year-old leader, dressed in a suit (the first time he had been so dressed for any group, he told us), joined us at 8:52 P.M.

He stood at a microphone accompanied by an outstanding woman translator who had worked with him for 20 years. She mimicked his facial expressions as well as the emphasis of his verbal presentation. He finally finished answering questions at 10:12 P.M., at which time he mixed with Time Newstour participants at cocktails and dinner until 1:15 A.M.

Castro seemed in excellent health, despite rumors of a stroke the previous year. He had forsaken his beloved cigars, but imbibed quantities of martinis and wine. We were not surprised to be told that he remained an inexhaustible talker, with an "average" conversation lasting three hours ... often conducted in the dead of night. He still devoted several hours a day to routine matters in his office as President of the Council of State, where his bookshelves displayed his eclectic tastes ranging from hydroponics to romance novels.

My impressions of Castro could be summarized in how I would answer the question: How do you turn a less-developed country into a lesser-developed country?

- Win a revolution against a corrupt regime.
- Champion the independence of Cuba for Cubans.
- Pick a losing economic system called Communism.
- Count and grow dependent on the champion of that system—the USSR.
- Be seduced by Santa Claus Russia, who sends equipment and oil in exchange for sugar priced above the world market price.
- Be a charismatic leader, who sees himself not as the last of the old communist leaders, but as the first of the future communist leaders of lesser-developed countries.
- Maintain total control for 36 years.
- Spend your time after age 69 rationalizing your life and working to prove that the rest of the world is wrong.
- Enjoy the power that comes with the office.
- Take credit for everything good in Cuba. Blame external forces, especially the U.S., for every problem.
- Refuse to recognize that mortality may intervene, while denying the need for leadership succession.

Castro appeared to have enjoyed the visit, however. He sent to the plane boxes of cigars (at a value we estimated at $120 apiece) and bottles of rum for each person on the Newstour ... with his calling card.

VIETNAM—1985 AND 1995

Pham Van Dong—Time Newstour, 1985

Like Castro, Vietnam's 80-year-old leader, Pham Van Dong, had plenty of blame for the U.S., which he held "morally and materially" responsible for Vietnam's plight. He had all the charm of an overzealous character actor playing a Nazi General in a World War II movie. He was a tough old man, and unquestionably in charge.

As part of our visit, we were required to go to a war museum and to Ho Chi Minh's mausoleum. The latter included a gruesome display of Ho Chi Minh's embalmed body, frozen and vacuum-sealed like a can of coffee. Prominent at the museum were wax dummies of U.S. soldiers in their uniforms.

The museum also displayed a bicycle with bags of rice hanging over the seat. The bicycle couldn't be ridden but its wheels could carry 200 pounds of rice with a person walking alongside it. Above the bicycle was an aerial picture of what looked like a long row of ants—actually Vietnamese people going down the Ho Chi Minh trail, wheeling their bikes with provisions for the troops. We also visited Ho Chi Minh's home, a small A-shaped building on the grounds of the large pretentious former home of the French Governors General.

We shook our heads to see his "Pentagon"—a table, a dozen chairs, and three telephones. From that frame house and with his people wheeling rice to the troops on their bicycles, he had managed to embarrass the U.S. for something we should never have been involved in. He had called the shots in the Vietnam War and won!

The leaders of Vietnam whom we met—Pham Van Dong, his vice-chairman, and his foreign minister—were single-minded and consistent. No matter how we phrased the questions, we got the same answers:

- Our system may be slower to get started than others in Asia; but mark our words, we will be way ahead in 2020 (yes, 2020!).
- We will not tell you what percent of our GNP is spent on defense, so why do you keep asking?
- We want to have foreign investment and high technology development, but it must be done within our Socialist system. We must avoid a divergence of wealth between rich and poor. Our people like to work for the benefit of the state.
- We have a population problem (58 million and counting) but we will overcome it (an assertion unaccompanied by an explanation).
- Our problems are not the result of our system or our planning process. They result from 30 years of war. The U.S. is morally and materially responsible for the state of our country and its economy.

It seemed ironic to consider how much better off the Vietnamese probably would have been had they lost the war. The U.S. would have been helping to rebuild Vietnam's economy as we did for Japan following World War II.

Do Muoi—Time Newstour, 1995

Our *Time* experts' briefing on Do Muoi, General Secretary of the Communist Party of Vietnam, read as follows:

Do Muoi was born in Hanoi on February 2, 1917. He began his revolutionary activities at 19 when he joined the Popular Front Movement against the French. He was sentenced to 10 years in jail by the French in 1941, but after just four years in Hoa Lo Prison—later known as the Hanoi Hilton—he escaped.

Despite a lackluster reputation for most of his career, Do Muoi has become a surprise favorite among foreign leaders in the past few years, while solidifying his power base as Party boss. He is known more for his dogged determination than his flair, and indeed, until he was named General Secretary for the Party in 1991, he had never distinguished himself as more than a loyal functionary. But in Vietnam, unlike China, as a top Vietnamese bureaucrat said recently, "charisma comes with office."

The man we met was senile, repetitive, evasive in answering our questions, and generally unimpressive. Three times he said that, rumors to the contrary, he did not think that the U.S. was trying to overthrow his government. If he was aware of the bustling street trade and happier lives around him, he did not indicate it. He seemed to have acceded to the market system as a trade-off that enabled him to sustain the power and perks of Communist Party leadership.

But if Do Muoi was unimpressive, the 10 years since my previous visit to Vietnam had brought about changes I would not have believed had I not seen them. The rest of our visit to Vietnam was a revelation. Hanoi had gone from grim to happy in many ways, including these:

1985	1995
Mao suits—for everyone.	Mao suits only for the leaders we interviewed—others in bright colors and varied styles.
Nothing I wanted to buy in few drab shops.	Everything imaginable for sale at bargain prices—like Hong Kong 30 years ago.

1985	1995
Not much play.	Badminton games everywhere a court could be squeezed in—also, arm wrestling.
Foreign investment limited to China and Russia.	Foreign investment mostly from the West at a rate of $1 billion per month.
Dollars are scarce.	Dollars are everywhere—it's the shopping currency.
Bicycles, bicycles, bicycles.	Motor bikes, motor bikes, motor bikes—and still plenty of bicycles.
Food unappealing.	Fresh vegetables everywhere.
Children with vacant stares.	Smiles and "hellos" from the children, waving at our buses.

PHILIPPINES—1985 AND 1988

Ferdinand Marcos—Time Newstour, 1985

Everyone and everything in the Philippines was focused on President Marcos. That was hardly surprising since he had been a virtual dictator under martial law for 20 years. We were told that he was the cause of every problem, and we were told that he was the solution to every problem. The U.S. builds up the importance of our president, but we can't compare in that respect to the Philippines of that time. Marcos's health was discussed like baseball in the U.S.

We found Marcos excessively proud—an arrogant man yet to come to grips with his own mortality. He bristled at suggestions that his regime had failed. He admitted no mistakes during his 20 years in the presidency. He repelled suggestions for change. Marcos himself described his rule: "I am the golf pro. I know where the sand traps are. No one else can tell me how to play my course." His wife Imelda was absent on a visit to Russia while we met with her husband in Malacanan Palace.

Because of what we had seen and experienced elsewhere on that trip, I could not restrain the comparisons in the question I addressed to Marcos:

> We have been to South Korea and Taiwan before coming to the Philippines. I am struck by the similarities of the three. All three have instituted martial law to combat Communist threats. All three have suffered through the recent oil-shock and World War II. All three have had a rapid growth in population. All three have large military budgets. All three envy the natural resources of other countries. But there is one big difference. South Korea and Taiwan have kept the state out of business, either as central planners or owners. Will your economic recovery reject central planning and economic cronyism?

Marcos rationalized. He attributed the economic miracles of Korea and Taiwan to their allowing some to become rich before others, a policy he rejected. He excused his nation's lack of economic progress with his view that the poorest needed help first. He added that the Philippines had distributed wealth before the country had earned it.

Marcos was very concerned about the impression he was making on our group. One of his young staff members asked many of us, one on one, what we thought of the president. Most of the group apparently said that we were not impressed with his answers to our questions. As a result, our agenda was suddenly changed and we were invited back for an unscheduled second session with Marcos. He was no more successful selling himself the second time.

Corazon Aquino—Ford Foundation, 1988

President Cory Aquino was the favorite topic of conversation three years later, as Marcos had been during my first visit to the Philippines. People could agree that Aquino was no Margaret Thatcher, but after that there was little consensus. Most agreed that she had poor advisors, but disagreed on which advisors failed her. They agreed that she had wasted her post-election honeymoon period, but disagreed on what she should have done with it. They agreed that her administration was in jeopardy, but disagreed on whether the threat came from the right or the left.

This meeting instantly refreshed my memory of my 1985 contact with Aquino as part of the same Time Newstour during which I had encountered Marcos. Following my 1985 visit, I had described her as an attractive and likable but inexperienced housewife who would have difficulty governing a country. While none of us knew it at the time, Marcos was three months from being expelled from the country; and Cory Aquino was three months from accepting, fatalistically, a call for which neither her religious faith nor her experience had prepared her.

As part of this second trip, we were invited again to Malacanan Palace. This time, our tour encompassed the private living quarters of the Marcos family, which I had not seen when I met Marcos three years earlier. We saw the ostentatious assembly of shoes and dresses that made Imelda's wardrobe look like an overstock at Neiman Marcus. The palace tour was carefully arranged to remind all visitors of the greed and thievery of the deposed dictator and his wife.

Aquino remembered our previous meeting and reminisced about neither wanting nor expecting to be a candidate for that upcoming election. She was grateful for the Ford Foundation's support in her country, and was surprised to learn that the University of the Philippines was the largest recipient of Ford Foundation funds of any grantee outside of the United States.

I ended my trip with my earlier assessment of Cory Aquino changed only in one regard—she was now more experienced. I found her an honest and caring person, with a fatalistic acceptance of the responsibility thrust upon her and a strong religious faith. She told us that her decisions came to her following prayer. To a person, the Ford Foundation trustees felt admiration tinged with sadness. None of us had any desire to be in her shoes.

MEXICO—1989

Miguel de la Madrid—Former President of Mexico

Jim Evans, the former head of the Union Pacific Railroad and a former fellow director of AT&T, once invited me to Bohemian Grove as his guest. My stepson Frank Phillips describes it as "the place corporate executives go to pee in the woods with George Schultz."

Miguel de la Madrid, former president of Mexico, was a special guest at the Grove that year and was staying in our camp. I walked around with him, discussing the same questions with which I had pressed his predecessors. I had previously met both Presidents Echevaria and Lopez Portillo, each of whom had always either denied that there was any issue with corruption in Mexico or claimed that it was isolated at the lower levels of the police, customs, or the immigration service. When I asked de la Madrid, he said, "It is a problem. And the only thing I know is that I have to do what I do when I clean house. When I clean the steps, I start sweeping at the top."

I told him how much I admired him. In contrast to most Mexican presidents who left office with significant personal wealth accumulated in office, de la Madrid was working at a publishing house upon completing his term of office, and returned to live in the house he had occupied before becoming president.

THE INFLUENTIAL

While it is easy to divide people into the all-powerful and the not-at-all-powerful, some striking people fall somewhere in the middle. Here are three.

POLAND—1981

Lech Walesa—Time Newstour, 1981

Of course it is tempting to put Walesa in the category of Powerful and Famous; and he is, at least to some degree, a household name. At our meeting, I realized that he was the first revolutionary I had ever personally met. But that meeting suggested his ultimate limitations, and it became clear that Solidarity was a political movement dressed up to look like a union.

Walesa was small in stature but extremely charismatic and a naïve believer that "right will prevail." At 37, his experience was limited to the shipyard in Gdansk, the Solidarity "Union," and enduring an autocratic Polish government. He had a good sense of humor and he chain-smoked.

Walesa told us:

- We have been lied to so often by the Polish government that we don't trust them anymore. There are rumors of trains transporting our food to Russia. We have no food. Like the husband who has cheated five times, there is no basis to believe the excuse.

- Our currency is so worthless, it won't buy glue to paper the wall with.
- Poland will recover when workers control investment and industrial plant operations.
- We are not against Marx and Lenin. We just want to get rid of the rules and do what is good for the people.

I asked Walesa about self-management and how resources would be allocated—would it be through prices or through a new central planning government? His answer began, "In our self-management system, a mayor would get together with his Solidarity leaders and they would decide how many pigs they needed, which roads to fix, etc., through local bargaining. A representative would be sent to the district level with a list of their needs. Bargaining at that level would determine…" One of his advisors interrupted him before he could finish his long-winded and terribly naïve answer.

I realized that Solidarity was designed to strike at the heart of Communism. While Communism was supposed to give the workers power, bad management had led to workers understanding that, whatever the system was called, it didn't represent them. At the same time, our Newstour group seriously questioned whether the inexperienced, provincial Walesa would be able to do any better. Time Newstour participants, hoping to find a hero, left very disappointed.

CHINA—1987

The Imam of Xian—Ford Foundation, 1987

A visit to Xian and the newest "wonder of the world" is designed to impress. It was memorable to see some of the 6,000 life-size terra-cotta soldiers and horses created before 200 B.C. and discovered by farmers digging a well. The soldiers and horses were the creation of an emperor's enormous ego and a belief that the earthly world could accompany him in the afterlife. We were astounded to see the features and details of each soldier's face, uniquely modeled after an individual soldier of that day.

Xian was also home to a great mosque, built in 749 A.D., which had somehow survived the Cultural Revolution. The Imam was a member of the People's Congress and received funding from the state.

As we left, I referred to the Imam as the Jerry Falwell of Xian. He lacked only television. As it was, he gave us a personal tour, repeating several times that all Muslims want is peace. I asked, "Would you explain how the Ayatollah Khomeini is working for peace?" The Imam's answer: "Each Muslim works for peace in his own way."

His tour took our group to a beautifully carved wood-paneled prayer room in the mosque which, he explained, was only for men. He was making a special concession to us to let the women in our group view it. We asked if women were ever permitted to worship there. "No," he answered. When we asked where Muslim women worship, he replied, "Muslim women pray at home." As we walked out of the mosque, Enid Schoettle, a Ford Foundation program staff member, turned to Jane and said, defiantly, "I got back at him. While we were in the men's prayer room, I prayed!"

PERU—1986

Hernando De Soto—Ford Foundation, 1986

Until I met Hernando De Soto, I thought that Peruvian researchers were reporters of the past and that predestination was the motto of the nation. A brain drain had been followed by a capital drain in Peru, and I began to wonder whether the

Ford Foundation should have a program, much less an office, there at all. One academic we met insisted that Peru no longer had any entrepreneurs.

Jane and I visited three supermarkets, an experience that readily dispelled the nonsense of a dearth of entrepreneurship, but I was really impressed when I met Hernando DeSoto. We connected instantly and discovered in each other a "breath of fresh air." While DeSoto's research was criticized because his approach was perhaps not rigorous, he made a powerful case that bureaucracy and controls were what was getting in the way of more abundant entrepreneurial activity. He had demonstrated by actually doing it that it took 267 days to get formal approval of a new small business, and even that included a couple of unavoidable bribes along the way. It is not surprising that, in De Soto's estimate, 60-plus percent of Peruvian business was in the "informal" sector (the black market).

Unlike many academics, De Soto was committed to seeing his views influence policy. Like a well-behaved Saul Alinsky, he was organizing the underclass to demand that the government get off their backs. He had even persuaded a local Communist mayor that Marx would have been against Peru's bureaucratic inertia because it held down the rise of the poor!

THE NOT FAMOUS, NOT POWERFUL, BUT STRONG

POLAND—1981

The Gruchala Family—Time Newstour, 1981

Unimpressed with Lech Walesa, we left Gdansk to visit a rural farm. The Gruchalas—a farmer, his wife, daughter, son-in-law, and three grandchildren—received us with as much excitement and as lavish a display of food as if we were the president or the pope. Our interpreter looked at the roast duck, chicken, pork cutlets, and plentiful vegetables and said, "Jesus, I don't believe it." We felt guilty as we remembered the empty shelves and food lines we had seen elsewhere in Poland.

Gruchala had built everything himself: a 75-acre dairy farm with eight cows, three pigs (probably four before we came), mechanical milking and refrigeration, and awards for milk production filling the wall. A picture of his hands on the wall might have better told the story of the lack of fertilizer, or fuel, or a new tractor—anything, in fact, to spend his Polish *zlotys* on. He had only a small pile of coal and was number 4,500 on a list from which less than 1,600 had as yet received fuel. We asked how he could get through the winter. He pointed to the trees of the nearby forest.

The evidence of their hard work was straightforward. The family's politics were more complex. Gruchala himself had spent five years in a German concentration camp and did not want to discuss politics. He dismissed Walesa with the statement: "He has no education or experience.'" His son, a Walesa fan, disagreed.

On my return to Chicago, I sent a box of staple groceries from Jewel to say thank-you to the Gruchalas. In that family we had seen the strength and pride of Poland.

INDONESIA—1989

A Good and Honest Farmer—Ford Foundation, 1989

Many expensive irrigation projects in Indonesia were planned and installed by foreign engineers without consulting the affected farmers. All that fancy expertise, in fact, had not worked. What *had* worked was the trial and error of centuries of farmers and their descendants dividing up water supplies with the help of their Hindu priests. Irrigation engineers and computer analysis had proved to be a poor substitute for the traditional approach developed from trial and error.

Religion was an integral part of all Bali farming. A small stone shrine stood at virtually every rice paddy, irrigation source, and water redistribution point. The mountain lakes, the source of the water, were the sites of pre-growing-season ceremonies. Almost every home had a white or yellow rag hanging from a bamboo flag pole to pay homage to a favorite god, in return for which good crops were expected.

We met a farmer who headed a *subak* (an irrigation system) that served hundreds of rice farmers, each with only about an acre of land. The "helpful" work of World Bank engineers had produced a particularly trying time for the subak we visited. Theory had failed, inappropriate gates had been installed, and concrete canals had been misplaced. The farmer, head of the *subak,* had patiently and personally redone the work of the World Bank engineers and redirected the water that had been misdirected to him and his fellow farmers.

This farmer's income came from his farm at the tail end of the irrigation system. Yet, he worked innumerable hours as *subak* leader. "Do you get paid?" we asked. "No," he said. "I will get my reward when I am reincarnated as a better person in the next life."

PERU—1986

Peru Mujer—Ford Foundation, 1986

In an unforgettable visit with Peru Mujer, an advocacy group for women, we met some extraordinary women who worked in Lima's shanty towns. The shanty towns were crowded with migrants from the surrounding mountainous areas who lacked access to voting, work, education, or health care, mainly because they lacked the primary document required for access—a birth certificate. Most of the shanty town residents had been born in circumstances unlikely to result in their receiving a birth certificate. Getting one cost $30-$40, a month's wage; and, even with ready money, birth certificates took four months or longer to process.

Peru Mujer's leader described how they helped these shanty town residents pay for and make their way through the application process so they could secure birth certificates and have access to social services, work, and, importantly, the right to vote. Peru, a self-described democracy, had excluded millions of low-income citizens from the voting rolls for want of a birth certificate, in a way reminiscent of the old U.S. South's laws that restricted the vote to those who owned land.

We will never forget going to visit the organization's leader as she sat in her "office," which more closely resembled a cardboard washing machine box. She had a shoe box for a filing system and a single dilapidated manual typewriter. Sadly, the day we visited—we heard later—her husband came home drunk, beat her, and destroyed her typewriter. Her crime was talking to us. All we could do was feel terrible and replace her typewriter.

BANGLADESH—1987

Grameen Bank Loan Holders—Ford Foundation, 1987

Jane and I had read about the Grameen Bank before going to Bangladesh, so we knew that a loan was granted to one member of a six-person group. We also understood that subsequent loans to others in the group depended on beginning repayment of the first loan and that 98 percent of the loans were being repaid. Group pressure served as a substitute for collateral.

Only when we visited three centers of women (six groups of six women constitute a center) and sat with them on grass mats in their thatched-roof huts, did we understand the extraordinary impact of the program.

Particularly for women in Bangladesh, belonging to the group was as important as receiving a loan. Though they had started their micro-loan program with men, the Grameen Bank now worked only with women. "Income earned by women is spent on the family; income earned by men is spent on themselves— probably on another wife or a motorbike," we were told.

The sense of belonging and support provided by group membership was revolutionary in the Islamic world of Bangladesh, where a husband could divorce his wife simply by telling her so three times; and landless, ignorant women are kept frightened and pregnant. The entire loan process made the group and center members feel good about themselves. The tears and anxiety that came with holding the equivalent of $60 in their hands for the first time in their lives turned into the pride of repaying the loan and qualifying for a second and larger one. Participants enjoyed talking about how much courage it had taken to join their groups in the first place.

We were told of one situation in which a group had been physically prevented from meeting three times before they succeeded in getting together for the first time. It was not uncommon for village leaders to warn the women that Grameen would take them away from their families and make them slaves if they did not repay the loans.

We saw so many positive effects of the borrowing program.

Saving had become a part of these women's lives. Members were not allowed to come to monthly meetings unless they brought their one or two *takas* (three to six cents) to be added to the group's savings account. When we asked whether they were now eating better, one member answered, "Yes, and thanks to our savings, we were not worried about eating even during the recent severe flood. That never happened before." Group members protected their dog-eared savings records as we might our passports.

When women group members could finally think about something other than hunger, they started developing an interest in family planning. All were learning to sign or draw their signatures. Some, realizing that others had taken advantage of them in business dealings, were learning to read and write.

The help of the Bank enabled preschool education for very young children and remedial education for older children, preparing the next generation to be literate.

Housing improved. House loans were available to one or two members in each center. The group decided on its own which member needed or deserved improved housing the most. I had the privilege of cutting the ribbon for a new house which would be inhabited for the first time the day we were there. The family was so proud because the house had a corrugated galvanized roof. It may have cost $300 to build.

We had the opportunity to meet with Dr. Muhammad Yunnus, the modest, charismatic, humorous, and creative founder of the Grameen Bank and winner, with the bank, of the 2007 Nobel Peace Prize. He gave credit to the Ford Foundation for providing funding to Grameen. One example of his creativity was the way he had found to distribute seed packets to the women who borrowed money from Grameen to lease farm land. To simplify distribution, every seed packet was sold for one *taka* (three cents). Like a Bangladeshi F.W. Woolworth, Yunnus had thought of selling packets of expensive seeds with fewer seeds and packets of inexpensive seeds with more seeds, so that all the packets could be sold at the same price.

Our visit convinced us that it is possible to teach the poorest illiterate person to borrow, invest, repay, and join the economic system. In Bangladesh, in contrast to much of the developed world, new participants in the system were being taught that credit was used for producing income rather than for acquiring possessions. Bangladesh lacked resources and could not afford welfare. We couldn't help asking ourselves how much more we might be able to accomplish in the U.S. if we had started with Grameen Bank-style micro-loans and the self-confidence fostered by the process, instead of welfare payments.

CHINA—1989

Family Responsibility Farm—Ford Foundation 1989

As we had learned in our meeting four years before with Deng Xiaoping, collective farms had been replaced by family farms in China. The process was called Family Responsibility. Individual families could now keep much of the proceeds of their labor, which they could sell at market prices, after selling a designated portion of their crop to the government for lower, controlled prices.

One farm wife, whose husband was the local school's math teacher when he wasn't farming, explained that only 15 percent of their grain had to be sold to the government. Family Responsibility, she said, had really improved their lives. She showed us around the small brick building in their courtyard, which the family shared with goats and chickens and caged rabbits. The family had one appliance—a window fan—and a single electric light over the bed. The oven used for baking bread was on one side of a dividing wall, the family bed on the other side. The coals from the oven heated the bricks under the bed, and provided some warmth in the otherwise unheated house when nighttime temperatures dropped to near-freezing.

Our visit to the village had not been pre-arranged; we just dropped by. Following our visits to individual homes, we assembled to meet the leaders of the village. General Obasanjo, a Ford Foundation trustee from Nigeria (who has served three terms as president of his country), spoke for our group. After a greeting and expression of thanks for the hospitality, the general (a huge man wearing his dashiki) asked, "If we were from your government, what would you ask us for?" The immediate answer: "I would ask you to go away! But before you left, I would ask you never to bring back collective farming. Since we divided up our land, we have all been doing better and I have saved almost enough to buy a television set!"

Six weeks later, Jane and I heard about Tiananmen Square. Watching the protests, we thought of that farmer, wondering whether he had been able to buy that television set and if he could have watched those dramatic events. I think he probably would have been pro-government and anti-protester for fear that any change in government might lead to a change in what was really important to him ... his ability to profit from his Family Responsibility farm.

CHAPTER 20

BLUE LIGHT BLUES

It was Harry "Pete" Cunningham's vision that turned the Kresge Variety Stores into Kmart Corporation. Pete foresaw that variety stores—whether they were called "Variety Store" or "5¢ and 10¢ Store" or "Five and Dime"—would be squeezed in the middle between drug stores, which added variety store products to the pharmacy; and discount stores, which offered more choices and lower prices in a big-store format. Pete didn't open the first discount store—that honor belongs to Ann & Hope in Rhode Island, who started off trying to sell their excess inventory of ribbons in a warehouse site. But Pete was a pioneer of the discount store format, and Kresge grew dramatically under his leadership.

I met Pete through meetings at the Harvard Business School when I was president and then chairman of Jewel. At one point, Pete suggested that perhaps Jewel and his company, still called Kresge at the time, should talk about merging. Jewel had so much going on then that we didn't follow through on Pete's suggestion. I often wonder how things might have changed for both companies had we gotten together back then.

When Pete retired as chairman, he made one of what I consider two unfortunate career errors. He appointed a triumvirate to share leadership of the company—the top lawyer, the top real estate executive, and the top merchant. As

307

he told me, each had strengths that complemented those of the others; and by combining them, the composite was the kind of person he wanted to run the business.

As it turned out, the worst, rather than the best qualities of the three combined, and conflict resulted. I am told that the disagreements created such lack of direction and leadership that the board, even though it lacked experienced retailers, recognized the need to act. The board then chose Ben Fauber, who had been running Kmart's West Coast operation, to take over as CEO. The company fared better under his leadership.

Pete's other unfortunate error was to perpetuate the tradition of long-term store service prior to giving talented people management responsibility. He thought that extended experience in the store environment was necessary to prepare someone to lead the company. Pete's own path to the top in the Depression years of the 1930s included a number of years in stores. Thirty years later, that no longer worked.

Many years after I met him at Harvard Business School meetings, I would see Pete again when he and I both had homes at Lost Tree Village in North Palm Beach, Florida. Pete had retired as chairman of Kmart and was no longer on the board, but still wielded influence. In 1985, Pete told me that Ben Fauber, Kmart's chairman, was retiring and that the company was looking for a successor. He asked me if I would be interested in being Kmart's CEO.

I said no. Jane and I had recently married, and I had established a new pattern in my life. I had climbed the CEO mountain once and did not need to do it again. Pete then asked if I would consider going on the board. To that I said yes.

It would be my first retail board since Jewel, and I thought it would be fun. There was no conflict, as ample time had passed since my retirement from Jewel.

One of the first things I was asked to do on the Kmart board was to serve on a succession committee. With the exception of "young" Don Perkins at age 58, the committee was composed of septuagenarians. The other three members of the succession committee—Carl Gerstacker, chairman of Dow Chemical; Ed Liddy, retired chief financial officer of Ford; and Paul McCracken, a University of Michigan professor and former head of the President's Council of Economic Advisors—were all distinguished, bright, and able people. They knew little about retailing.

Ben Fauber had given the succession committee a list of six names of people in the company he thought were possible successors. True to Kmart tradition, every one of the six candidates had started their careers in the Kresge stores, as Pete Cunningham had done when he graduated from college. Five of the six had remained in store jobs 15 years or more before moving into a management job.

The exception was Joe Antonini, who had taken on a management role after "only" 12 years. Kmart's approach was so different from what we had put in place at Jewel! At Jewel, we insisted on high potential MBAs "getting their hands dirty" in the stores. The difference was we had them do it for one year, not for 12 or 15. In hindsight, I concluded that this difference was the principal reason for Kmart's eventual failure and Jewel's success.

At Kmart, Antonini's 12-year stint in the stores was "the fast track." Being brand new on the board and brand new on the committee made it difficult to do what my gut told me would have been right—to look outside the company. Instead, we chose an insider. Joe Antonini was the strongest choice, and the board agreed that we would do our best to help him succeed.

Joe's early years as a CEO were successful. However, he might have been doomed to failure by the people and management practices he inherited. Ironically, it was those very people and practices that had brought him to the role. Only reluctantly did he finally begin to change the people and the management practices—and by then it was too late.

I was committed to helping Joe succeed. I encouraged him to look at the food business as an addition to Kmart. He agreed, and the result was Super K, a very attractive effort to sell a combination of food and Kmart merchandise. The first Super K was opened before the first Sam's Club, Wal-Mart's version of the food-discount store, and was a great sales success.

I also tried to help him bring in good people from outside the business. One of the people was Ron Floto, a former Jewel executive and a great example of the way Jewel attracted and developed people.

During the 1970s, I had served on a regional committee to help select White House Fellows—a role I thoroughly enjoyed. I was so intrigued by the benefits of sending an outstanding young person to Washington for a year that I urged a Jewel talent, Peter Cook, to apply. Peter was selected and served in the Department of Transportation with Ron Floto. Ron had gone to West Point and had been injured in Vietnam; Peter spoke enthusiastically about him. We invited Ron to come to Jewel as a trainee.

When American Stores acquired Jewel, Ron left to become CEO of a chain of stores in Florida, which is where he was when I was urging Joe Antonini to bring people like him into Kmart. Ron came in to run the Super K stores.

A third way in which I tried to help Joe was urging him to hire McKinsey Consultants to help with strategic planning issues. Joe heeded the advice and brought in a consulting team headed by Mark McGrath. The McKinsey study's conclusion showed Kmart that they could sell staple groceries within the Kmart store and make a good return on the space used while attracting customers to the stores for the discounted values in the grocery department.

But, as Kmart growth declined, Joe, with board support, became enamored of diversification. Kmart bought Borders, Sports Authority, Office Max, Builders Square, Waldenbooks, and Pace Warehouse Clubs, among other specialty retailers. Kmart even tried to buy Costco, but ended up selling Pace to Wal-Mart instead. The specialized retail businesses that Kmart acquired were good businesses, for the most part—except for Builders Square—but it turned out that there wasn't enough synergy to add any extra value. Each business did well or poorly on its own. Overall, the company's earnings continued to decline, primarily because of the decline of the core Kmart operation. Diversification came to be viewed by investors as a distraction.

At that point, investment bankers sold Joe on the idea of issuing tracking stock for each of the specialty retail companies, in order to capture their true market worth. Tracking stock is a hybrid stock intended to follow the fortunes of a subsidiary while it is still fully owned by the parent. I reluctantly went along with the proposal, although I expressed my concern about the potential conflicts for board members in attempting to serve the divergent interests of different shareholders in the subsidiaries and the parent company.

The transaction involved a complex spin-off of some shares in each company—the complexity of the transaction is indicated by the fact that the proxy statement for the special shareholders meeting was two inches thick. Investors were angry about the underperformance of the company and its core operation, and the vote failed to carry. Kmart management was stunned. It was the beginning of the end for Joe at Kmart.

After Joe's failed effort with tracking stock, institutional investors became more vocal and more negative. Over time, much of the board itself shifted from "help mode" to being increasingly critical. Members of the board included Dick Munro, retired chairman of Time Warner, whom I had recommended; and Joe Califano and Lilian Affinito, whom Joe had introduced to the board, having gotten to know them on the Chrysler board. Other directors included Joe Flannery, former CEO of BF Goodrich; Jim McDonald, the retired president of General Motors; Willie Davis, a former Green Bay Packers tight end and media executive; Enrique Fala, former chief financial officer of Dow Chemical; and Gloria Shatto, president of Berry College in Georgia.

Every meeting of the Kmart board over two years kept coming back to the same question: Would Joe make it or should we replace him?

The vociferousness of the investment community's criticism intensified and was epitomized in one meeting with an investment management firm, which demanded to see Joe Antonini and some directors. Jim McDonald and I went with Joe to the meeting.

We started the meeting by telling the group that we were prepared to listen to them and, at some point, we were also prepared to excuse Joe from the room so that they could say whatever they wanted. The senior member of the firm responded, "We don't want the son of a bitch to leave the room! We want him to hear everything we have to say!"

Under such pressure, the board eventually reached a compromise—Joe would step down as chairman of the board, but would remain president and chief executive officer. We hoped that the approach would give us time to help Joe turn earnings around while removing him as the lightning rod for investor dissatisfaction. I would take on the chairman's role, although, as I said in an interview with *Crain's Detroit Business* in January 1995, it was not "what I expected to be doing at this point in my life."

Splitting the CEO and chairman's roles had one well-publicized precedent at the time. We would pattern our approach at Kmart after the role that John Smale, former chairman of P&G, had taken at General Motors when he became non-executive chairman of that board. When the concept of a non-executive chairman first came up, I sought advice and input from John on his role at GM.

As non-executive chairman, my role would be to serve as tutor and counselor to the president. The chairman wouldn't run the company and certainly would not be its external spokesperson.

A cartoon that appeared in *Crain's Detroit Business* in late January showed Antonini with me sitting on his shoulders. Antonini is saying, "He ain't heavy, he's my Chairman." I genuinely tried to help Joe and spent considerable time on Kmart business.

Our biggest problem was that we hadn't bought Joe the time we had hoped for. While the response to my taking over the chairman's role may have been positive, the pressure from the investment community for a quick turn-around was intense and unrealistic. The criticism became an onrush that we couldn't hold off. By March, we gave up, and, with the unanimous support and on behalf of the board, I asked Joe for his resignation.

It was a challenge to find a new CEO for the company. Kmart was in trouble and there were not a lot of people who wanted the job. Spencer Stuart conducted the search, and I was struck by the fact that no fewer than one quarter of the suggested people on the initial list they developed were former Jewel executives. It made me realize that too few other retailers had spent the necessary time and effort developing people.

One of the people eventually added to the prospect list was Floyd Hall, who had led the Target stores in their early days. He had also been CEO of Grand Union, taking it out of bankruptcy and making an excellent financial return for Jimmy Goldsmith, a successful international financier, who told us that Floyd was the best executive he had ever worked with. Others had high praise for him, as well. The major difficulty was that Floyd's wife did not want to leave New Jersey and, at one point during the discussions, he turned us down.

Not long after that, I got a message from Floyd that the press was after him because they had heard that he was a candidate for the CEO job at Kmart. He wanted to know what he should do. I told him, "I hope you will tell them what you told me— which is that you couldn't take the job because your wife didn't want to move. I hope that you won't do or say anything that will make it harder for us to find the person we need because we're obviously still searching." He agreed. He then added that his son had come to him and said, "You really wanted that job, didn't you?" We were back talking again.

I tried to hold things together during the search for a new CEO. It took us 11 weeks—exactly 77 days—from the time I received Joe's resignation until we announced that Floyd Hall would be Kmart's new CEO. It also happened that the annual meeting took place during that time period, and I had to chair it. I couldn't announce anything, although I was hoping we would get to a final agreement with Floyd soon. The mood of the shareholders meeting was angry; I tried to calm them down by agreeing with them. "I'm angry too," I told them.

Not long after the annual meeting, we were able to announce that Kmart had a new chairman and CEO. I was relieved.

There had been a number of discussions within the board about how we could help Floyd be successful as chairman and CEO, and I thought there was agreement at the board level that I would continue to help Floyd when he came into Kmart. I would not maintain the same time commitment I had given as non-executive chairman during the search, but I would serve as chairman of an executive committee and become a lead director to help the new CEO. That plan was presented at the first board meeting Floyd attended and was unanimously approved.

It was a surprise at the next board meeting when, as we were considering approval of the minutes of the previous board meeting, Joe Flannery, who had missed the earlier meeting, said that he wanted to re-open the issue. I left the room and the board rescinded the resolution. When I came back in and learned of the decision, I said, "Thank you. I've been evaluated and I will leave the board." I resigned from the board effective in December, exactly 10 years after I had joined it.

Kmart filed for bankruptcy seven years later. I don't know if things would have played out differently if the executive-committee-chairman plan had remained in place. There were certainly those who thought I could have made a difference. One of those was John Smale, who wrote to Walter Elisha the month I resigned from Kmart's board, "I know Don Perkins agonized about the situation at Kmart. Frankly, I think the board would have been well advised to keep Don as non-executive chairman for a longer period of time than they did."

When Floyd Hall left Kmart, the company's stock was less than half the 12 5/8 level where it had been when he started. About two years after the board chose Chuck Conaway to be Floyd's successor, Kmart filed for bankruptcy.

One of the things Conaway did was put a low-price program in test stores and then roll it out chain-wide before the test was completed. I am told that the board agreed to the test, but was not informed in advance of the roll-out. Wal-Mart responded predictably by lowering their prices. Jewel had responded the same way two decades before when National Tea started a price war in Chicago (Chapter 6). We had taken them on, knowing that we had more staying power than they had—and that it was less expensive to retain share of market than it would ever be to regain it.

The price challenge was a blip in Wal-Mart's financial history. It bankrupted Kmart.

Most people point to physical reasons Kmart faltered ... the condition of the stores, poor stocking, poor logistics. These were just the visible symptoms. The real problem was people. Wal-Mart did a much better job finding and developing people. In fact, Sam Walton talked about the fact that Wal-Mart copied Kmart. He copied everything that was good and then did it better. Kmart simply did not have the talent developed in the business to manage its growth or to recover from its setbacks.

I expressed some of my frustration with the Kmart experience when I gave a speech in October 1995, accepting an award as Director of the Year from the National Association of Corporate Directors. It is perhaps even a little ironic that the previous recipient of the award was John Smale. I observed, in my speech, that the short-term imperatives of mutual-fund and pension-fund managers were increasingly in conflict with the longer-term views of individual owners of a corporation's shares and the directors of the corporation. This, I emphasized, was a recipe for tension. And in Kmart's case, it had not been a healthy tension.

In that speech, I recalled my simplistic view of my responsibility as a director three decades earlier—that my job was to represent shareholders. Over the years, I had begun to ask myself some questions about fiduciary responsibility. Did shareholders mean long-term or short-term holders of the company's stock? Did shareholders mean employee shareholders or arbitrageurs? My view of shareholders was certainly influenced by the fact that, when Jewel was acquired by American Stores in an unfriendly takeover a few years after I retired, 60 percent of the shares cashed in at the conclusion of the takeover had been held for less than six months.

Over the years, I redefined my role as a director. I concluded that my responsibility is to do everything possible to assure the long-term health of the enterprise. In this approach, I have to thoughtfully consider all of a corporation's constituencies ... shareholders (both large and small), but also other stakeholders, including employees and management, unions, suppliers, communities ... and even future constituencies, such as future employees. All of these groups are impacted by board decisions ... and by board failures.

Chapter 21

Adventures with Ventures

Parson Group
(Current Assets) 1994-2002
Neodesic 1997-2000
Nanophase 1998-present
Potomac Partners 1998-2002
Luminant 1999-2000
Cantilever 1999-2005
Arasys (CS Tech) 1999-2005
RoundTable Healthcare
Partners 2000-present
Blue Ridge Partners 2002-present

Between 1997 and 2002, I reached the various retirement ages for the major corporate boards on which I served. Instead of being the end of my corporate life, however, these retirements have been the beginning of another "next phase." Once again, "being repotted" is an apt characterization of my involvement with intriguing and always promising but only occasionally successful small ventures. Big or small, companies still require independence and judgment on their boards, and ventures benefit from the years of business experience and the personal networks of their board members.

I have invested time and money in ventures when I thought the management was smart and talented and honest and hardworking. Some of the ventures have been sold at a profit; others have been subsumed into other entities or terminated. The jury is still out on a few of them. They have had several attributes in common—all had management with a high degree of integrity—and all were fun to work with. And, all of their CEOs and boards had to listen to my Alfred Sloan story.

Steve Dubrul, a Lehman Brothers investment banker and Jewel board member, was the source of the Alfred Sloan story. Steve was between his two years at the Harvard Business School when he worked as an intern at General Motors. He was assigned to "carry bags" for Alfred Sloan, the famous founder of modern management at GM. After one meeting Steve attended with him, he said to Sloan, "You didn't like that idea, did you?" Sloan replied, "No, it's the dumbest idea I've heard in a long time."

Steve asked why Sloan hadn't stopped the discussion. Sloan's answer: "Young man, someday you will understand how expensive it is to develop a chief executive officer." I have repeated this story many, many times to young leaders with whom I have worked and to their board members who need to understand that CEOs are developed, not hatched.

• • •

PARSON GROUP

The Parson Group started in the early 1990s with a much catchier name. The company, which provided temporary and project staffing to finance, tax, and accounting departments, was originally called Current Assets. My acquaintance with Jeff Louis, one of the major investors in Current Assets and the stimulus for my involvement with the company, goes back to his childhood. And my acquaintance with his family can be traced to the close friendship that Phyllis and her parents had with Jeff's grandparents.

When Phyllis was in high school, her mother became ill and was hospitalized for an extended period of time. Henrietta and Jack Louis, close friends of the Babbs, asked Phyllis to stay with them for what turned out to be six months. (Jack Louis co-founded an advertising agency, Needham, Louis & Brobry; and Henrietta inherited a third interest in Johnson Wax from her father, Hib Johnson.) The Louises were very kind to Phyllis and me when we moved to Chicago.

John, the oldest son and Jeff's father, later became ambassador to the Court of St. James under President Reagan, an appointment that ended when, it was said, Nancy Reagan preferred someone else.

Not long after I joined the board, we discovered that the Current Assets name was being used by a company in California. The West Coast firm declined to sell the name, so Current Assets became the Parson Group. There was a lot of concern within the company about the name change.

My reaction was that a name means whatever you make it mean. I remember that when Jewel acquired Osco, many thought it a terrible name. But over time, Osco came to have a very positive meaning to drug store consumers. The change from Current Assets to Parson Group was easy and successful.

Parson was an interesting business and a tough one. Recruiting the talent and finding companies that needed the kind of help the firm provided wasn't easy. One of the approaches we took as a board was a bit out of the ordinary—we assigned a board member as mentor to each member of management. I mentored the CEO, Dan Weinfurter.

Six years after the initial investment, we sold Parson Group to a British firm for $55 million. This was a significant accomplishment for Dan Weinfurter. With a 20 percent compound annual return, it turned out to be a good investment.

● ● ●

NEODESIC

As I reached Illinova's retirement age of 70, Wally Scott, a professor in the business school at Northwestern (Kellogg) and a fellow member of the Illinova board, asked if I wanted some new young people to work with. That led to my investing in and joining the board of Neodesic.

Neodesic had been formed by one of Wally's students at Kellogg—Charlie Kwon. Charlie had met two computer "geeks" with NASA contracts to develop the use of natural language to direct robots. He thought he could work that talent into creating an interactive sales management program. It was difficult for me to judge the software program they developed, but Charlie was impressive.

Unfortunately, the idea never totally took off. When the business had used up about three quarters of the money raised for it in the angel round of funding, Charlie and his associates turned the program into a web site for independent truck owners.

Neodesic did well enough with the truck owners' web site that, when they did run out of money, they were able to sell the site for shares in an Internet company. The software itself was traded for shares in a second company, and Neodesic was dissolved.

• • •

NANOPHASE

Nanophase was founded to commercialize a process originally developed at Argonne National Laboratory: the creation of nano-size (billionths of a meter) materials. One way to describe the minute size of a nanocrystal is to think of stacking them on top of each other. With one nanocrystal for each of the almost 300 million people in the U.S., the stack would measure about 11.5 inches!

Nanoparticles produced by Nanophase are found in sunscreen and other personal care items marketed through BASF; in high-quality semiconductor applications of customers of Rohm & Itaas; in industrial paints and coatings sold through BYK Chemie; and in interior and exterior architectural paints and coatings produced by Behr. In its early years, Nanophase had to learn that there was limited demand for nanoparticles alone. However, when surface-treated or dispersed in appropriate solutions, they became viable in manufacturing processes.

When Nanophase's chairman, Len Batterson, approached me in 1998 about joining the board, I was intrigued with the technology and thought it would be another desirable learning experience. The company had already raised $35 million in an IPO the year before I joined the board; so at least, I thought, I wouldn't have the problem of raising money for the venture. Had I done better due diligence on the company, I probably would have declined the invitation. Joining the Nanophase board would lead to one of my most bizarre board experiences.

As I came to understand the people better, I learned that Bob Cross, the CEO, in addition to being a personal friend of Batterson, was under fire. The venture capitalists on the board were critical of Bob while Batterson was his ally.

It was generally agreed that we needed to bring additional, stable talent into the business and to the board. Since Bob Cross had the chairman's support, the only acceptable approach initially was to bring in a strong number-two person. The Spencer Stuart search yielded an outstanding candidate named Joe Cross (no relationship to the CEO); and, in order to get him to take the job, I promised I would stay on the board to help him.

In December 1998, not long after we brought Joe on board, he called me saying that he wanted to see me. When he arrived at my office, I was surprised to see that he had the top salesperson and the CFO with him. They were all highly agitated. They proceeded to share with me their concerns about the CEO's lack of realism.

When the three managers left my office that Friday, I immediately called the board chairman, Len Batterson, and asked him if I could talk to him in confidence. He said, "Of course."

I explained the situation. I told him that I thought he and I should visit with these three managers and that Bob Cross should not be involved in the conversation. Batterson agreed.

The next Tuesday, I got a frantic phone call in the middle of a Lucent board meeting in New York from one of the three Nanophase executives with whom I had visited four days previously. Bob Cross had fired all three of them that morning and had them escorted from the office by the local police. They said that these dramatic events were triggered by a phone call that Bob Cross had received. Joe Cross and his two colleagues were incredulous. I was even more so. The only person with whom I had discussed the situation was the board chairman.

I asked to have a special board meeting. We had only 24 hours before we would have to go public with the three firings. I left my Lucent board meeting in New York to participate by telephone in the special Nanophase board meeting, having talked to the other directors and our legal counsel in the meantime. The board was composed of Len Batterson; Bob Cross; three venture capitalists; Dick Siegel, the inventor of the company's original process; and me.

By a vote of five to two, we rescinded the firings of the previous day. By a vote of five to two, we dismissed the CEO. By a vote of five to one, since Bob Cross was no longer CEO or a director and could no longer vote, we installed Joe Cross as CEO and elected him a director. It is rare for a board to view a CEO's actions as that board did.

A few months later, in March, Batterson resigned from the board. As a consequence, 13 months after joining the board, I became its chairman. I talk to Joe Cross a number of times a week and have brought other independent directors onto the board, including Jerry Pearlman and Jim McClung, former leader of the world-wide chemical business at FMC.

More so than any other board on which I have served, the Nanophase board has involved opening doors to corporations around the world to have them understand the company and its products. Nanophase may be the only company in the world, other than large multi-product chemical companies, that can produce and coat nano-materials in commercial quantities. I have personally opened doors to companies like Xerox, Colgate Palmolive, P&G, 3M, Armstrong International, Kodak, Ace, and Corning. Not all have led to business relationships, but the high-level contacts have facilitated a more prompt answer than would otherwise have been the case.

An interesting outcome of networking came about when I accidentally learned that Art Kelly (the venture capitalist who had the "meaningful conversation" with a Chicago State University student—Chapter 17) was a member of the German BASF board. Although BASF was Nanophase's largest customer, we had never been able to have a high-level relationship to investigate broader business opportunities. Thanks to Art, those doors were opened.

In late 2003, Altana, a German pharmaceutical and chemical company, made an investment in Nanophase. Altana told us that they had looked at 400 possible companies, visited more than 60 of them, and chose Nanophase as the most developed of any they had seen. Their $10 million investment was a substitute for cost and time they would have had to devote to research to develop nano-materials on their own for their chemical coatings business.

Not many days after the Altana investment money was in the bank, Art Kelly called and asked if I knew about Susanne Klatten, the majority shareholder of Altana. I did not. Art told me about her and the fact that he sits next to her on two corporate boards, BMW in Germany and DataCard in Minneapolis. After we laughed about the serendipity of these relationships, Art made a memorable comment which I have relayed to the Nanophase board and management. Art praised Susanne and added, "You have the right address in Germany." At a dinner with her, I was impressed—she was the "right person" as well as the "right address" in Germany!

Nanotechnology has captured the imagination of investors; and Nanophase stock sells at a multiple of revenues. The company has yet to produce a profit.

I feel confident that demand for the kinds of nanoparticles produced by Nanophase will grow dramatically and that Nanophase is positioned to enjoy that growth.

• • •

CANTILEVER

Cantilever was a story of outstanding people fighting an uphill battle to bring a venture to profitability—Julie Goonewardene, the CEO of the company, and her husband, Jim Wallin, a computer genius who developed a software program they called the Readiness Engine. The Readiness Engine was designed to work across a variety of legacy IT systems within a company, bringing information together in a way that forces decisions.

The program had success at Cummins, helping that company identify and resolve warranty issues much sooner and enabling accounts receivable staff to spend their time taking action versus gathering information. The ratio of time spent researching issues to taking action has gone from 80/20 to 20/80, and accounts receivable have been reduced from 7 to 5.8 percent of sales.

While Cantilever showed promise of success, the money ran out before cash flow became positive and before seemingly imminent contracts were signed and producing revenue. The technology works, as the experience at Cummins demonstrates, and the people are outstanding—but the climate for systems investments was too difficult.

In early 2005, Cantilever was sold to one of its directors as an alternative to closing it down completely.

• • •

ARASYS (FORMERLY CS TECH)

Like Cantilever, CS Tech (as Arasys was originally called) was founded to commercialize computer programs. In this case, the programs helped companies manage all aspects of their printed material on an outsourced basis. What CS Tech demonstrated is that computer-aided management of printed material, such as financial or insurance sales material, is especially attractive to financial services companies operating in 50 different states, each of which may require different materials.

In those businesses, materials go in and out of date—times 50—and it can be difficult to get the right state-specific materials to the right salespeople and the right customers. Allstate seemed to be the breakthrough client that would enable Arasys to reach cash flow breakeven. Interestingly, the decision-maker at Allstate was someone I had worked with at Northwestern University on the capital campaign before she left to take a position at Allstate. It is indeed a small world, and this is another example of benefits from volunteering, not to mention the need for and the importance of networking in venture involvement.

The question we had to confront as a board in late 2002 was whether the company's growth would be limited by the modest amount of positive cash flow the business might generate, or whether we should seek a major investment to grow faster. Accepting venture capital money would bring some significant changes to the business, including losing control.

Gary Arakelian, Arasys's founder, technical whiz, and original leader, decided that, in order to grow, he had to give up much of his ownership and control of the business. Business founders typically have great difficulty doing that, but as one of the venture capitalists put it in a letter to Gary, "This process has been one of the most civilized and professional that I have undertaken in my career so far as vc [venture capitalist]... I look forward to partnering with you." Gary took pride in that affirmation and sent me a copy with a cover note thanking me for my mentoring and guidance "both explicitly and by example" in dealing with people. That was the high point of what turned into a failure.

Arasys raised $6.5 million from Sigma Partners, a highly successful Boston-based venture capital firm. But solving Allstate's problems was, in retrospect, an anomaly. Despite hiring a sales force and eventually a new CEO, sales results were not achieved. The business, which at one time seemed to have so much promise, failed. I resigned from the board in 2005, and the company was dissolved two years later.

• • •

POTOMAC PARTNERS/LUMINANT/BLUE RIDGE PARTNERS

Jim Corry is the common denominator in three ventures in which I have participated, beginning with Potomac Partners. Jim and I met in 1982, when I was recruiting volunteer talent from Arthur Andersen, Booz Allen Hamilton, and McKinsey to work on the Commercial Club's study of jobs in Chicago that would lead to the founding of the Civic Committee (Chapter 17). Jim was one of the impressive people Arthur Andersen contributed to the project when I asked for help.

After the jobs study, I didn't see Jim again until 15 years later, when I found myself sitting with him on the back porch of my home (the porch and the solarium being the oft-used sites for mentoring discussions—the choice dependent on the season). Jim came to talk to me about Potomac Partners, the company he founded to develop web-based applications using the Internet in new and creative ways. Potomac Partners worked with companies like Phillip Morris, United Airlines, and Wells Fargo.

The applications they developed addressed business process problems, rather than just being marketing tools, and the business grew as long as the dot-com world was growing. I enlisted an advisory board for Jim at Potomac Partners, including John Richman, retired chairman of Kraft (also a Yale classmate and a dear friend); Ellen Marram, former president of Nabisco and then Tropicana; and Jerry Pearlman.

Along the way, Jim had an opportunity to fold Potomac Partners into a roll-up of eight purportedly similar companies; the roll-up was called Luminant. In the course of the roll-up, I joined the Luminant board. Unfortunately, six of the eight companies turned out not to be any good. Luminant's creator, a former McKinsey consultant, was not effective, and the board was so ineffective that I tried to quit.

Instead, I ended up becoming chairman and was able to bring Jerry Pearlman and John Richman onto the board. We appointed Jim Corry CEO. Within 90 days, Jim reduced expenses by 75 percent and managed to give the company hope for survival. Had Luminant continued to grow at the same rate it had during its first year, it might have survived, but volume declined and the remaining liabilities didn't change.

The legacy of debt held by those who had sold their companies to Luminant for deferred cash payments threatened to take the company under in the declining sales environment the business faced. We put the company into a pre-packaged bankruptcy where it was sold to a competitor.

Not long afterwards, Jim came to visit with the idea for his next venture—Blue Ridge Partners. My first reaction, was to say, "Your last idea cost me so much, I'm not sure I can afford to listen to you." But I always bet on good people like Jim Corry, and I agreed to chair the advisory board for Blue Ridge Partners.

After doing consulting work with various twists, BlueRidge discovered a niche...consulting focused on increasing revenues. The offering has been particularly attractive to private equity firms whose efforts have more typically been to reduce costs. Their work begins with interviews with current, past, and lost customers; current and prior employees; and competitors. Mystery shoppers place telephone orders. After assembling information from the "Nine Voices of the Market," the opportunities for revenue improvement become apparent and corrective work begins.

Blue Ridge Partners is a virtual company, in that the consultants can live anywhere. Moreover, by not hiring people until the business needed them, the company had positive cash flow from the time it went into operation.

Seeing Jim's approach to virtual offices succeed is one of the experiences that helped me when I decided to give up my office in downtown Chicago and to work from home. After almost 30 years of maintaining an office at Jewel and another 20 years of officing in the Loop, the year 2001 marked the move to my virtual office. I would not have needed a Loop office for my first 20 post-Jewel years except for two reasons—the demands of my civic and not-for-profit involvements and the lack of electronic substitutes for proximity.

My longtime assistant, Marilyn Kaderabek, and I now get everything done electronically that we once did when we sat 20 feet apart in a traditional office set-up. We had the opportunity to practice the approach when I started to spend more time in Florida, while she still worked from our Loop office. Now, she works from her home, and it makes little difference whether I am north or south.

For someone whose business school class sessions from 1949 to 1951 never included the word "computer," I am amazed and amused to be able to enjoy the electronic virtual office of today.

• • •

ROUNDTABLE HEALTHCARE PARTNERS

RoundTable Healthcare Partners is the creation of a talented and experienced leader who also happens to be the grandson of the person from whom I bought my home in Winnetka in 1965. Lester B. Knight, III, the CEO of RoundTable, was the number-two person at Baxter Laboratories under Vern Loucks.

When Baxter's acquisition of American Hospital Supply failed to realize the synergies that had been projected for it (projected by Baxter, not by American Hospital Supply, whose CEO, Karl Bays, was a director of Jewel and a good friend), Baxter decided to spin it off under the leadership of Lester Knight. Lester ran the company (Allegiance) for a few years, sold it to Cardinal Health, and then set out to determine what he would do next.

He sat on our porch in Winnetka to discuss his range of possibilities. A very capable leader with significant expertise and experience in health care, Lester assembled a team beginning with two operating managers who had worked with him at Baxter and Allegiance and a mergers-and-acquisitions manager from a banking firm in Chicago. The venture was named RoundTable Healthcare Partners.

The company's purpose has been to buy, revitalize, and grow businesses related to health care. In a period of less than a year ending in 2002, Lester and his associates raised $400 million, selling the basic soundness of their idea and their operating experience. Lester asked me to be on his advisory board with Si Cathcart (a former Jewel director and mentor of mine, now deceased); Lester's father, Chuck Knight (who very successfully ran Emerson Electric); Lester Crown (chairman of Henry Crown and Company); and Ned Jannotta (managing partner at William Blair).

The initial investment was in a business that recycles and reconditions used hospital supplies and equipment. The recycled equipment can save money for hospitals and patients. The second investment was in Sabex, a generic drug company from Canada which was planning to come to the United States, a market that is very well understood by the RoundTable team. The Sabex investment was sold to Sandoz, an international pharmaceutical company. The return from this single sale assures the success of the entire fund.

A third major investment came from my networking. I brought Lester together with Rod Goldstein, CEO of Frontenac (a Chicago-based venture capital firm) in the solarium of my home. Out of the discussion came an interest on the part of RoundTable to acquire the health care equipment companies of the Marmon Group, a Pritzker family investment. In addition to the Hyatt hotels and numerous other investments, the Pritzkers owned seven medical equipment companies. The experience of RoundTable's management team did wonders for a business so decentralized that, even under common ownership, the companies did not work together and, on occasion, even competed.

• • •

Reflecting on my experiences with ventures, I am struck by the role that networking has played in my ability to contribute. It has often beeen possible for me to initiate a contact or a request out of personal experience. It would be a cold call for someone else. And importantly, the contact is most often a plus for both parties. All of the ventures with which I am involved have been opportunities to work with outstanding people, to become acquainted with fascinating business opportunities and issues, and to stay active. This latest version of "being repotted" has been an extraordinarily good way to stay active in the phase of life I call my "life of variety."

CHAPTER 22

A BRAND NAME IN CORPORATE GOVERNANCE

T he continued strength and acceptance of corporations in our country will be more assured if independent, outside boards of directors provide checks and balances and oversight of management. I made this statement not in 2002 after the corporate scandals epitomized by Enron, but in 1983 when I retired from the Jewel board. I added that oversight, complete with the requisite checks and balances, was something that the Jewel board exercised exceptionally well.

In fact, as I have become fond of saying, all the corporate governance practices that seem like good ideas post-Enron were understood to be good ideas pre-Enron. My views on corporate governance have matured through the years and draw on my experiences on a variety of boards, but the inclusion of outside directors and board independence were top priorities from early in my career.

From the time that I could influence Jewel beginning in the 1960s, I worked with George Clements on increasing the independence of the Jewel board of directors. The only truly independent board member at that time was Vernon Jannotta, a descendent of the Ross family, which had founded Jewel. Most of Jewel's directors were officers of the company. Jewel's non-management directors then included Jim Allen, chairman of Booz Allen Hamilton, and Ed McDermott of McDermott, Will and Emery. Booz Allen did consulting work for Jewel and McDermott, Will and Emery did legal work, so neither Jim nor Ed was independent by today's standards.

Two of the directors were from Jewel's original investment bankers—Stan Miller from Goldman Sachs and Steve Dubrul from Lehman Brothers. A representative of each of these firms had served continuously on the board since the company went public in 1916. Having our investment bankers on the board had been a tradition, but it was awkward when the company issued stock and their firms set the issuing price. It reminded me whose payroll they were on.

As George Clements and I thought through the talent we wanted on the Jewel board, two criteria stood out. We needed good, experienced advice and counsel, and we wanted a truly independent board. I was reflecting on what I was learning about corporate governance. In my first two board experiences, Inland Steel and Kodak, I was one of a minority of independent directors, and board meetings were too much like management meetings. I also looked at the Jewel board as a very inexpensive way to get outstanding talent helping us at Jewel.

We attracted deans of the Harvard Business School (first George Baker and later Larry Fouraker) to the board. Over the course of the years, we also had Jim Olsen, when he was chairman of AT&T; Karl Bays, CEO of American Hospital Supply; Si Cathcart, chairman of ITW; Father Ray Baumhart, president of Loyola University; and Dick Ogilvie, following his service as governor of Illinois.

We also wanted women on the board, so I asked for candidate suggestions and met Jewel Lafontant. When Jewel resigned to become U.S. Trade Representative, we added Barbara Scott Preiskel as a director. The Jewel board was Barbara's first. She was a graduate of Wellesley and the Yale Law School (at a time when African-American women were far from the norm) and a vice president of the Motion Picture Academy of Arts and Sciences. We were impressed, and she turned out to be such an outstanding director that I later recommended her for the Ford Foundation board. She would also serve on the GE board.

We recruited Lou Gerstner (later CEO of IBM), who was running much of the travel and credit business at American Express at the time, and others whose advice, counsel, and independence were tremendously helpful to Jewel. One Sunday, I read in the paper that Bob Reneker, CEO of Swift (Esmark), was retiring. It would have been a conflict to have named him to the board prior to that time, because Jewel was a customer. Bob was just five years away from Jewel's mandatory retirement age, but I reasoned that I would like to have Bob's help and counsel for five years.

My reasoning was similar when Art Schultz retired from Foote, Cone & Belding. Art looked at our advertising and public relations with a thoughtful and challenging eye and was an outstanding director. He so impressed Walter Elisha at Jewel that Walter invited him to join the Springs Industries board when Walter became CEO there.

One of the changes we made to enable us to recruit outstanding outside directors was to the board's meeting schedule. Instead of meeting monthly, as many companies did, we met only four times a year. When we did meet, however, we wanted the directors' time for a full 24 hours. We would start with committee meetings one afternoon and finish up with the board meeting the next day.

Although Jewel wasn't a very big company at the time, this strategy helped us attract outstanding but very busy people to our board. Between meetings, I sent out a weekly communication with the sales results of the major parts of the business compared with those from the previous year and anything else I thought would be of interest. Not a week passed without directors being reminded of their Jewel involvement.

We sent out a board report before each meeting written by the heads of each operating company and unedited by me or by any corporate staff member. Every board meeting agenda was planned with an hour set aside for directors to talk about whatever *they* wanted to discuss. Because of the information they had received from the operating heads, it was never very hard to start the questions and discussion.

Whenever a director was critical of one of the Jewel companies, that director was invited to spend a day in that business. We paid a per diem to directors to do that. The director would then come back and report firsthand to the board on his/her observations. I didn't implement this policy just to promote disclosure and good corporate governance; I was also acting from the purely selfish desire to garner all the help I could get!

In 1970, when I was elected chairman, the fifteen-member Jewel board included ten current or former employees and three directors whose firms did work for the company. The only two completely independent outside directors were Si Cathcart, chairman of Illinois Tool Works, and George Baker, Larry Fouraker's predecessor as dean of the Harvard Business School. When I left the board in 1983, the board consisted of three members of management (Wes Christopherson, Dick Cline, and Walter Elisha) and nine very independent directors.

The importance of help and oversight from a strong independent board cannot be overstated. Directors can see ideas and issues that those in the business may not, because they are so close to it. For example, one time when we were discussing the Osco Drug business, thoughtful, perceptive Ray Baumhart said, "We spend so much time and effort auditing the money in the business. Shouldn't we be spending more time and effort auditing the drugs in the business?" I thought it was a brilliant comment, and we increased our controls over and audits of prescription drugs.

Father Baumhart provided another example of independence when the proposal for the American Stores acquisition of Jewel came to the board a few years after I retired. He was the only director who voted against the acquisition; he voted against it because he felt it was wrong for the people in the business. He knew his vote would not change the outcome, but he voted his conscience.

Si Cathcart of ITW and Karl Bays of American Hospital Supply were both outstanding directors. Both had much more extensive business experience in Mexico than Jewel people did, for example, which was helpful when Jewel was getting involved with Aurrera. They were cautious because they had trouble believing that our partners, the Arangos, were as straightforward and honest as they appeared (and, in fact, were—Chapter 6).

Having directors with the stature of those on the Jewel board helped us recruit new MBAs into our management program, as well as provide employee relations benefits. Barbara Preiskel was a great symbol for and communicator to women and minorities in our business, a real plus given the nature of the employee population in Jewel stores.

Bob Reneker provided wise counsel many times. One of those times was when Jewel's auditors, Touche-Ross, asked me to write an article about what a chairman and CEO should expect from his/her board. When I sent my thoughts to Bob, he asked me why I didn't also describe the other side of the relationship—what the board should expect from the CEO. The work I did on that led to a *Harvard Business Review* article, published in 1979, the year before I stepped down as chairman and CEO. In that article, I wrote:

> If I were to try to pick out one element that is most important in the successful functioning of a chairman and a board in the interest of a company and its shareholders, that element would be attitude. Congress can write laws, the SEC can issue regulations,

and advocate groups can demand representation. But nothing is as important as a chairman who wants counsel and able directors who desire to be and in fact are both challenging and helpful.

A board of directors can contribute minimally if it acts as a necessary legal entity tolerated by the chairman. On the other hand, a board can contribute a great deal if it acts as a truly diverse group of informed and interested counselors, advisers, and directors of management.

I described what I felt were the primary expectations in my relationship with the Jewel board—the components of attitude that would contribute to a successful relationship. I said that there were both obvious expectations and less obvious ones, some of the less obvious ones being:

- They expect me to remember that I am a company employee.
- They expect me to operate in a style consistent with genuine concern for people.
- They expect regular communication about problems as well as achievements.
- They expect me to show respect for their time.
- They expect a certain quality and style of board meetings.
- They expect me to welcome their involvement and oversight.

When it came to describing the CEO's expectations of the board, the cornerstone of the list was independence, but the list detailed other elements characterizing that "challenging and helpful" attitude so vital in a director:

- Complete independence.
- A lack of need for the Jewel board seat (another dimension of independence).
- Appreciation for the human as well as the financial aspects of our business.

- Recognition of the very distinct differences between the daily responsibility of management and the periodic responsibility of directors to evaluate plans and results (avoiding micro-management).
- A sense of what's significant.
- Challenge to management thinking.
- A genuine interest in Jewel.
- A willingness to participate in an active discussion and take a position, even if it is in the minority.

I have had a number of opportunities in recent years to distill and share my conclusions on the role of directors. The ideal director, I believe, would answer "yes" to the following questions:

- Can you say that your independence is never compromised by a need for prestige or income, or by loyalty to an individual who invited you to join the board?
- Have you told the CEO your concerns about the corporation and his or her administration of it?
- Do you avoid trying to micro-manage the corporation from a board seat?
- Have you shown your belief in the future of the corporation by taking some or all of your director's compensation in company shares?
- Do you spend enough time learning about the corporation and its industry to question the reasonableness of the management's plans and projections?
- Do you refrain from speaking on behalf of the company or discussing board deliberations outside of the board room?
- Are you making a contribution to the board's consideration of strategy, top management succession, and executive compensation?
- Are you willing to vote as a minority of one on a board issue?

- Are you prepared to find a replacement for a fellow director who is not pulling his or her weight?
- If necessary, are you prepared to replace a CEO?

One of the opportunities I have had to promote and participate in discussions of corporate governance issues in recent years has been a series of corporate governance conferences that evolved from my service on the advisory board of Spencer Stuart.

In 1986, about the time Jane and I were married, I was on 12 boards and certainly wasn't looking for anything else to do when I got a call from Tom Neff at Spencer Stuart asking me if I would consider joining their advisory board. The other members of the board were outstanding—including Reg Jones (the former head of General Electric) and R.J. Miller, the retired dean of the Stanford Business School. The fact that they met only twice a year—once in Bermuda, where Jane could accompany me—made it easier to say yes.

As an advisory board, we discussed Spencer Stuart's searches and companies that might need a search. However, the most important discussions were strategic. One key issue the advisory board helped resolve was whether Spencer Stuart should remain private or go public. In 1999, at the peak of the boom stock years, Spencer Stuart's two primary competitors—Korn Ferry and Heidrick and Struggles—both went public.

When asked for my thinking on the subject, I remembered back to the early 1970s when Booz Allen Hamilton had gone public as a way to buy out Jim Allen's ownership in the business. I had been asked to be a director, the only outside director, of the new publicly traded company. Despite the fact that Jim Allen was on Jewel's board and had been a mentor to me, I politely declined, citing how much I had to do at Jewel.

Within a few years, Booz Allen's stock price declined dramatically and they realized what a mistake it had been to take the company public. A personal services firm, by its nature, has a very difficult time with transparency in disclosures, the pressure of quarterly earnings reports, and stock options that would inevitably be under water at some point. The partners at Booz Allen borrowed money to take the firm private again.

With the benefit of that and similar history lessons, the Spencer Stuart advisory board was unanimous in feeling that the firm should remain private. The company is better off today as a result of that decision.

In its efforts to help the firm attract the attention of CEOs, Spencer Stuart held conferences with expensive speakers but found that the right people did not attend. What CEOs wanted in the late 1980s was to talk about something they really cared about such as corporate governance, an area where they were newly under attack. I also recommended getting the Kellogg School of Management at Northwestern and Booz Allen Hamilton involved, because that would heighten the credibility of the conference.

The first conference, jointly sponsored by the three organizations, was held in 1990, and was specifically designed to bring institutional investors together with corporate directors. It provided a successful forum for the two groups to air and discuss issues. Succeeding years have witnessed even greater success, prestige, participation, and a fascinating evolution in the topics we have addressed. The 17th annual conference is scheduled in 2008.

At the conference that took place on the heels of the Enron revelations and similar corporate scandals, I introduced a session entitled "How can boards be revitalized given the customary expectations of tenure of most directors?" with three thoughts and three questions:

Thoughts:
- Peers are uncomfortable criticizing or evaluating each other.
- Once an individual joins a board, there is seldom a process to improve his or her quality of participation.

- Director turnover initiated by the CEO gives the CEO too much control over the board, but director turnover initiated by the board too rarely happens.

Questions:
- Isn't it intellectually dishonest to re-slate a continuing director who has not been evaluated by his or her peers on the board?
- While most boards evaluate their CEOs, are many doing a good job of evaluating their directors?
- Are you comfortable that each member of your board could protect your interests if deposed in important and potentially expensive litigation?

My bias was contained in my questions. Most board members expect to continue to be re-slated at annual meetings until they reach a mandatory retirement age, assuming one exists. Typically it requires some unusual form of non-performance for an existing board member to be dropped from a proposed re-election slate.

Today, the compensation committee has to explain how the CEO was paid and why. This process has led to better evaluations of CEO performance than formerly was the case, because it is hard to explain why a board compensated a CEO as it did without some kind of evaluation.

The board nominating committee process could be similar. I have suggested that the members of the nominating committee (composed entirely of independent directors) should sign their report in the annual proxy statement stating that each of the members of the board being presented to shareholders has been evaluated, and that each is worthy of support.

Often, the first step in instituting a board evaluation process is to overcome the resistance of sitting directors. At one corporate governance conference, I explained it this way:

> The biggest challenge of the evaluation process is to get directors interested in it. Many if not most directors do not

want to be evaluated. Some say that they are concerned about interfering with the collegiality of boards. I think in the post-Sarbanes-Oxley era, it is no longer sensible to try to preserve the "collegiality of boards."

Where I have been able to persuade boards that we ought to have an evaluation process, we begin by discussing the qualifications of the directors we want. In this way, we set the standard against which some evaluation process would be developed. We then work out a series of questions, including questions that relate to the way the chairman runs the board, the way the board operates, the way the committees operate, and conclude with evaluations of the individual directors. Boards accept the first three of those pretty easily. It's evaluating individual directors which causes tensions to surface.

On one board where I was proposing evaluation, one of the directors said, "Don, judge not lest ye be judged!" I was so taken aback by the biblical rhetoric of the comment that I didn't have the right answer, which would have been, "I'm perfectly willing to be judged!"

Then, of course, the question is "Who gets the information? Who assembles it? Doesn't this become fodder for discovery in a lawsuit?" I find it illogical to suggest that it is better not to have an evaluation process because the result might become subject to discovery than it is to have one that improves and develops board member contributions.

When our first governance conference was held, Enron, Adelphia, and WorldCom were closer to being start-up companies. Today, they are infamous examples of corporate governance failures. In 1990, the hot topic was how to align management compensation with shareholder interests. The unintended consequence of the stock-related plans that many companies began to put in place has been compensation levels that have gotten out of hand, that are unpredictable and, at times, egregious.

One major change since that firest conference has been a shift of power from the CEO to the board. Because directors are now predominantly independent, the balance of power is shifting to those independent directors. And along with power, come increased demands for time and participation. As I said at one conference:

> In 1990, most active and retired CEOs wanted to be directors of other companies. Since then, the recognition of the amount of work to be done by directors and of the liabilities they may face has led to a sea change. For much of the time that I served on a dozen or so corporate boards, I had a 98.5 percent attendance record. I kept track of that in case anybody ever asked me about it at an annual meeting. And I did that in 60 percent of my available work time. Today, it would probably take 120 percent of my available time—an impossible task.

One participant in the 2003 conference was Raymond Troubh. Ray has had the unenviable task of picking up the pieces of the board at Enron. Ray had served as a strong, independent director of companies such as Becton-Dickinson, Health Net, and Time Warner, on whose board I served with him. Ray once referred to that experience, saying, "The first time I heard 'corporate governance' as an expression was from Don Perkins, 20 or 25 years ago on the Time Warner board."

> He has been a fighter for corporate governance from the beginning. He took a lot of abuse, verbal and other, because he pushed certain reforms on various boards, and those reforms are finally being recognized.

I am proud of that description. The fact that I have become something of an activist on corporate governance issues led Doug Gray, a friend, recently to tell me that I was becoming a "brand name in corporate governance." I do not claim that status. I can claim more than 350 cumulataive years as a director of corporations and and a similar number serving on boards of not-for-profit organizations. I have interacted with CEOs and I have chaired boards. I can claim some strongly held feelings about what I think is right, and what I know, from experience, works. And, I can claim the willingness to speak my mind—whether that be in a boardroom or at a governance conference or mentoring an individual CEO or board member.

Pre-or post-Enron, the words with which I started the chapter still hold true: "The continued strength and acceptance of corporations in our country will be more assured if independent outside boards of directors provide checks and balances and oversight of management." It has been gratifying to observe the positive effects of that principle being not only more broadly recognized, but put into practice.

CHAPTER 23

MENTORS

I n December 1999, I received a letter from Tom Jorde, whom I had not seen in over 20 years. This is what he wrote:

Dear Don,

As the millennium draws near, I write to salute and thank you for all you did for me to make my life so wonderful. It has been many years since we have talked, but I will never forget that fateful visit to your office in Barrington, when you thought you were going to meet a successful college junior, but instead found a rather precocious high school junior at your doorstep. There are few CEOs who would ever have been as welcoming and enthusiastic as you were.

The lightning bolt in my life that you delivered was your question, "Are you going to Yale?" No one from my high school in Castro Valley had ever applied to an Ivy League college. But you knew my grades and what I had accomplished, so you pushed me ...

Yale changed my world. I went on from the undergraduate program to Yale Law School. I had an opportunity to clerk for Justice Brennan, practiced law in San Francisco for five years, and then joined the law faculty at the University of California at Berkeley (Boalt Hall Law School) ... I also formed an economics consulting firm. Ten years later, Law & Economics Consulting Group went public with an IPO on the NYSE. Unexpectedly, six months later, we were acquired by the Metzler Group. All of a sudden, paper wealth became liquid. American capital markets are quite extraordinary! As a result, I have now been able to resume full-time teaching at Boalt and devote my attention to charities and seeing what I can do to help others.

Among my first gifts were $1 million to Yale and $1 million to Boalt. I tell you this not to boast, but so that you can share in my joy at being in a position now to make such gifts. You were responsible! Thank you!

Everything Tom Jorde accomplished he accomplished through hard work, education, and his own abilities. What I did for him was ask questions and give advice that no one in his immediate sphere could offer, at a time when he was making important decisions. In other words, I did for Tom what Judge Mix had done for me. The same is true for others I have talked with, encouraged, and challenged—in short, mentored—over the years.

Mentoring the Tom Jordes of the world was the best way I could express my gratitude to the people who mentored me and provided the important role models in my life. Many of them have already appeared in my narrative. One of the most important was George Clements, my Jewel predecessor. During the period of time that I was executive vice president and president of Jewel, George included me in every strategic consideration about the business.

Mentoring also involved helping me see that the principles embodied in the Jewel Concepts (Chapter 7), which may have seemed corny when I first heard them, were really the right way to run a business. George was a very unselfish person. I never heard him put himself ahead of the organization in terms of what should be done or what was fair.

The Jewel Concepts put into words the business philosophies of Frank Lunding, George Clements, and me. Not only were they guidelines for me during my Jewel years, but they stayed with me in my years of board service. The need to develop people ... the need to have some part of compensation relate to an individual's personal achievements ... the need to understand and relate to customers ... and, of course, the management approach required by the upside-down organization chart ... all these were examples of the Clements and Lunding mentoring influence on me. Numerous managers with whom I have worked have been challenged by me to live up to principles like these.

One concept that George encouraged me to embrace was decentralization with local control. He pointed to the fact that, when an outstanding Chicago-area retail location became available, A&P, with its headquarters in New York; National, with its headquarters in Minnesota; and Kroger, with its headquarters in Ohio, all had to go through the ritual of headquarters approval—while Jewel was signing the lease for the property. Jewel managed its business by deciding at the beginning of the year how many stores would be built and how much we would spend on capital, rather than by micromanaging location by location as we went through the year.

Across the company, we always tried to make sure that process did not interfere with getting things done. Having independent operating companies with strong leadership gave us confidence that, if something needed to be done for customers, Jewel people could respond quickly. This practice was a contrast with organizations that were more hierarchical and didn't trust their people, as Jewel did.

Of course, we didn't always agree about everything. I remember when I was buying the house in Winnetka, George said, "I guess you can spend your money any way you like, but it's a very expensive house." And neither he nor Frank Lunding thought that it made sense for me to announce up front that I would limit my tenure as chairman to 10 years. But I always appreciated George's candor, judgment, and counsel.

The mentoring relationships at Jewel stimulated a fair amount of discussion beyond Jewel when they became the subject of a 1978 *Harvard Business Review* article called, "Everyone who makes it has a mentor." The article comprised interviews with three generations of Jewel management: Frank Lunding, George Clements, and me.

The article noted the young ages at which each of the three of us became leaders at Jewel and then passed the baton to the next generation well before typical retirement age. "That simple fact epitomizes what is now a Jewel tradition; young people shall be given their heads to challenge the organization to grow," as the article put it.

I like that description because it sets up mentoring as a two-way street. It is not just about an older, more experienced mentor showing his or her mentee the ropes and sending up alarm signals when danger looms. It is also about ensuring the appropriate development experiences, an environment in which the younger, less-experienced mentee has the ability to impact the organization and improve it while he or she grows into a leadership position. George didn't single me out at Jewel. He did make certain that a number of us had the experiences that would let us develop into the best possible managers we could be.

This characterization of mentoring at Jewel brings to mind the innumerable times I have been in a board or committee meeting reviewing the talent of a business when someone says, "But he (or she) is only 35 …" or whatever age was relevant. At that point, I always ask, "What were *you* doing at 35?" Virtually anyone who is a CEO or board member or a senior member of management had some significant responsibility at a young age. Unfortunately, as people are successful and get older, they seem to forget that someone took a risk with them when they were "that age."

Sometimes assuring that young people have those developmental experiences can cost money. George must have been recalling the $50,000 he agreed to invest in my failed effort to put home shopping catalogs in Jewel stores when he said in the same *Harvard Business Review* interview, "Young people absolutely have to have the freedom to make mistakes. Just so they aren't too big. What was more important, me being right or Don learning?" George was really saying the same thing that Alfred Sloan said to Steve Dubrul (Chapter 21) when he observed that it can be expensive to develop a CEO.

When I started at Jewel, I knew that George would be the toughest nut to crack. Frank Lunding would naturally be impressed with my education, but George, who had just one year at the University of Illinois, was skeptical and thought I might be over-educated for the business.

As George described it to the *Harvard Business Review*, "The only other thing I had to do besides give him experience was to get him—you know 'the bright boy right out of the Harvard Business School'—accepted in the organization." I knew that I had finally won George over when he called me in one day and asked, "How do we get some more talent like you into the business?"

The charge from George to figure out how to bring new talent into the business gave rise to the Jewel corporate sponsorship program. I built on my early post-business-school experience at McCann Erickson and the training program that Don Booz had arranged for me at Jewel.

The program we developed involved assigning each MBA that we recruited to a member of senior management who would serve as a "sponsor"—the term that we used instead of "mentor." Not every member of management made a good sponsor, but most did and those were the people who served in the role.

As candidates came through during the interview process, they would meet with a number of us, including several who were potential sponsors. Once the new MBA was on board, the sponsor's job was to check on his or her mentee from time to time, visit regularly with him or her, provide feedback on performance, and participate in his or her placement in the business when the year of training and exposure to our businesses was completed.

The sponsorship program was a great selling point for the talent we wanted to attract to Jewel. I would say to the young people we were trying to recruit, "We're going to do something for you that I don't think any other companies will offer. We're going to arrange for you to see all parts of this company. When you finish your training, you will have seen the breadth and variety in Jewel and understand it better than anyone short of those at the top of the business."

Each trainee would get to know people throughout the business in the course of working in several different areas or companies. Each one would also have a good relationship with a senior member of management, his or her sponsor. Those friendships paid dividends for Jewel and for the individuals throughout their careers.

At the end of the training year, the various operating companies would bid on the graduates of the corporate sponsorship program. The bidding did not involve salary, which had already been set. The bids were the development programs the operating companies were prepared to put in place. Each operating company that wanted a trainee would have to articulate what they would commit to do to help the person develop and grow.

When we initiated the corporate sponsorship program, most Jewel operating people thought it was a dumb idea. But as soon as they saw it in operation and saw the people rather than the concept, they forgot their objection to the program and wanted the talent. The program took hold and turned out to be more than a powerful recruiting tool. It was also a great retention tool. Graduates of the corporate sponsorship program were likely to see Jewel as their career.

Some of the early objections to the corporate sponsorship program came from concerns that it would confer "crown prince" status on those in the program. We addressed that concern, although I have to say that having an active program to recruit MBAs produced a very interesting phenomenon at Jewel.

When other Jewel young people started seeing the quality of the MBAs that were coming into the business, they realized that having an MBA was an advantage. Many Jewel people began taking advantage of Jewel's tuition assistance program to get their MBAs in the evening programs at the University of Chicago, Northwestern, and elsewhere. Some did so without having graduated from college.

We addressed the "crown prince" concern with the creation of the Management Development Council. Key people in the business could appoint those employees they thought were every bit as good as any of the new MBAs to the council—a total of a dozen employees at a time.

I would get the council together at the start of each year and say, "This is not a scout troop, and we're not appointing a scoutmaster." No one from management acted as an overseer. The council elected its own leader (and it was always fascinating to see who was elected). We gave the council members a half-day per month off, paid for dinner, and gave them the power of subpoena for anyone in the organization. We gave them access to Jewel's directors—something that impressed the directors as much as the council members. They were to use this time to their best advantage and to increase their knowledge of the business.

Membership in this group proved to be something very desirable and led to friendships and learning across corporate lines that otherwise would not have happened. It was, for its members, a development experience not unlike the corporate sponsorship program. It also silenced the critics and the charges that we were creating crown princes.

While George Clements stands out as a mentor, he was not my first mentor at Jewel. The first was Don Booz. In addition to being my primary corporate contact when I was in training, Don lived not far from me, and we would commute to Barrington together whenever both of us were in town.

Those car rides gave us the chance to discuss just about everything that was going on in the business and to speculate on how we would change things if the decisions were ours. The talks during those car rides are one reason that I became fond in later years of asking young people at Jewel, "Have you reorganized the business lately?"

Don was very bright, but caustic. He was a critic of almost everything he saw. His insights were always right in direction, but he would express his views as extremes. He had trouble giving balance to his observations.

Although Don did not enjoy general acceptance at Jewel, I will always be grateful for his mentoring. I also appreciated his endless supply of colorful "sayings," which expressed his philosophic outlook on people and what made them tick, such as:

> **Saying #1:** The question that has not been asked cannot be answered.
> **Saying #2:** Those who name their chickens seldom eat them for Sunday dinner.
> **Saying #3:** Every man gets the wife he deserves.

I have often referred to Don and his sayings, quoted or occasionally paraphrased.

Another mentor at Jewel was Bob Updegraff, one of Jewel's early outside directors (he also was a director of other companies, including retailer W.T. Grant). Bob had gone to work directly out of high school, yet he was as good with words as anyone I have known and a very wise man.

In addition to providing me with the motto I keep posted near my desk—"A Calm Temperament Expectant of Good"— he gave me much sage counsel. Whenever I see a cluttered highway billboard that is hard to read, I think of Bob. When he came to our offices to work with us, he would toss our route sales material on the floor, stand over it and then ask, "Can you read it from here?"

One day when I was talking with Bob, I must have said something like, "I can't figure out why they're doing that," referring to some management decision that didn't make sense to me. Bob said, "What you really ought to do when you have a thought like that is write it down on a piece of paper. Keep your list of the things that make you say, 'I can't figure out why they're doing that.' Someday, when you're in a position to change things, take the list out and read it."

I have had mentors in the corporate world outside Jewel, as well. Two that I would name as among the most significant were Irwin Miller at Cummins and Charlie Brown at AT&T. Perhaps I should call them role models. In any event, I admired them and observed how they handled people: how they brought them into the business, let them get their hands dirty, and then gave them other jobs to do, while they showed their support and trust.

Charlie Brown's foresight and ability to plan ahead were illustrated in June 1980, two years before the divestiture plan at AT&T was approved and three and a half years before it was implemented. With the approval of the FCC (Federal Communications Commission), he divided AT&T into two parts, one regulated and the other deregulated. This gave Charlie a chance to observe some of his people in a competitive environment before he knew for sure what the ultimate outcome of the various legal and regulatory attacks on the company would be.

I also learned a lot from observing Irwin Miller. I especially remember a comment Irwin made, years ago, as he was reflecting on some of the bad business actions of the time. He said, "We are losing our freedom not because of some monster government, but because we (businessmen) have abused our freedoms when we had them." This was long before the tragedies of Enron, Arthur Andersen, WorldCom, and HealthSouth.

I admired the way Irwin and Charlie worked with their boards, especially in the very difficult situations each of them encountered. Both Irwin and Charlie were the antitheses of the desk-thumping, dictatorial, imperial chairmen I saw hurt other companies. They were just genuinely good people and fun to work with. They reinforced what came naturally to me—that it is far better to be yourself than to strike a pose when it comes to managing and leading people.

Over the years I would find that, in the same way I watched and learned from George Clements, Irwin Miller, and Charlie Brown, others were watching me, particularly when I retired from Jewel at the age of 53. At that time, I began having discussions with many sitting CEOs or other high-ranking people in business and other institutions about "what it was like" to leave the CEO job at an early age. I could have called them the "Life after CEO" discussions; I'd be very surprised if I haven't had at least 100 such conversations.

Setting aside the question of whether they could afford to leave their CEO job (an issue I always reminded them of), I would say something like, "I have two questions for you, and I don't want to hear your answers because I won't know whether to believe them or not. Instead, answer these two questions for yourself, and you will have a much better understanding of what you want to do and why. The first question is, 'At this point in your life, what are you trying to prove?' And the second question is, 'Who are you trying to prove it to?'" I can't tell you how many people I have met in my life who were still trying to prove themselves to their deceased parents.

Some of those with whom I have had this type of discussion were in the executive outplacement program at Jannotta-Bray (the outplacement firm founded by Joe Jannotta and Bud Bray—later merged with Right Associates). Jannotta-Bray provided me with office space during the early 1990s in return for which I counseled their most senior clients. In these conversations, the first question I learned to ask was, "Are you angry?"

Some people were so angry about losing their jobs that they couldn't start to work on their futures. As if dealing with someone going through a divorce, I would counsel people that as long as they were angry, they were unlikely to make progress in moving to the next phase of their lives.

Whether talking with an outplaced manager who was ready to move on or a current CEO thinking of his or her future, I often offer my thoughts on the "phases of life." Retirement is like an admission of mortality for many in the corporate world. And admitting that we are mortal is not something that comes easily to active executives. But the end of one's corporate reign is not the end of life; there are other phases. I have said to many people, "You have the prospect of living longer than your predecessors did. You really ought to think about what you're going to do from 65 to 85 with the same energy and dedication you have used deciding what you will do until age 65."

As I think of mentoring, my relationship with John McCarter has been typically satisfying. I first became acquainted with John when he was named director of the Illinois Bureau of the Budget in the Ogilvie administration. I learned that John has a great deal to recommend him. He graduated from Princeton and the Harvard Business School and was a White House Fellow. He is also a natural leader and a genuinely nice person.

John and I have discussed his career decisions over the years—when he went from directing the Illinois Bureau of the Budget under Governor Dick Ogilvie to DeKalb, an agribusiness company (now part of Monsanto), where he spent 17 years …when he went from DeKalb to spend 13 years as a consultant and manager at Booz Allen Hamilton, the management consulting firm where he had worked before joining the Ogilvie administration … and when he went from Booz Allen Hamilton to the Field Museum of Natural History, where he has served with distinction for more than a decade.

I will always remember our conversation when John was considering the Field Museum offer. After we discussed the creativity of the board members who sought him out, I asked if he could afford the decrease in income. His answer was that he could. My advice then was that he should go for it. One of the benefits, I added, was that age 65 would then pass as just another birthday. John would already have determined what he would be doing in the "next phase" of his life. John is the envy of many younger people who see the variety in his career as something they would like to emulate.

Like John McCarter, I am a believer in variety in careers and in life. I did not stop working when I retired from Jewel. What I did was trade one title in on what I like to refer to as a "life of variety." Although I am undoubtedly guilty of rationalizing my own life, I have found that, with my life of variety, the typical corporate retirement age of 65 went by with hardly any notice.

Having a diverse array of activities and involvements also makes it easier to "dial down" as that makes sense. Corporate leaders, doctors, lawyers, and others who are busy and successful cannot do their jobs at less than 100 percent. With multiple activities, all of which are part-time, it is no longer a choice between 100 percent and nothing. And perhaps the most important advantage to a life of variety is that it develops a much broader person—with benefits both for the individual and those around him or her. I cannot imagine what I would be like if I had stayed at Jewel and not had the extraordinary experiences I have enjoyed during "retirement."

A life of variety seldom happens by itself; it requires planning and effort. Those who wait until they are 65 to announce to the world that they are available for other activities have to be either lucky or prominent in order to easily assemble their array of new involvements. I have challenged any number of executives to get involved in civic and not-for-profit activities, in anticipation of the time they will be able to enjoy a life of variety."

I have also challenged CEOs to set a deadline for completing their tenure as CEO. Without a deadline, the succession process does not get started. Successors don't have the chance to develop if the CEO is viewed as staying in the role for an indeterminate time. A CEO doesn't develop people if he or she really wants to be there forever.

I have also mentored many people who have not yet reached the top of the mountain, but were in early or mid-career, typically when they were looking for a job. When I meet with young people in mid-career, I tell them, "If I were in your shoes, I wouldn't just be looking for a job. I would look for the kind of company and the kind of people that help you figure out not only what you're going to do from now until you retire, but what you're going to do after that." A company that encourages civic involvement may be more valuable to the life of someone in mid-career than an extra $10,000 in salary.

As I look back at those who were mentors to me and those whom I have mentored, there are clear connections, many stemming from education or volunteering. From skipping the third grade and Judge Mix, to Yale to Irwin Miller to Cummins Engine to the Ford Foundation. From the Harvard Business School to Amory Houghton and Corning Glass to TBG, as well as to George Putnam and the Putnam Funds, and most importantly to Jewel and Chicago. From the United Way to Charlie Brown to AT&T to Lucent. From Dick Ogilvie to Jim Thompson to the SSC to the Illinois Coalition. From the Chicago Community Trust to Leadership Greater Chicago. From Governor Rhodes to "Jobs for Metropolitan Chicago," to the Civic Committee to Leadership for Quality Education.

As I wrote at the beginning of my memoir, the branches start off distinct and end up in a bramble of connections. It *is* almost true that everything that happened to me in my life has been influenced by, if not the result of, education or volunteering.

Chapter 24

A Living Philosophy

I put my personal philosophy on paper for an address I delivered in November 1979 to the Chicago Sunday Evening Club, an organization whose mission was to positively influence people's spiritual, moral, and religious lives. The principles I articulated then have withstood the test of the intervening 25-plus years, and I would not change them today. Here is what I wrote, and here is what I believe:

> Each of us spends a lifetime trying to live up to a personal philosophy ... one which gives meaning to an existence ... and satisfaction in response to an inner urging to live for a purpose greater than self-gratification. What is my philosophy? What are my beliefs?
>
> *I believe in the human need for self-determination.* We all show greater desire and energy to accomplish something that we think of as our own idea. The best political leadership—the best business leadership— the best leadership for social change—begins with an understanding of the human need for individual pride, creativity, and expression ... in an increasingly crowded world. Somehow, to order oneself is always freedom. To be ordered by another can feel like enslavement.

I believe in the dignity and power of the human spirit.
Things get done in this world because people believe
in themselves—and in their organizations—and in the
desirability of reaching clearly understood goals. Simple
achievements—or difficult ones—are possible when
physical and mental powers are unleashed by the greatest
of human powers—the human spirit. True leadership
talent learns that the toughest jobs can be accomplished
by a group of people who have three things going for
them: appropriate authority—patient support from their
leaders—and an understanding of the potential of the
human spirit.

***I believe that the satisfactions of leadership come from
helping others to get things done and changed*** … and
not from getting credit for doing and changing things.
For years our company's management style has been
keyed to decentralization and has been called the "first
assistant philosophy." Each management person thinks
of himself not as the desk-pounding, domineering boss,
but as the first assistant to those who "report" to him in
a typical organizational sense. Thus we mentally turn our
organizational charts upside down and challenge ourselves
to seek ways in which we can lead—by helping … by
teaching … by listening … and by managing in the true
democratic sense … with the consent of the managed.

I believe in the wonder of youth. Far from being a cross
I bear, the challenges of the young are something I delight
in—the challenges to the establishment and to the status
quo that I too often find myself protecting. Without
detracting from the wisdom that years bring, I have no
problem choosing the enthusiasm … the idealism … and
the just plain energy … of the young in spirit … over
the tired prejudices … the false pride … the personal

concerns ... and the weariness we often find in those who are uncomfortable with change. Solutions to the oldest or newest of the problems man faces won't come from those who are old enough and wise enough to "know it can't be done."

I believe that I am my brother's keeper—not in a busybody sense—but in the sense of believing that my family and my business are not truly healthy unless my community is healthy. I believe this also in the personal sense that my conscience will not be comfortable with what my apathy will endure. And in the political and social sense that our nation cannot be as aptly measured by the well-being of the average as by the ill-being of the disadvantaged.

I believe in the greatness of our country—but not because we can out-produce ... or out-accumulate ... or out-fight any other country. I believe that the greatness of our nation is found in the ability of our political system to change the rules by which we live to meet the needs of each new era—and the ability of the system to preserve freedom of opportunity with resulting social and economic mobility for all. In the preservation of these capabilities, our Constitution remains a living Constitution.

I believe in the strength of the family. Each of us has a very human need for the strength ... the fun ... and the satisfaction that comes from loving and being loved in a family. There are other benefits, too. It's hard to grow mentally old with children around. It's unlikely that success will add to the swelling of the head when your family understands your weaknesses, perhaps even better than your strengths. And, most importantly, the compassion so needed in our outside-of-the-home activities is most naturally taught and nurtured in a family environment. Mankind would be much better off if only it weren't so difficult for humans to extend such compassion beyond the home and the family!

These are beliefs—elements of a philosophy—but they are just disjointed ideas without an adhesive to bind them together. What is that adhesive for me? It is the God-given good fortune that smiles on ... a man whose predecessors and associates have so developed a business philosophy that his business goals of service and value mesh with his social concerns ... a man whose business and social involvements are supported by good health ... a man whose personal concerns mesh with the interests and desires of his family. As I have considered what I would say to you this evening, it occurred to me that I wish nothing more for my own children than they will be able to develop their own living philosophy with the benefit of a similar adhesive.